B53 035 156 5

easy
Windows® 8

Mark Edward Soper
Sherry Kinkoph Gunter

800 East 96th Street
Indianapolis, Indiana 46240

ONLINE CONTENT

APPENDIX A
Windows Essentials 2012

APPENDIX B
Windows Media Center

CONTENTS

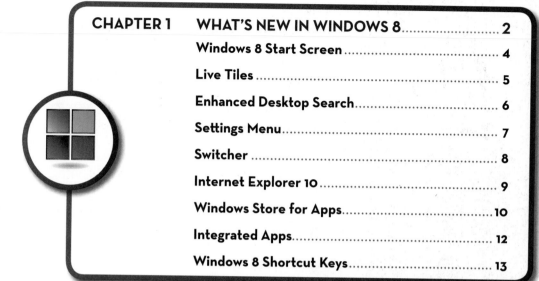

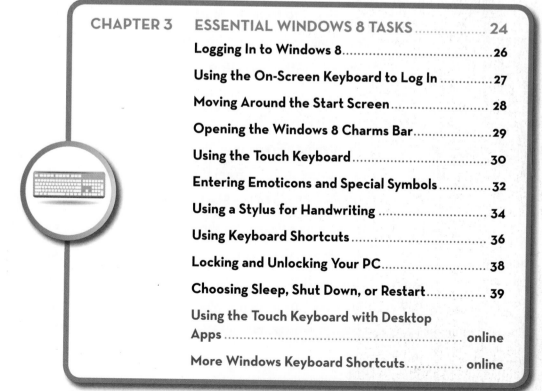

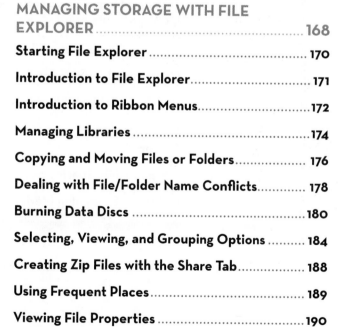

ONLINE ELEMENTS

Appendix A: Windows Essentials 2012

Appendix B: Windows Media Center

EASY WINDOWS® 8

ISBN-13: 978-0-7897-5013-6
ISBN-10: 0-7897-5013-9

Library of Congress Cataloging-in-Publication data is on file.

Printed in the United States of America

First Printing: November 2012

TRADEMARKS

WARNING AND DISCLAIMER

BULK SALES

Que Publishing offers excellent discounts on this book when ordered in quantity for bulk purchases or special sales. For more information, please contact

U.S. Corporate and Government Sales
1-800-382-3419
corpsales@pearsontechgroup.com

For sales outside of the U.S., please contact

International Sales
international@pearsoned.com

Editor-in-Chief
Greg Wiegand

Acquisitions Editor
Michelle Newcomb

Development Editor
Joyce Nielsen

Managing Editor
Sandra Schroeder

Senior Project Editor
Tonya Simpson

Indexer
Erika Millen

Proofreader
Sarah Kearns

Technical Editor
Vince Averello

Editorial Assistant
Cindy Teeters

Book Designer
Anne Jones

Compositor
Bumpy Design

ABOUT THE AUTHOR

Mark Edward Soper has been using Microsoft Windows ever since version 1.0, and since 1992, he has taught thousands of computer troubleshooting and network students across the country how to use Windows as part of their work and everyday lives. Mark is the author of *Easy Microsoft Windows 7*, *Teach Yourself Windows 7 in 10 Minutes*, and *Using Microsoft Windows Live*. Mark also has contributed to Que's *Special Edition Using* series on Windows Me, Windows XP, and Windows Vista; *Easy Windows Vista*; *Windows 7 in Depth*, and has written two books about Windows Vista, including *Maximum PC Microsoft Windows Vista Exposed* and *Unleashing Microsoft Windows Vista Media Center*.

When he's not teaching, learning, or writing about Microsoft Windows, Mark stays busy with many other technology-related activities. He is a longtime contributor to *Upgrading and Repairing PCs*, working on the 11th through 18th and 20th editions. Mark has co-authored *Upgrading and Repairing Networks*, Fifth Edition, written several books on CompTIA A+ Certification (including two titles covering the new 2012 exams), and written two books about digital photography, *Easy Digital Cameras* and *The Shot Doctor: The Amateur's Guide to Taking Great Digital Photos*. Mark also has become a video content provider for Que Publishing and InformIT and has posted many blog entries and articles at InformIT.com, MaximumPC.com, and other websites. He also teaches digital photography, digital imaging, and Microsoft Office for Ivy Tech Corporate College's southwest Indiana campus in Evansville, Indiana.

DEDICATION

Once again, for the love of my life, Cheryl.

ACKNOWLEDGMENTS

Many people have enabled me to be the lead author of this new Windows book, and I want to tell my readers, "Thanks for continuing to read my work." But, there are many others I need to thank for this opportunity.

Thanks first and always to God, whose encouragement (often conveyed through the encouragement of my wife, Cheryl), has been a constant presence in my life.

I started using Windows back when it was a graphic overlay over MS-DOS, and there are plenty of people who helped me learn more about Windows through the years. Thanks go to Jim Peck and Mayer Rubin, for whom I taught thousands of students how to troubleshoot systems running Windows 3.1, 95, and 98; magazine editors Edie Rockwood and Ron Kobler, for assigning me to dig deeper into Windows; Ed Bott, who provided my first opportunity to contribute to a major Windows book; Scott Mueller, who asked me to help with *Upgrading and Repairing Windows*; Ivy Tech Corporate College, Bob Cowart, and Brian Knittel, who have continued my real-world Windows education. And, of course, the Microsoft family.

Thanks also to my family, both for their encouragement over the years and for the opportunity to explain various Windows features and fix things that go wrong. Even though some of them have joined the "dark side" (they have Macs), we are all still loving each other and laughing about the differences.

I also want to thank the editorial and design team that Que put together for this book: Many thanks to Michelle Newcomb for bringing me back for another *Easy* series book, and thanks to Joyce Nielsen, Vince Averello, and Tonya Simpson for overseeing their respective parts of the publishing process. Thanks also to Cindy Teeters for keeping track of invoices and making sure payments were timely.

I also want to thank Sherry Gunter for coming in late in the process to help with several of the early chapters so we could bring this book to you on a timely basis.

I have worked with Que Publishing and Pearson since 1999, and this is the best year yet. I'm looking forward to many more.

WE WANT TO HEAR FROM YOU!

As the reader of this book, *you* are our most important critic and commentator. We value your opinion and want to know what we're doing right, what we could do better, what areas you'd like to see us publish in, and any other words of wisdom you're willing to pass our way.

We welcome your comments. You can email or write to let us know what you did or didn't like about this book—as well as what we can do to make our books better.

Please note that we cannot help you with technical problems related to the topic of this book.

When you write, please be sure to include this book's title and author as well as your name and email address. We will carefully review your comments and share them with the author and editors who worked on the book.

Email: feedback@quepublishing.com

Mail: Que Publishing
          ATTN: Reader Feedback
          800 East 96th Street
          Indianapolis, IN 46240 USA

READER SERVICES

Visit our website and register this book at quepublishing.com/register for convenient access to any updates, downloads, or errata that might be available for this book.

INTRODUCTION

WHY THIS BOOK WAS WRITTEN

Que Publishing's Easy series is famous for providing accurate, simple, step-by-step instructions for popular software and operating systems. Because Windows 8 is the biggest change in Windows in years, *Easy Windows 8* is here to help you understand and use it. Whether you're a veteran Windows user or new to Windows and computers, there's a lot to learn, and we're here to help.

Easy Windows 8 makes learning the essential features of Windows 8 painless and enjoyable. We spent months learning how Windows 8 works, what's similar to previous versions, and what's brand new. All of this information has been condensed into an easy-to-read visual guide that gets you familiar with this newest Microsoft creation in a hurry.

We won't waste your time discussing obscure operations that not even help desk workers or Windows geniuses ever use. Instead, our objective with *Easy Windows 8* is to give you a solid grounding in the everyday features you need to make your computing life better, more productive, and even more fun.

HOW TO READ *EASY WINDOWS 8*

Someday I might take a stab at writing the "great American novel," but *Easy Windows 8* is thoroughly grounded in fact. We've spent countless hours working our way through Windows 8's features to bring you this book.

So, how should you get started? You have a few options, based on what you know about computers and Windows. Try one of these:

- Start at Chapter 1, "What's New in Windows 8," and work your way through.
- Go straight to the chapters that look the most interesting.

- Hit the table of contents or the index and go directly to the sections that tell you stuff you don't know already.

Any of these methods will work—and to help you get a better feel for what's inside, here's a closer look at what's in each chapter.

BEYOND THE TABLE OF CONTENTS— WHAT'S INSIDE

Chapter 1, "What's New in Windows 8," provides a quick overview of the most important new features in Windows 8. If you're reading this book mainly to brush up on what's new and different, start here and follow the references to the chapters with more information.

Chapter 2, "Upgrading to Windows 8," is designed for users of Windows 7 or previous versions who are upgrading to Windows 8. This chapter covers the process and helps you make the best choices along the way.

Chapter 3, "Essential Windows 8 Tasks," shows you how to log in to Windows 8, how to use the touch keyboard or handwriting interface, how to use shortcut keys, how to lock and unlock your computer, and how to shut it down or put it into sleep mode.

Chapter 4, "Using the Windows 8 User Interface," helps you understand how to use the new tile-based user interface on the Start screen. Learn how to start programs, switch between programs, close programs, and search for files and programs.

Chapter 5, "Browsing the Web in the New UI," provides step-by-step instructions on how to use the new features in Internet Explorer 10.

Chapter 6, "Enjoying Media with the Windows 8 UI," shows you how to use the new Music, Video, and Photos apps.

Chapter 7, "Staying Connected with Windows 8 Apps," helps you use the new Mail, Messaging, Calendar, Maps, and Weather apps to stay in touch with the world around you.

Chapter 8, "Customizing the Windows 8 Start Screen," shows you how to pin folders and websites to the Start screen, how to change its background, and how to rearrange tiles. You'll also discover how to change your lock screen, Start screen, account picture, and time zone settings.

Chapter 9, "Using the Windows 8 Store," takes you on a tour of the new Windows 8 online app store. Learn how to search for apps, download free apps, and buy new apps and Windows components.

Chapter 10, "Playing Games with Windows 8," helps you take advantage of the new Windows 8 connections to Xbox 360 and learn how to download, install, and enjoy free games available at the Windows Store.

Chapter 11, "Running Desktop Apps," helps you run and manage programs that run from the Windows desktop, use the new features in popular accessory programs, and print files.

Chapter 12, "Managing Storage with File Explorer," helps you manage files, folders, and drives.

Chapter 13, "Networking Your Home with HomeGroup," shows you how to use the HomeGroup feature to set up and manage a network with Windows 7 and Windows 8 computers. This chapter also helps you understand which network functions can be performed from the Start screen, and which ones run from the Windows desktop.

Chapter 14, "Working with Photos from Your Desktop," helps you import photos into your Pictures library, use the Windows Photo Viewer, and use SkyDrive for online photo and document storage and sharing.

Chapter 15, "Working with Music from Your Desktop," helps you use Windows Media Player to play, rip, and burn music CDs.

Chapter 16, "Browsing the Internet from Your Desktop," shows you how to use Internet Explorer 10's desktop-only features for tab, home page, and favorites management.

Chapter 17, "Adding and Using Multimedia Features," introduces you to Windows Essentials 2012's new Photo Gallery and Movie Maker and to Windows Media Center. Learn how to add these components to Windows so you can use them to edit, share, and enjoy photos and videos.

Chapter 18, "Advanced Configuration Options," shows you how to add a second display, personalize your desktop, manage devices and printers, and add more features to Windows 8.

Chapter 19, "User Accounts and System Security," introduces you to different ways to set up a Windows 8 login for users, how to add additional users, and how to use parental controls to keep an eye on what young users are up to.

Chapter 20, "Protecting Your System," shows you how to keep Windows 8 updated, protect your files, create a restore point, and check for spyware.

Chapter 21, "System Maintenance and Performance," helps you improve system speed and solve problems that can prevent your system from running properly.

Baffled by PC and Windows terminology? Check out the Glossary!

Appendix A, "Windows Essentials 2012," which is online, discusses the major features of Photo Gallery, Movie Maker, Messenger, Mail, and other components and where to learn more.

Appendix B, "Windows Media Center," which is online, discusses customization options and where to learn more.

Also be sure to check out the additional tasks available online in PDF format at quepublishing.com/register.

Enjoy!

Chapter 1

WHAT'S NEW IN WINDOWS 8

Microsoft Windows 8 is the eighth generation of the world's most popular desktop and laptop computer operating system. Tablet computers and smartphones have made computing power more widespread than ever before. Windows 8 is designed to be the first operating system that's equally at home on traditional desktop and laptop PCs as well as tablets and smartphones. In fact, Windows 8 functions very much like Windows Mobile 8, the new version of Microsoft Windows for smartphones.

What makes Windows 8 intriguing isn't just the new touch-friendly interface—behind the scenes, it is also more powerful than Windows 7. In a way, Windows 8 is two operating systems in one. For media consumption and casual web browsing, the default Windows 8 tile-based interface is slick and easy to navigate. Also, whenever you need to create, edit, or manage your system or its content, you're just a couple of clicks or a fast text search away from the familiar Windows desktop and its enhanced tools.

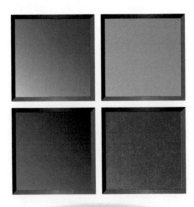

The Windows 8 Start screen includes live updates and provides quick access to mail, news, search, pictures, and other programs.

Switcher enables you to easily switch between open programs.

Use Charms to access search, share, devices, and other program settings.

Internet Explorer 10 features built-in search to help you quickly find matching websites.

The new Windows Store includes Windows 8 apps you can purchase or download for free.

The All Apps menu provides easy access to Windows 8 apps and Windows desktop apps.

WINDOWS 8 START SCREEN

When Windows 8 starts, the new Windows 8 Start screen appears. Use your touchscreen, touchpad, or mouse to scroll horizontally through the tiles to access the programs or features you want.

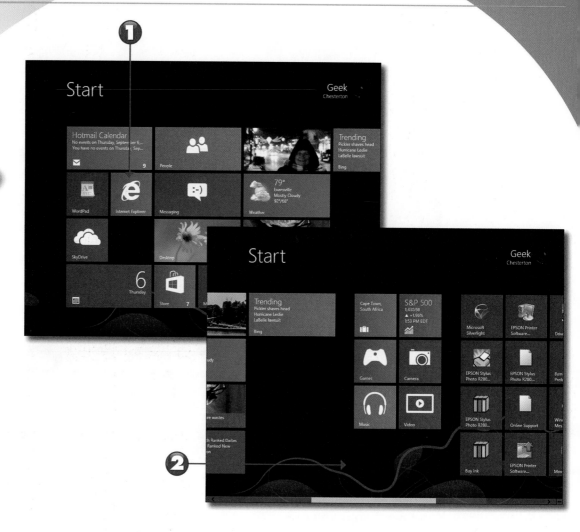

1 Click or tap a program tile or icon to start it.

2 Scroll to the right to see more program tiles.

NOTE

Windows 8 Start Screen To learn more about working with the Start screen, see "The Windows 8 Start Screen" in Chapter 4, "Using the Windows 8 User Interface." ■

LIVE TILES

Many of the programs shown on the Start screen are live tiles—some display a live preview of their contents, while others display a live preview after you start them. This section highlights some of these live tiles; other live tiles include the Travel and Finance tiles.

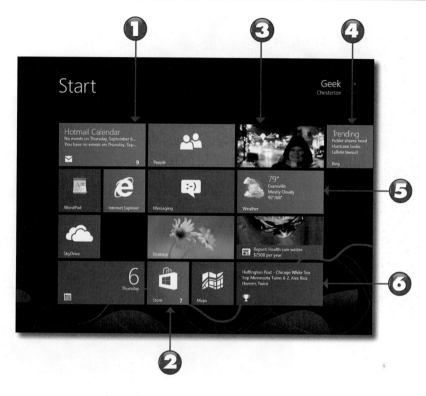

Start

1. Hotmail Calendar provides a live feed of events if you sign in with your Microsoft account.

2. After you install programs from the Windows Store, the store notifies you of updates for those programs.

3. The Photos tile cycles through the photos in your Photos library.

4. Bing displays trending searches.

5. Configure Weather with your preferred location for the current conditions and forecast.

6. The Sports tile features the latest stories from the world of sports.

End

ENHANCED DESKTOP SEARCH

Windows 8 makes searching for specific files or programs easier than ever before. Just start typing from the Start screen, and Windows 8 automatically opens the Search window. The Search feature categorizes your search and remembers previous searches to save time.

Start

End

1. Type text to search.

2. The Search box opens and displays the text you type.

3. Matching apps (programs) are listed in the left pane.

4. Click **Settings** to see matching settings.

5. Click **Files** to see matching files.

NOTE

More About Searching To learn more about the Search feature, see "Searching for Files," and "Searching for Apps and Programs," both in Chapter 4. ■

SETTINGS MENU

The most common settings in Windows are even easier to view and change with the Windows 8 Settings menu. From this menu, you can change the appearance of the Start screen, adjust tile settings, get Help information, and access other PC-related settings.

1 Hover the mouse pointer over the lower-right corner of the screen.

2 Click **Settings**.

3 Choose the setting or category you want to change—Start is selected by default.

NOTE

Customizing Other PC Settings To learn more about changing PC settings in Windows 8, see Chapter 8, "Customizing the Windows 8 Start Screen." ■

SWITCHER

When you open one or more programs in Windows 8, you can see live thumbnails of these programs on a vertical bar at the left side of the display. To use this new Windows 8 feature, known as Switcher, click a thumbnail in the Switcher to switch to that program.

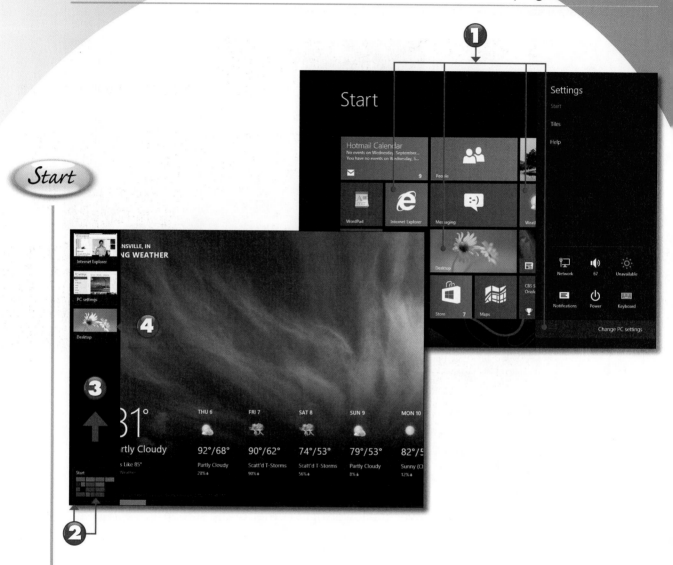

① Start some apps from the Start screen or desktop.

② Hover the mouse pointer over the lower-left corner of the screen, and click the **Start screen** thumbnail.

③ Move the mouse pointer toward the upper-left corner of the Start screen.

④ Click a live thumbnail to switch to that program.

End

INTERNET EXPLORER 10

Windows 8 includes Internet Explorer 10 (IE10), the latest version of Microsoft's popular web browser. When launched from the Start screen, IE10 provides a streamlined view of the Web. When you start IE10 from the Windows desktop, the program offers full support for plug-ins and tabbed browsing.

Start

1. Click **Internet Explorer** from the Start screen.

2. Enter the website address (URL) or part of the website name.

3. If one of the suggested sites is the one you want, click it.

4. The website opens.

End

NOTE

Web Browsing in the New UI To learn more about using Internet Explorer 10 from the Start screen, see Chapter 5, "Browsing the Web in the New UI." ■

WINDOWS STORE FOR APPS

With Windows 8, getting new software is just a few clicks away, thanks to the new Windows Store for Apps. You can quickly download and install free applications. Purchasing applications is just as simple.

Start

1 Click **Store** from the Start screen.

2 Click the app you want to download.

Continued

3 Click **Install** to download the app.

4 The app is added to the Start screen.

End

NOTE

Shopping at the Windows 8 Store For more details about shopping for apps at the Windows 8 Store, see Chapter 9, "Using the Windows 8 Store." ■

INTEGRATED APPS

Windows 8 includes new versions of familiar apps for use from the Start screen or from the classic Windows desktop. Only a few are visible from the Start screen, but it's easy to locate more apps on your system.

1 Right-click a blank area on the Start screen.

2 Click **All apps**.

3 Windows 8 apps are listed first.

4 Scroll to the right to see apps you installed as well as desktop apps.

End

NOTE

Running Desktop Apps To learn more about using desktop apps in Windows 8, see Chapter 11, "Running Desktop Apps." ■

WINDOWS 8 SHORTCUT KEYS

Windows 8 includes new shortcut keys you can use to start Windows desktop apps and utilities. One of these helpful shortcuts enables you to quickly access a list of common Windows desktop applications.

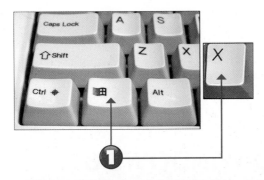

Start

1) Press the **Windows key** and the **X key**.

2) A list of Windows desktop programs appears.

3) Click a program.

4) The program opens on the Windows desktop.

End

Chapter 2

UPGRADING TO WINDOWS 8

If you're using Windows 7, upgrading to Windows 8 is easy—you can run the installation process from the Windows 7 desktop. Windows 8 lets you bring along your installed Windows 7 applications and adds them to its Start screen for easy access. Your documents, photos, videos, and other files also come along for the ride. In this chapter, you discover how easy it is to upgrade to Windows 8.

Launch the Windows 8 installer
from the Windows 7 AutoPlay
dialog box.

Personalize the
Windows 8 desktop.

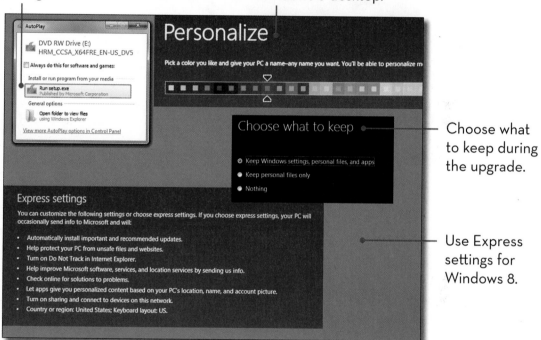

Choose what
to keep during
the upgrade.

Use Express
settings for
Windows 8.

STARTING THE INSTALLATION

To install Windows 8 on a computer running Windows 7, you should start Windows 7 and then launch the installation process from the Windows desktop. Follow these steps to start the process from Windows 7.

Start

Insert the Windows 8 DVD into the optical drive on your computer.

Click **Run setup.exe** from the AutoPlay dialog box.

Continued

NOTE

Checking for App Problems During the Upgrade During the upgrade process, Windows 8 checks your system for applications (programs) that might cause problems with the installation. Depending on the problem, you might need to uninstall the application before continuing the upgrade, update the application after the upgrade is finished, or reinstall the application after the upgrade. ■

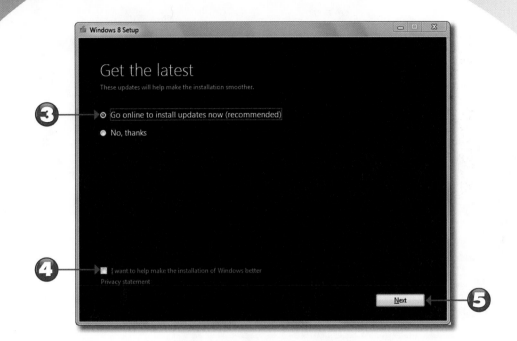

③ Click **Go online to install updates now**.

④ Select **I want to help make the installation of Windows better**.

⑤ Click **Next**.

Continued

TIP

Starting the Upgrade Manually If the AutoPlay dialog box shown in step 2 doesn't appear, open Computer, navigate to the optical drive where the Windows 8 disc is located, view the contents of the drive, and double-click Setup.exe. ■

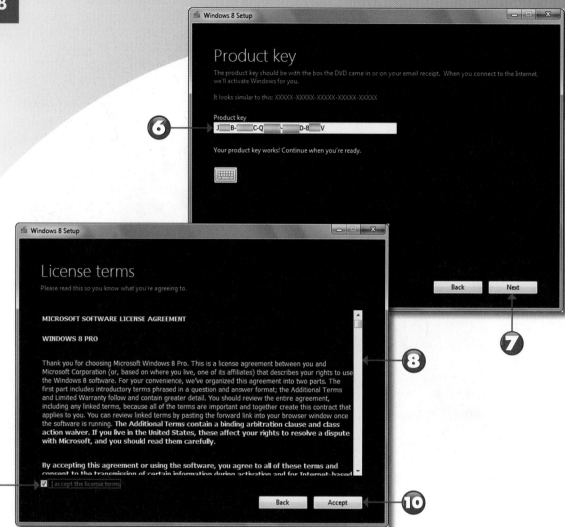

6 Enter the product key.

7 Click **Next**.

8 Scroll through and read the license terms.

9 Click the **I accept the license terms** checkbox.

10 Click **Accept**.

Continued

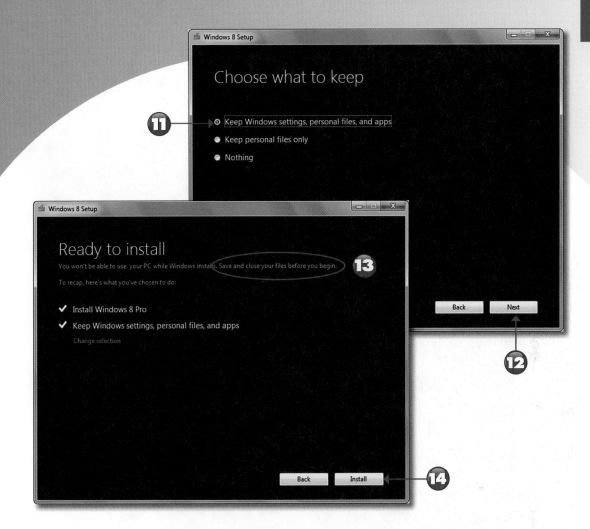

11 Select **Keep Windows settings, personal files, and apps**.

12 Click **Next**.

13 Make sure you have saved and closed your files.

14 Click **Install**.

End

NOTE

Windows 7, Vista, and XP Upgrade Differences You can start the installation process the same way if you upgrade from Windows Vista or XP to Windows 8. If you upgrade from Windows Vista, you can keep your Windows settings and personal files. If you upgrade from Windows XP, you can keep only your personal files. With either Windows Vista or Windows XP, you will need to reinstall your apps or install updated versions after you upgrade to Windows 8. ∎

COMPLETING THE INSTALLATION

Windows 8 does most of the work during the installation process and restarts your computer a few times. However, near the end of the installation process, you will be prompted to provide a few responses.

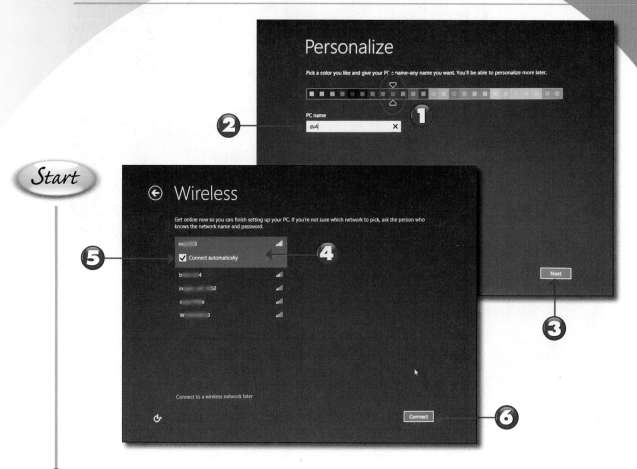

1 Select the Start screen color scheme you prefer.

2 If prompted, enter a name for your PC.

3 Click **Next**.

4 Select your wireless network.

5 If you want to connect to your network manually, clear the **Connect automatically** checkbox.

6 Click **Connect**.

Continued

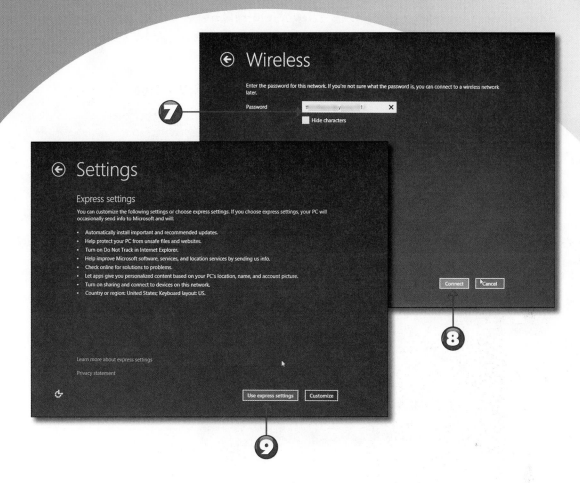

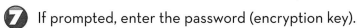

7 If prompted, enter the password (encryption key).

8 Click **Connect**.

9 Click **Use express settings**.

Continued

NOTE

No Wireless Connection? If you use a wired Ethernet connection to a broadband modem or you use a dial-up modem, skip to step 9. If you have a wireless connection but prefer to set it up later, click the Connect to a Wireless Network Later Link (refer to the bottom of the screen shown in step 4). ■

TIP

Seeing What You're Typing To see the characters of the encryption key as you type them, clear the Hide Characters checkbox shown below the password in step 7.

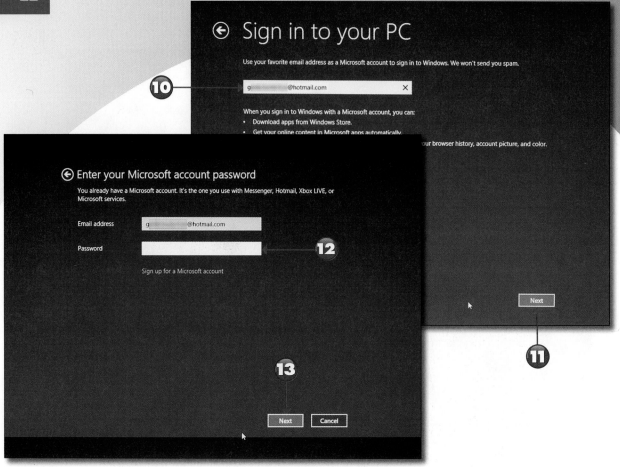

10 Enter your preferred email address for your Microsoft account.

11 Click **Next**.

12 If you entered a Microsoft account email address, enter your password.

13 Click **Next**.

Continued

NOTE

What is a Microsoft Account? Windows Live, Messenger, Xbox 360, and Hotmail accounts are all Microsoft accounts. If you enter a different email address in step 10, it will be used to identify your Microsoft account. ■

NOTE

Getting a Microsoft Account If you don't have a Microsoft account, you can get one by clicking the Sign Up for a Microsoft Account link. ■

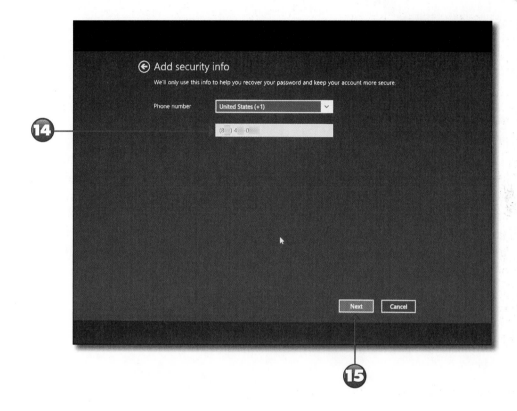

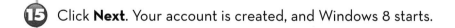

14 Confirm or enter security verification information, as necessary.

15 Click **Next**. Your account is created, and Windows 8 starts.

End

NOTE

Logging In to Windows 8 If there is only one user on your system, Windows 8 will log you in automatically. If there is more than one user, you will need to select the user and log in manually. To learn how to log in to Windows 8, see Chapter 3, "Essential Windows 8 Tasks." ■

NOTE

Software and Hardware Compatibility In general, software and hardware that works with Windows 7 will also work with Windows 8. Check out the Microsoft Windows 8 page at http://windows.microsoft.com for more information. ■

Chapter 3

ESSENTIAL WINDOWS 8 TASKS

The new Windows 8 user interface is like nothing you've seen before on a PC. Whether you're a newcomer to Windows or an experienced user of previous versions, Windows 8 provides a new way to enjoy local and web content on your PC. You'll notice the changes as soon as you log on to the system. In this chapter, you learn how to log in, how to interact with the new user interface through a mouse, keyboard, or touch interface, how to lock your computer, and how to shut it down.

Login Screen

Preparing to put the computer into low-power sleep mode.

Charms Bar

Entering symbols with the touch keyboard.

Using the handwriting panel.

Displaying the Run dialog box with Windows key+R.

LOGGING IN TO WINDOWS 8

To log in to Windows 8, you must know the username and password (if any) set up for your account. If you installed Windows 8 yourself, be sure to make note of this information when you are prompted to provide it during the installation process. You also log in to Windows 8 when you are waking up the computer from sleep, unlocking it, or restarting it.

Start

11:10
Tuesday, August 28

Geek Chesterton
gee_____@hotmail.com

Sign-in options

① Press the **spacebar**, click your mouse, or tap your touchscreen or touchpad.

② Type your password.

③ Press **Enter** or click the arrow. The Start screen appears.

End

NOTE

Seeing Your Password To see the characters you are entering, click the eye icon next to the arrow in step 3. You must enter one character before the eye icon is visible. ∎

USING THE ON-SCREEN KEYBOARD TO LOG IN

You can also use the Accessibility menu's on-screen keyboard to log in. Here's
how to open and use this menu.

1 Click the accessibility icon.

2 Click **On-Screen Keyboard**.

3 Click each character in your password.

4 Click the **Enter** key and the Start screen appears.

NOTE

Forget Your Password? Check the Hint If you are using a local account (as
you specified during the Windows 8 installation) and mistype your password,
a password hint is displayed if you provided one during installation. ■

MOVING AROUND THE START SCREEN

The Start screen appears after you log in. In this lesson, you learn how to navigate the Start screen.

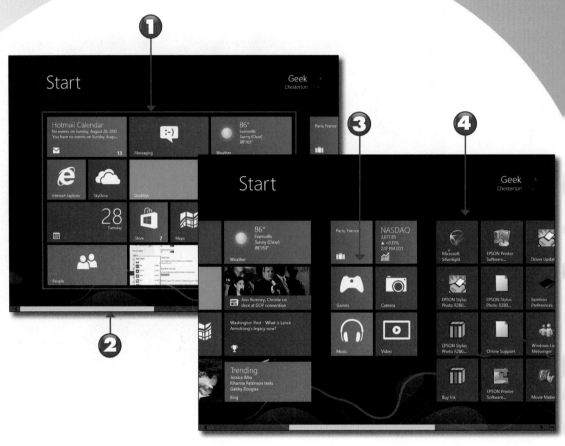

Start

1 Internet-enabled and social-media program tiles are on the left side of the Start screen, as is the Windows Desktop tile.

2 Click and drag the scrollbar to the right.

3 Notice the media programs.

4 Tiles for Windows desktop programs appear toward the right side of the Start screen.

End

TIP

Scrolling with a Touchpad or Touchscreen You can also scroll by using the scroll gesture for your touchpad or touchscreen, which is typically two fingers held together. ■

OPENING THE WINDOWS 8 CHARMS BAR

Windows 8 includes a Charms bar with five charms: Search, Share, Start, Devices, and Settings. You'll use these charms for many tasks throughout this book. If you want to access the on-screen keyboard or stylus, you must open the Charms bar first. Here's how.

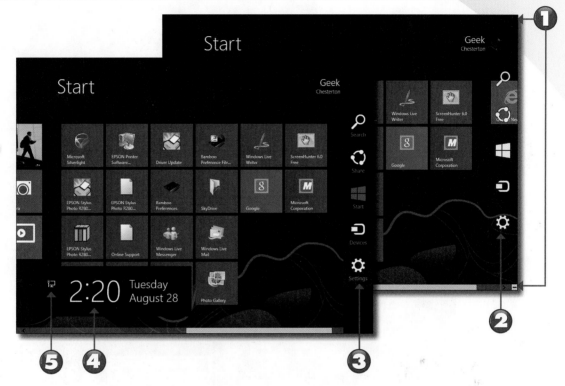

1 Hover the mouse or point to the upper-right or lower-right corner of the screen.

2 The Charms bar appears on the right side of the screen.

3 Move your mouse or pointer into the Charms bar to select an option.

4 Note the current date and time.

5 The network connection status appears here.

End

NOTE

Date, Time, and Network Connection Status The date, time, and network connection status appear when you move your mouse or pointer into the Charms bar in step 3. ■

USING THE TOUCH KEYBOARD

If you have a tablet computer or a PC with a touchpad (either integrated or connected externally), you can access the touch keyboard from the Settings charm and use it for text entry and searches.

Start

1 Click the **Settings** charm.

2 Click **Keyboard**.

3 Click **Touch keyboard and handwriting panel**.

Continued

NOTE

Accessing the Touch Keyboard from the Desktop The on-screen keyboard is also available from the Desktop taskbar. ■

4 Click characters and they appear in the Search box.

5 Matches are displayed in the left pane as characters are typed.

6 Click to switch to uppercase keys.

7 Click to switch between text and numbers or symbols.

8 Click to switch to another symbol set.

9 Click to backspace.

End

TIP

Configuring the Touch Keyboard Click Change PC Settings (available from the Settings charm) and select General to make changes to how the Touch Keyboard works. ∎

ENTERING EMOTICONS AND SPECIAL SYMBOLS

The Windows 8 touch keyboard also makes entering emoticons and special symbols easy. Here's how to use this feature to enhance your messages and documents.

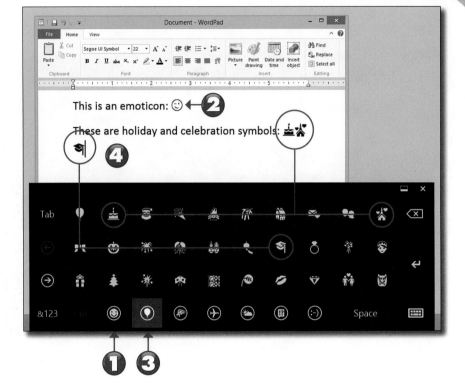

Start

(1) The **emoticon** key.

(2) An emoticon entered from the emoticon keyboard.

(3) Click the **holiday and celebration** key.

(4) Click holiday and celebration symbols from the holiday and celebration keyboard.

Continued

5 **Food** key and characters.

6 **Travel** key and characters.

7 **Sky and weather** key and characters.

8 **Icons** key and characters.

9 **Character emoticon** key and character.

10 Click to hide keyboard.

End

USING A STYLUS FOR HANDWRITING

If you're more comfortable with a stylus than with a touch keyboard, Windows 8 has you covered. Here's how to switch to and use the stylus.

Start

1. Click the **keyboard** icon.

2. Click the **stylus** option.

3. Write the text you want to insert.

Continued

4 Click **Insert** after the text is recognized.

5 The text is inserted into your document.

End

USING KEYBOARD SHORTCUTS

Windows 8 offers more keyboard shortcuts than ever before. As you learn in this lesson, some keyboard shortcuts make working with the Start screen easier, while others super-charge the Windows desktop. These shortcuts use the Windows key in combination with other keys.

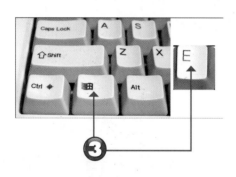

Start

1 Press **Windows key+C**.

2 The Charms bar opens.

3 Press **Windows key+E**.

4 File Explorer opens on the Windows desktop.

Continued

NOTE

More Keyboard and Mouse Shortcuts To find more keyboard and mouse shortcuts, open Help and Support from the Start screen and search for the keyboard shortcut. Look for the "What's new" article. ■

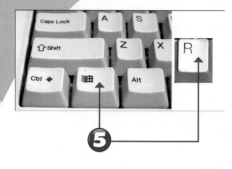

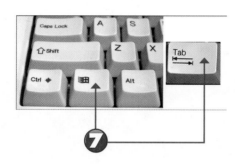

(5) Press **Windows key+R**.

(6) The Run dialog box opens on the Windows desktop.

(7) Press **Windows key+Tab**.

(8) Continue to press the **Tab** key—the shortcut toggles through running apps.

End

TIP

Selecting the App to Switch to with Windows key+T When the app you want to use is highlighted, release the keys. The app opens. ■

LOCKING AND UNLOCKING YOUR PC

If you have a password on your account, you can lock your PC when you leave it and unlock it when you return. Once again, the Windows key plays a part in this task.

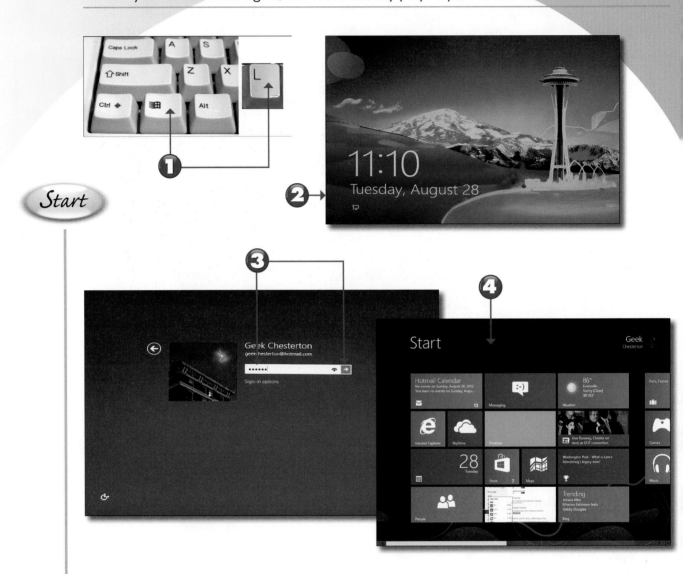

Start

1. Press the **Windows key+L** to lock your computer.

2. Press the **spacebar**, click your mouse, or press the touch keyboard or touchscreen.

3. Enter your password and click the arrow, if applicable.

4. Windows reopens on the screen, where you previously locked it.

End

CHOOSING SLEEP, SHUT DOWN, OR RESTART

When it's time to put away the computer, Windows 8 makes it easy. Want to go back to work (or play) right where you left off? Choose Sleep. Want to start from scratch the next time you start up Windows, or need to put away your PC for more than a few hours? Choose Shut Down. Need to restart the computer? Choose Restart.

Start

1 Move the mouse to either right corner or swipe in from the right.

2 Click **Settings**.

3 Click **Power**.

4 Click one of the options listed.

End

NOTE

Power Options Sleep puts the computer into low-power mode. Shut down turns off the power. Restart restarts the computer. You will need to log in again after choosing any of these options. ■

Chapter 4

USING THE WINDOWS 8 USER INTERFACE

The new Windows 8 user interface, or UI for short, is remarkably different from previous versions of the operating system. The Start screen greets you as soon as you log on to your computer. Before you jump in and start clicking and scrolling, take a few moments to orient yourself to the new interface. Much like learning your way around a new city, learning your way around Windows 8 takes a little navigating. You must figure out where to find the apps you need, and which direction to go to get you where you want to be.

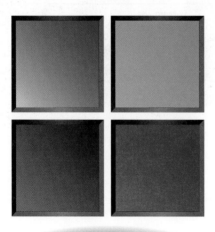

Start Screen

App Tiles

Charms Bar

Apps Bar

THE WINDOWS 8 START SCREEN

The starting point any time you log on to your computer is the Windows 8 Start screen. The Start screen displays all your app tiles—special icons representing installed apps, short for *applications*. You can also add tiles for desktop programs, such as Microsoft Word, or add shortcuts to web pages, contacts, and more. The Start screen is a jumping-off point for accessing apps, computer settings, and the traditional Windows desktop.

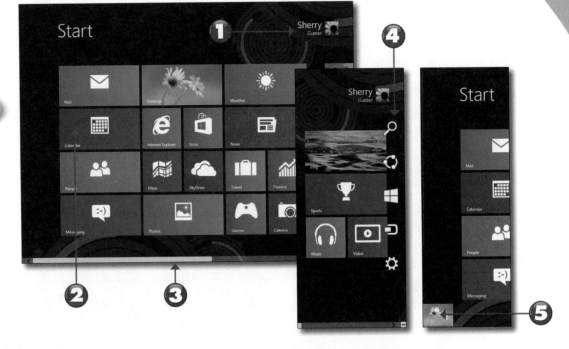

1 Click this area to switch users or edit your account picture.

2 App tiles appear as square or rectangular boxes, sometimes showing live data.

3 Use the scrollbar to navigate through the app tiles.

4 The Charms bar displays shortcuts for common tasks.

5 The corners of the screen are also active; move the mouse pointer to the bottom-left corner to view the Start screen or desktop thumbnail.

End

TIP

Quick Start Press the Windows key on your keyboard, or swipe the bottom-left corner and click or tap the Start screen thumbnail, to quickly view the Windows 8 Start screen. ■

OPENING AN APP

The app tiles on the Start screen represent applications installed on your computer. You can also add tiles for desktop programs, such as Microsoft Office programs. When you open an app, it fills the screen. The first time you use some apps, you might be prompted to activate your Microsoft account—just follow the onscreen directions to do so. You can use touch gestures to move around an app, or you can use the mouse and keyboard to interact with the program.

1 Display the Start screen.

2 Click the app you want to open.

3 The app opens in full-screen view. In this example, the Calendar app opens.

End

NOTE

Desktop Programs You can still use desktop programs in Windows 8, but they don't use the new touchscreen capabilities that the new UI apps do. Regular programs run in their own windows on the traditional Windows desktop and use the same controls found in other desktop software, such as a Ribbon of commands, and Minimize, Maximize, and Restore buttons. ■

SWITCHING BETWEEN APPS

Windows 8 apps do not close like traditional program windows. Instead, when you stop working with the app and go on to something else, the app remains suspended in the background, ready to pick up where you left off. This makes switching to other apps as easy as a click or tap away. You can display a list of open apps on the left side of the screen.

Start

1. Swipe the left side of the screen, or hover the mouse pointer in the top-left corner and then move it downward.

2. A list of recently used apps appear as thumbnail images.

3. Click or tap the app you want to open.

4. The app opens full screen to the previous task or screen you were performing.

End

TIP

Snapping Apps You can also reopen an app by dragging an app thumbnail from the list of open apps on the left and dropping it in the center of the screen—this is called *snapping*. ■

NOTE

Closing an App Although apps are suspended when you open another app, you can close them completely. Simply right-click on the app thumbnail and click Close. You can also grab the top of the app and drag it to the bottom of the screen to close. ■

COMPARING APPS WITH DESKTOP PROGRAMS

Windows 8 apps are designed to respond to touch gestures, use the full screen, and do not need window controls (Minimize, Maximize/Restore Down, and Close). Regular desktop programs run in their own windows on the traditional Windows desktop and employ the same controls found in other desktop software.

Start

1

2

End

1 An app fills the whole screen when open, and if you have a touchscreen computer, you can use touch gestures to navigate around the app features.

2 A program opens in its own window on the desktop and features the traditional Ribbon or toolbars, menu bar, and program window controls.

NOTE

No Touchscreen? If your computer does not use a touchscreen, you can still use the traditional methods for navigating around a program and using commands, namely the mouse and keyboard. You can use the mouse to click, drag, scroll, and right-click just as you did with previous versions of Windows. You also can use the keyboard navigation keys and shortcut keys to work with the computer. ■

VIEWING ALL APPS

The Start screen displays a variety of Windows 8 apps that you can scroll through to view what's available. However, not all apps and programs appear on the Start screen. To view other apps installed on your computer, including Windows accessories such as Paint and Notepad or Windows system apps such as File Explorer, display the All Apps screen. The All Apps screen lists your apps alphabetically.

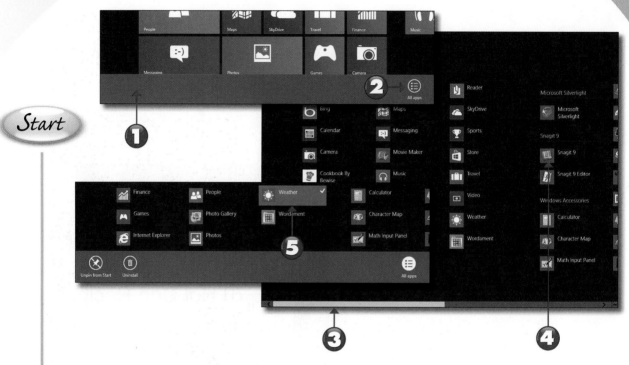

Start

① Swipe the bottom of the Start screen or right-click near the bottom edge to display the Apps bar.

② Click or tap **All apps**.

③ The All Apps screen opens; use the scrollbar at the bottom of the screen to scroll through your apps.

④ To open an app, click or tap it.

⑤ To view more controls for an app, right-click the app name to open the Apps bar.

End

TIP

Pinning Apps If you want to add an app or program to the Start screen, you can pin it using the Pin to Start button on the Apps bar. Learn more about customizing the Start screen in Chapter 8. ■

ZOOMING THE START SCREEN

Windows 8 starts you out with several preinstalled apps. As you add more apps and other items to the Start screen, you might need to zoom in and out to view all the app tiles or groups of tiles. You can use the Zoom control on the Start screen to quickly see all your apps at a glance. You also can use the Zoom view mode to create and name groups of apps.

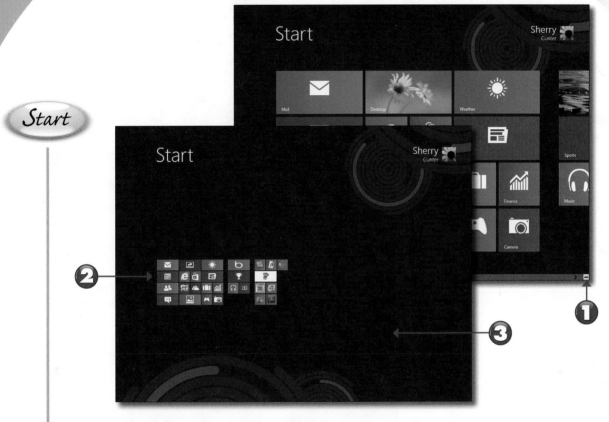

1 Tap or click the **Zoom** icon.

2 The Start screen zooms out.

3 Tap or click an empty area of the screen to return to normal view.

End

TIP

Grouping Apps You can move app tiles around on the Start screen and make groups. For example, you might want all your media apps in one group and all communication apps in another. You can use the Zoom view to select and name a group; simply right-click the group to display the Apps bar and then click the Name group command and assign a unique name. ∎

MOVING APP TILES

You can move app tiles around on the Start screen to position them where you want them. For example, you might want to move all the communication-based tiles into a group, or move a single tile for the app you use the most to the top of the group.

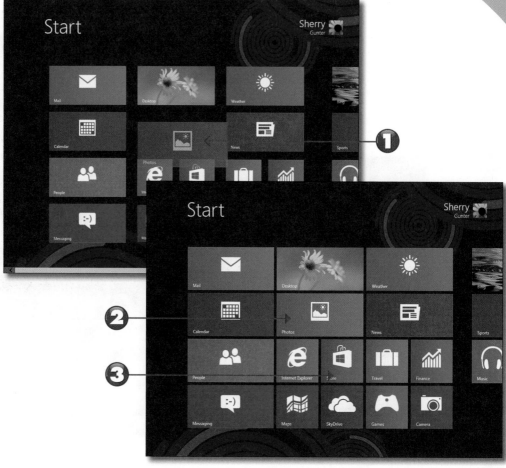

1 Click and drag the app tile.

2 Drop it where you want it to appear.

3 The Start screen adjusts the remaining tiles as needed.

End

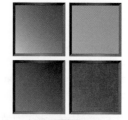

NOTE

Customizing Tiles You can move tiles into groups of related apps and give the group a distinct name. You also can resize some tiles. Learn more about customizing app tiles in Chapter 8. ■

WORKING WITH THE CHARMS BAR

You can use the Charms bar to access search tools, computer settings, and de-vices, as well as to share items and customize the Start screen. The Charms bar hides on the right side of the screen until activated. You can click a charm from the bar to open associated settings.

① Swipe the right side of the Start screen, or move the mouse pointer to the bottom-right corner of the screen and pause.

② The Charms bar appears.

③ Click a charm to open its pane.

End

TIP

Charms Bar Shortcut Press Windows key+C, swipe the right side of the screen, or hover your mouse pointer over the bottom-right corner any time you want to display the Charms bar. ■

SEARCHING FOR APPS AND PROGRAMS

You can easily search for apps and programs directly from the Start screen. Windows 8 immediately tries to guess what you're searching for and displays a list of possible matches on the All Apps screen.

1 From the Start screen, type in the first few letters of the app or program you want to find.

2 The All Apps screen opens and lists possible matches.

3 Click the app or program you want to open.

End

NOTE

More About the Desktop Remember, programs open into their own windows on the Windows 8 desktop. To learn more about using the desktop, see Chapter 11, "Running Desktop Apps." ■

SEARCHING FOR FILES

You can search for files on your computer using the Search feature on the Charms bar. The Search pane, when activated, lets you search for apps, files, and settings based on typed keywords.

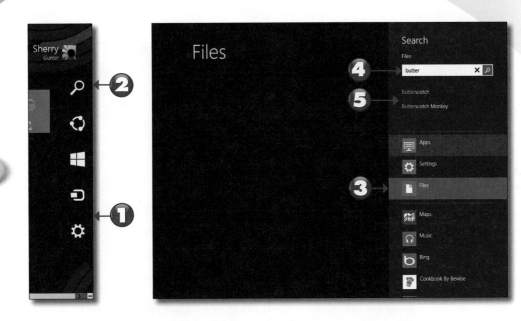

1 Display the Charms bar.

2 Click or tap the **Search** charm.

3 The Search pane appears. Click or tap the **Files** setting.

4 Click or tap the **Search** text box and start typing in the filename.

5 Possible matches are immediately listed beneath the Search box; click a name to open the file in the associated app or program.

End

TIP
Keyboard Shortcut You can quickly summon the Charms bar from the keyboard by pressing Windows key+C. ■

TIP
Using File Explorer You can also search for files using File Explorer, Windows 8's updated version of the Windows Explorer feature. You can access File Explorer from the desktop; press Windows key+D, and then click the File Explorer icon on the Desktop taskbar. ■

VIEWING SETTINGS

You can use the Settings pane to quickly view basic computer settings, such as volume controls, wireless connection, screen brightness, notifications, and power settings. For example, you can find the Shut Down command located among the Power settings on the Settings pane.

1 Display the Charms bar.

2 Click or tap the **Settings** charm.

3 The Settings pane opens.

4 Click or tap a setting to view associated controls.

End

NOTE

PC Settings Screen To find additional computer settings, such as personalization options, click or tap the Change PC Settings link at the bottom of the Settings pane. This opens the PC Settings screen, which offers more categories of computer settings and options. ■

FINDING HELP WITH WINDOWS 8

Anytime you run into difficulty using Windows 8, you can find assistance through the help files. With an online connection, you can access the Windows Help and Support center directly and look up topics you want to learn more about. The Help window works much like a browser window, letting you navigate from topic to topic.

Start

1. Type **Help** from the Start screen.

2. Click or tap **Help and Support**.

3. The Help window opens on the Windows 8 desktop.

4. To view a topic, click a link or category.

5. You can use the navigation buttons to move back and forth between Help pages.

6. Click **Close** to exit the window.

End

BROWSING THE WEB IN THE NEW UI

Windows 8 includes Internet Explorer 10 (IE10), the latest version of Microsoft's web browser. You can access IE10 from the streamlined new user interface (UI) or from the classic Windows desktop. This chapter shows you how to perform basic web-surfing tasks with IE10.

InPrivate Browsing

Pin a Website to the
Start Screen

Frequently
Used Websites

Search History

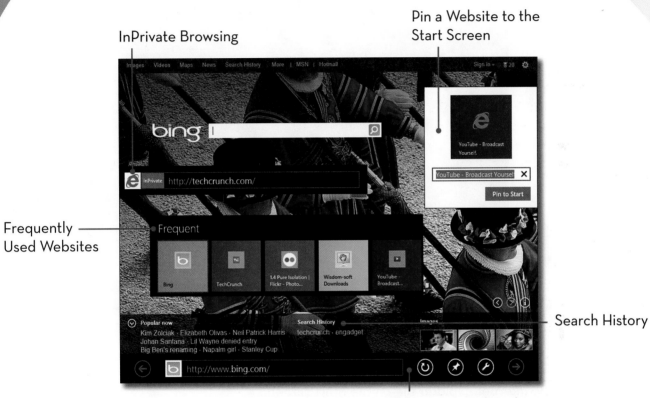

Address Bar and Tools

STARTING IE10 FROM THE START SCREEN

You can start Internet Explorer 10 from the Start screen of the new Windows 8 interface. The Internet Explorer tile is visible without scrolling, so you can launch it as soon as you log into Windows 8.

Click the Internet Explorer tile on the Start screen.

Type the URL in the IE10 address bar.

Use the IE10 Refresh button to reload the website.

Use the IE10 Pin site button to add a site to the Start screen.

Use the IE10 Tools button to find text or view the web page on the Windows desktop.

End

ENTERING A WEBSITE ADDRESS (URL)

Internet Explorer 10 includes a feature called AutoComplete. This feature displays the most common websites that match what you type in the address bar.

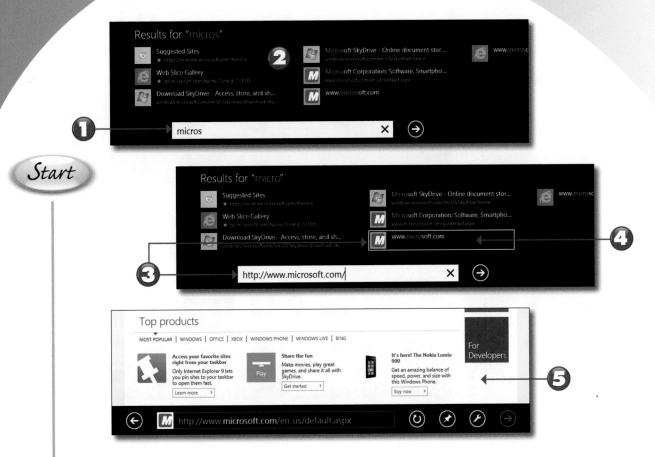

Start

1. Begin typing the name of a website. You do not need to include the "www."

2. IE10 displays the most popular websites with matching names online.

3. If you scroll through the list with your keyboard, the selected website is highlighted and placed in the address bar.

4. Click the website you want to open.

5. The website loads into your browser.

End

WORKING WITH TABS IN IE10

You can open a website link in a new tab and easily switch from one tab to another tab in Internet Explorer 10. Here's how to work with tabs in IE10.

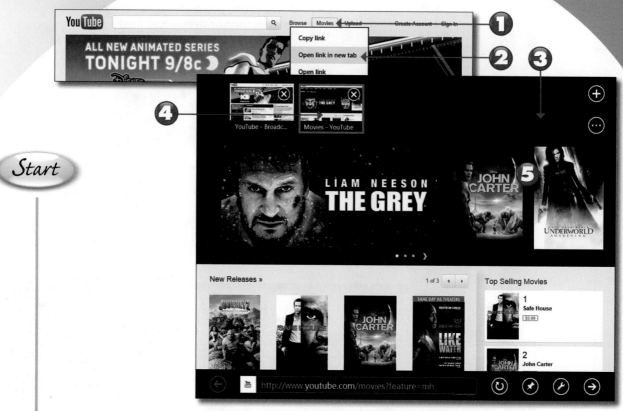

Start

1 Right-click a link.

2 Click **Open link in new tab**.

3 Right-click a blank area in the browser window.

4 Select the tab you want to display.

5 The tab appears in the main window.

End

NOTE

Tab Switching Repeat steps 3–5 to switch between tabs. ■

CREATING A NEW TAB IN IE10

With Internet Explorer 10, you can also create a new tab by using the New Tab button. Here's the process.

Start

1 Right-click a blank area on the screen.

2 Click the **New Tab** (+) button.

3 Enter a URL or click a thumbnail.

End

TIP

New Tab Keyboard Shortcut You also can press Ctrl+T in Internet Explorer 10 to add a new tab to the browser window. ■

USING INPRIVATE BROWSING

Internet Explorer 10 supports the InPrivate browsing feature originally introduced in IE8, but makes it easier to get to. Here's how to use it so you can surf and shop without leaving traces of your web activity behind.

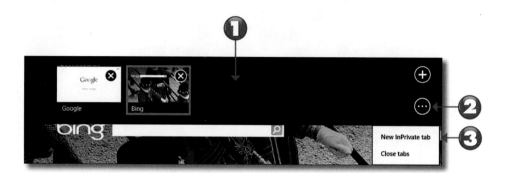

1 Right-click a blank area on the screen.

2 Click the **Tab tools** (three dots) button.

3 Click **New InPrivate tab**.

Continued

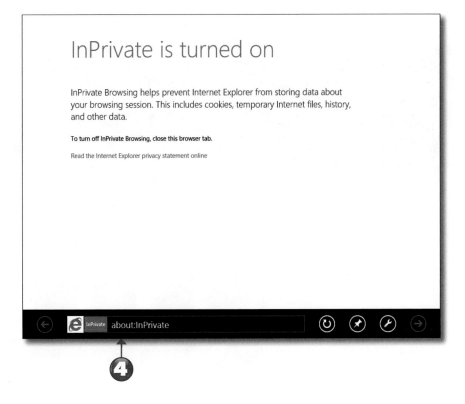

InPrivate is turned on

InPrivate Browsing helps prevent Internet Explorer from storing data about your browsing session. This includes cookies, temporary Internet files, history, and other data.

To turn off InPrivate Browsing, close this browser tab.

Read the Internet Explorer privacy statement online

InPrivate   about:InPrivate

4 The InPrivate tab opens. Enter the desired URL in the address bar.

End

NOTE

InPrivate Browsing and Browser History Your browser history does not list any sites you visited while using InPrivate Browsing. ■

REOPENING A FREQUENTLY USED WEB PAGE

Internet Explorer 10 enables you to choose from frequently visited pages right from the browser's address bar. Here's how it works.

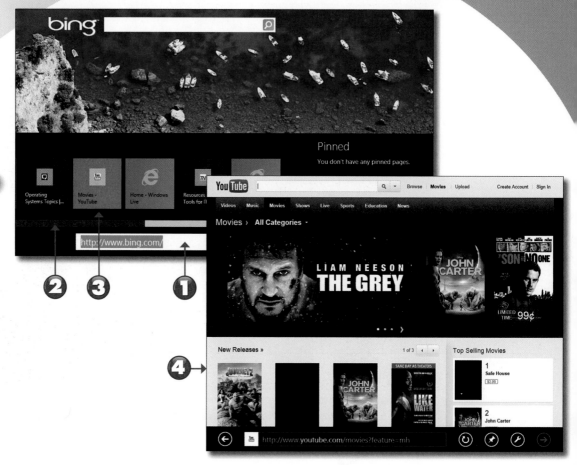

Start

1. Click the address bar.

2. Scroll to the right, if necessary, to view all Frequent pages in the list.

3. Click an icon.

4. The page opens.

End

NOTE

Building a List of Frequent Entries Microsoft pre-loads some web pages, so the Frequent list includes entries the first time you run IE10 from the Start screen. The pages you visit most often are added to the Frequent list. ■

REMOVING AN ENTRY FROM THE FREQUENT LIST

You can reduce the number of pages displayed in the Frequent list by removing unwanted entries. Here's how to omit entries from the list.

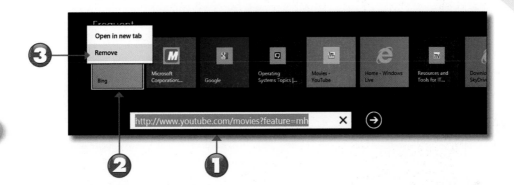

Start

1. Click the address bar.

2. Right-click the entry in the Frequent list that you want to remove.

3. Select **Remove**.

4. The selected item is removed.

End

PINNING A PAGE TO THE START SCREEN

Windows 8 makes getting to your favorite websites easy with the Pin to Start screen option. Here's how it works.

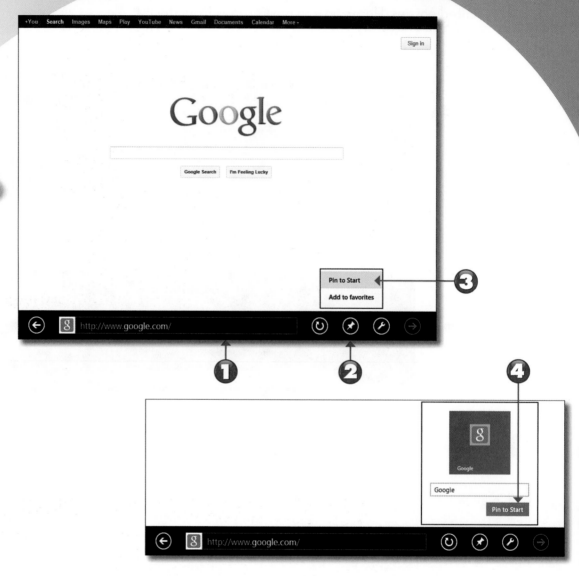

Start

1. Right-click the bottom of the screen.

2. Click the **Pin site** button.

3. Click **Pin to Start**.

4. Click **Pin to Start**.

Continued

5 The page is added to the Start screen.

6 The page is also added to the Pinned list.

End

UNPINNING A PAGE FROM THE START SCREEN

Sooner or later, pages you have pinned to the Start screen will no longer be as important to you. Thankfully, they're easy to remove.

Start

① Click the address bar.

② Right-click a page to remove and select **Remove**.

③ Click **Unpin from Start**.

End

CLOSING A TAB IN IE10

After you're finished viewing a tab—including an InPrivate Browsing tab—you can close it in Internet Explorer 10.

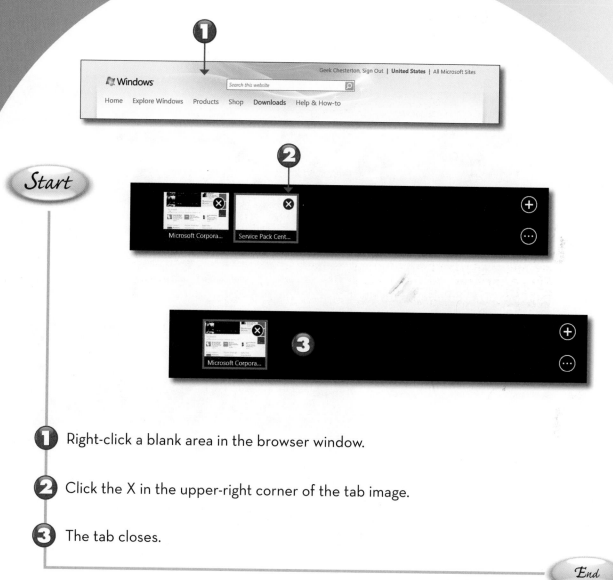

Right-click a blank area in the browser window.

Click the X in the upper-right corner of the tab image.

The tab closes.

CLOSING IE10

When you start Internet Explorer 10 from the Start screen, you drag the window to close the browser. Here's how.

1 Point to the top of the IE10 window. When the cursor changes to a hand icon, click and drag downwards.

2 Drag the IE10 window all the way down to the bottom of the screen until it disappears.

3 The Start screen appears.

TIP

Closing IE10 from the Keyboard You also can press Alt+F4 in Internet Explorer 10 to close the browser window. This shortcut closes all open tabs in IE10. ■

VIEWING A PAGE ON THE WINDOWS DESKTOP

Opening Internet Explorer 10 from the Windows 8 Start screen provides stream-lined access to IE10's most common features. However, if you want to set your home page, create a tab group, or print a web page, you need to display the web page in the Windows desktop version of IE10.

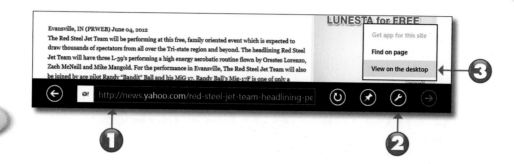

Start

1 Open a website.

2 Click the **Tools** button.

3 Click **View on the desktop**.

4 The page opens in IE10 on the Windows desktop.

End

NOTE

Closing the Desktop Version of IE10 When you're ready to close the Desktop version of IE10, click the Close button in the upper-right corner of the IE10 window. ■

NOTE

Advanced Features in IE10 To learn about advanced Internet Explorer 10 features available from the classic Windows desktop, see Chapter 16, "Browsing the Internet from Your Desktop." ■

Chapter 6

ENJOYING MEDIA WITH THE WINDOWS 8 UI

Among the many app tiles found on the Windows 8 Start screen are multimedia apps for viewing pictures, listening to music, watching videos, and other media tasks. You can use the Photos, Music, and Video apps, for example, to access media files. This chapter shows you how to tap into the multimedia content on your computer and find more content online.

Photos App

Web Camera App

Music App

Video App

PLAYING MUSIC

The new Music app in Windows 8 acts as a one-stop shop for your computer music needs, whether you want to listen to files on your computer or purchase more music online.

Start

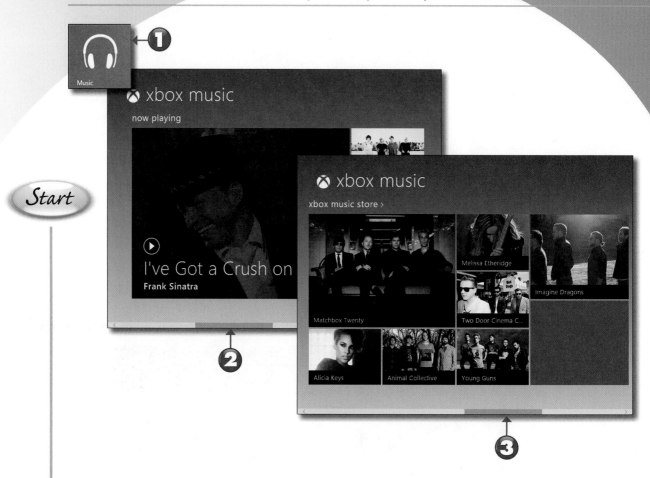

1 Click the **Music** tile.

2 Scroll to the middle to view featured or now-playing items.

3 Scroll to the right to view music store content and categories to peruse.

Continued

TIP

Sample It As you peruse the Xbox Music store, you can preview selections. Click an item to open it, and then click the Preview button to play a sample of the music. Learn more about buying music later in this chapter. ■

NOTE

Your Music Library Windows 8 includes a default folder—called the Music library—for organizing and storing your music files. You can view its contents using File Explorer on the Windows 8 desktop. Learn more about using File Explorer in Chapter 12, "Managing Storage with File Explorer." ■

 4 Scroll to the left to view your own music files.

5 To view an item, click or tap it.

6 To play a file, click **Play album**. You can also click a specific song from the list.

7 The Apps bar appears with playback and other controls.

End

TIP
Apps Bar Shortcut You can also right-click the screen or press Windows key+Z to display the Apps bar. ▪

NOTE
Change Your Preference If you prefer to view your own music files as soon as you open the Music app, you can change the default view. With the Music app open, press Windows key+C to display the Charms bar, and then click or tap Settings, Preferences. Switch the Startup view option to On. ▪

VIEWING VIDEO

You can use the Video app to view video clips on your computer, or search for online content available through the Microsoft Store.

Start

① Click the **Video** tile.

② Scroll to the middle to view spotlighted videos.

③ Scroll to the right to view more online content, including movies and television shows.

Continued

TIP

Preview It As with music selections, you can preview clips and movie trailers for some video content in the online store. Click an item to open it, and then click the Play Trailer button to play a preview clip. To buy the content, click the Buy link. ■

4 Scroll to the left to view your own video files.

5 To view a file, click or tap it.

6 Right-click to display playback controls on the Apps bar.

End

NOTE

Your Videos Library Windows 8 includes a default folder—called the Videos library—for organizing and storing your video files. You can view its contents using File Explorer on the desktop. Learn more about using File Explorer in Chapter 12. ■

BUYING MUSIC AND VIDEOS

You can shop for music and videos online from within the Music and Video apps. Both apps access albums, movies, and television shows. Using your Microsoft account, you can purchase items for downloading or streaming.

Start

1. Display the album you want to buy.

2. Click **Buy album**, or select a specific song and click **Buy song**.

3. Review the purchase details here.

4. Click **Confirm**.

5. Click **Done**.

Continued

TIP

Microsoft Points You can make your purchases using points you add to your Microsoft account. If you do not have enough points to make a particular purchase, the app directs you to an account screen where you can buy more using your credit card. To access account details, click the Settings charm and click Account. ■

⑥ Open the video you want to buy from the Videos app and click **Buy** or **Rent**. For TV shows, you'll see a View seasons option.

⑦ Review the purchase details and click **Next**.

⑧ Log on to your Microsoft account; type your password, and click **OK**.

⑨ Click **Confirm**.

⑩ Click **Done**.

⑪ Click **Play** to stream your purchase, or click **Download** to save it to your computer.

End

TIP

Search for It You can use the Search feature on the Charms bar to conduct an online search for a particular music artist, album, or video. Press Windows key+C to display the Charms bar, and then click the Search charm and type your search text. ■

VIEWING PICTURES

You can use the Photos app to view digital pictures stored on your computer, SkyDrive, Facebook, Flickr, or other devices you attach to the computer. You can choose a variety of ways to view your photos, including the default view, which automatically opens a photo in full-screen view.

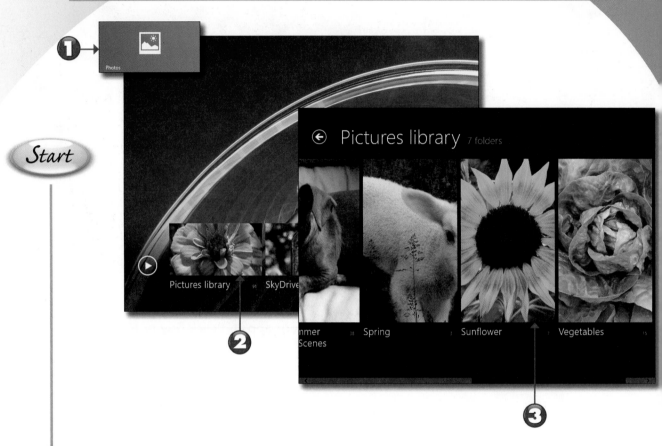

Start

Click or tap the **Photos** app.

Click the location of your photos.

Click the folder you want to view.

Continued

TIP

Importing Photos When you plug in a camera, the Photos app offers to help you import the files. You can also start the import from within the Photos app. Just right-click the Start screen or press Windows key+Z to display the Apps bar, and click Import to get started. ■

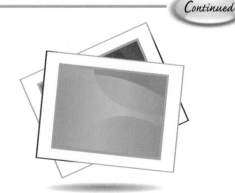

4 Click the photo you want to view.

5 The photo opens in full-screen mode. Press **Esc** to return to the Photos app, or click the navigation arrow.

End

TIP

Slide Show To view your photos as a slide show, right-click the screen or press Windows key+Z to display the Apps bar, and then click Slide show. ■

NOTE

Sharing Photos You can easily email a photo or series of photos directly from the Photos app. Right-click a photo to select it, and then press Windows key+C to display the Charms bar and click the Share charm. You can then choose to share the photo via email or SkyDrive. ■

UPLOADING PHOTOS WITH SKYDRIVE

You can use Microsoft's online cloud storage to save your digital photos and view them with the Photos app, as well as share them with others online, through your mobile device, or across computer platforms. You will need a Microsoft account to use the SkyDrive services.

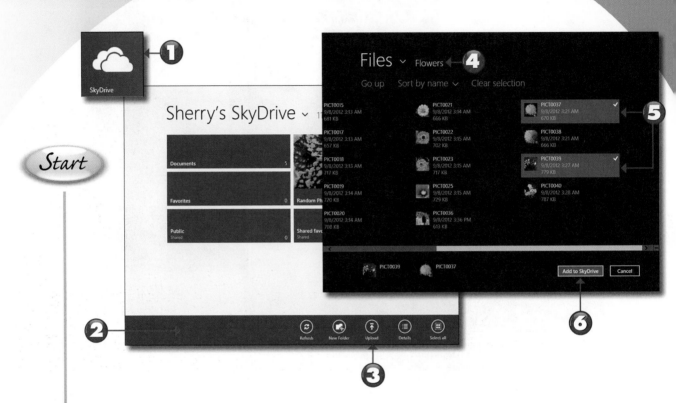

Start

Click or tap the **SkyDrive** app.

Right-click the screen or press Windows key+Z to display the Apps bar.

Click **Upload**.

Navigate to the folder containing the photos you want to upload.

Select the file or files you want to upload.

Click **Add to SkyDrive**.

End

GRABBING PHOTOS WITH YOUR WEBCAM

You can use your computer's built-in camera to take photos of yourself in front of the computer. You might use such a picture to email someone or to create an account picture. Pictures you take with the built-in camera are stored in a folder labeled Camera Roll in your Pictures library.

Start

1 Click or tap the **Camera** tile.

2 Click or tap the screen to take a photo.

3 Click the left navigation arrow to view the picture.

4 Right-click to view the Apps bar if you want to crop or delete the picture.

End

TIP

More Options! You can use the Timer option on the Apps bar to start a three-second delay before the photo is taken. You can use the Video mode button to record a video using the camera. To change resolution or audio devices, click the Camera options button. ∎

Chapter 7

STAYING CONNECTED WITH WINDOWS 8 APPS

The Windows 8 Start screen offers a plethora of apps to help you stay connected with friends, family, coworkers, and the world at large. This chapter shows you how to use the new email features, message friends, add contacts, schedule appointments, and look up places, weather, and news.

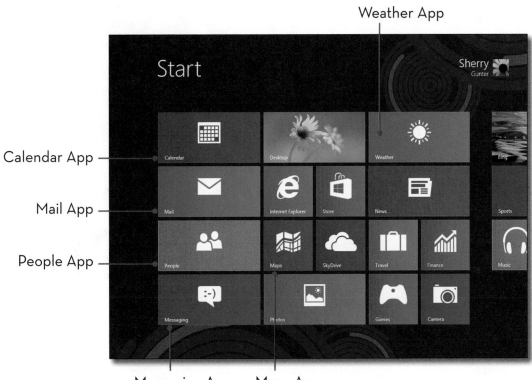

Weather App

Start

Sherry
Gunter

Calendar App

Mail App

People App

Messaging App   Maps App

SETTING UP EMAIL ACCOUNTS

You can use the Mail app to manage and organize your email tasks. You can use the app to send and receive email, send file attachments, and filter out junk email. The first time you use the app, you might need to set up your email account. You can add multiple email accounts to Mail, including your Hotmail, Gmail, Yahoo!, and Exchange accounts.

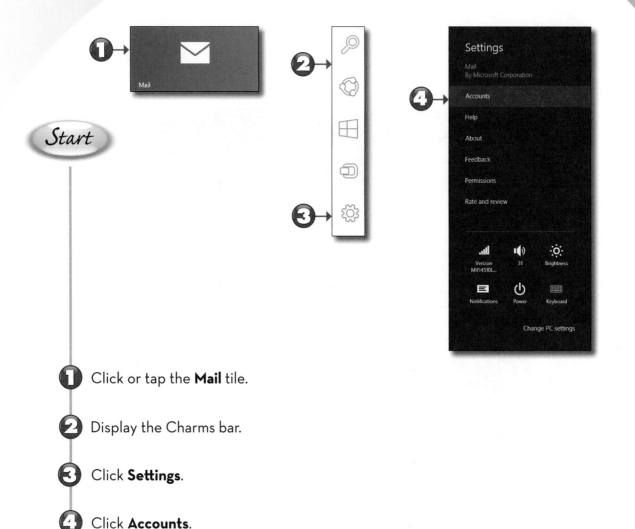

Start

1. Click or tap the **Mail** tile.

2. Display the Charms bar.

3. Click **Settings**.

4. Click **Accounts**.

Continued

TIP
Charms Shortcut You can press Windows key+C to quickly open the Charms bar. ■

CAUTION
Safety First Always be diligent regarding the unknown items you receive in your email accounts, particularly spam and phishing email. Spam is email that is sent out to thousands of accounts. Some spam can contain computer viruses. Also be wary of phishing emails, which are financial scams requesting credit card or bank account numbers from you on some pretext, only to ultimately steal from you instead. ■

 Click **Add an account**.

Choose an account type.

Type in your account email address.

Type in your password.

Click **Connect**. Mail adds the account.

End

NOTE

Creating a Free Email Account You can find free email services on the Web, including Hotmail and Google. You must sign up with an Internet service provider (ISP) to use Windows 8 Mail and set up an email address either with that provider or with some other source. You also must set up your account in Mail using the username and password you established with your email provider. ◼

NOTE

PDF Reader Windows 8 includes Windows Reader for viewing PDF apps. However, if you need more features, you can download or purchase alternatives from the Books & Reference category of the Microsoft Store. ◼

READING AND REPLYING TO EMAILS

You can easily read and respond to email messages from multiple email accounts in the new Mail app. You also can delete messages you no longer want, move messages into different folders, and save draft messages.

Start

Inbox
Drafts
Outbox
[Gmail]
    All Mail
    Important
    Sent Mail
    Spam
    Starred
    Trash
Personal
Receipts
Travel
Work
Gmail
Yahoo

Yahoo Inbox

Matt
RE: Fall Festival   4:17 PM

Matt
September 9, 2012 4:17 PM
To: Sherry

RE: Fall Festival

What time would you like to get started? I think the festival opens at 9 or 10.

Matt

From: sw
To: matt
Subject: RE: Fall Festival
Date: Sun, 9 Sep 2012 16:15:39 -0400

Sounds like fun! Count me in!

Sherry

From: Matt
Sent: Sunday, September 09, 2012 2:12 PM
To: Sherry
Subject: Fall Festival

Don't forget, the annual Fall Festival is happening this next weekend over in Willard Park. Would you like to

1 From the Mail app, click the account you want to check.

2 Click **Inbox**.

3 Click the message you want to read.

4 The message is displayed in the message pane.

Continued

TIP

Sync It To manually check your email, display the Mail app's Apps bar (press Windows key+Z), and then click the Sync button. Windows 8 checks your accounts and displays any new messages. ■

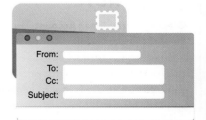

From:
To:
Cc:
Subject:

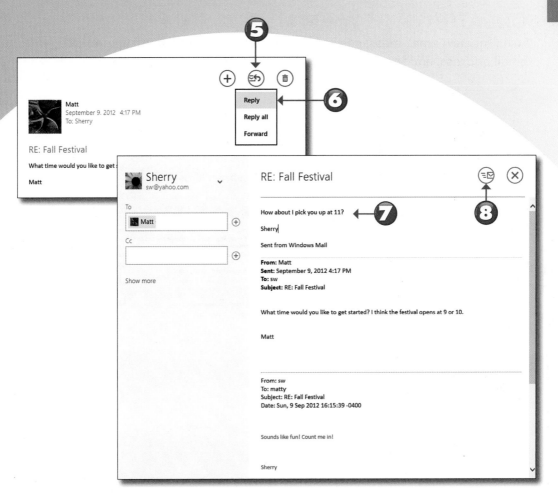

5 To send a reply, click **Respond**.

6 Click **Reply**.

7 Fill out your reply.

8 Click **Send**.

End

TIP
Forwarding a Message To forward a message, click the Respond button, and then click Forward. Mail adds FW: (short for forward) to the message subject line. ■

NOTE
Sent Folder Sent messages are stored in your account's Sent Mail folder. ■

CREATING A NEW EMAIL MESSAGE

Creating new email messages is surprisingly simple in Mail. All you need is the person's email address, and then you just add your own subject line and message text.

Start

① In your email account, click the **New** button.

② Type in the recipient's email address.

③ Type in a subject title.

④ Type in the message text.

⑤ Click **Send**.

End

TIP

Show More You can click the Show More link in the left pane to view options for adding a BCC (blind carbon copy) or assigning a priority level to the message. ■

TIP

Draft It If you are not ready to email the message yet, you can save it as a draft. Press Windows key+Z to display the Apps bar, and then click Save Draft. ■

ATTACHING A FILE TO A MESSAGE

You can attach a file to a message you want to send. File attachments, such as documents or pictures, are easily attached using the Attachments option on the Apps bar.

Press Windows key+Z to display the Apps bar.

Click **Attachments**.

Navigate to the folder containing the file you want to attach.

Click the file, and then click **Attach**.

The attached file appears with the message, ready to send.

NOTE

Opening File Attachments To open a file attachment, simply click the filename. The associated app or program opens to display the file. ■

CHATTING WITH THE MESSAGING APP

The Messaging app lets you chat with other users logged on at the same time as you. When you chat with someone via messaging, it happens in real time in a scrollable conversation. You can use the app to chat with Facebook users, Windows Live users, and more.

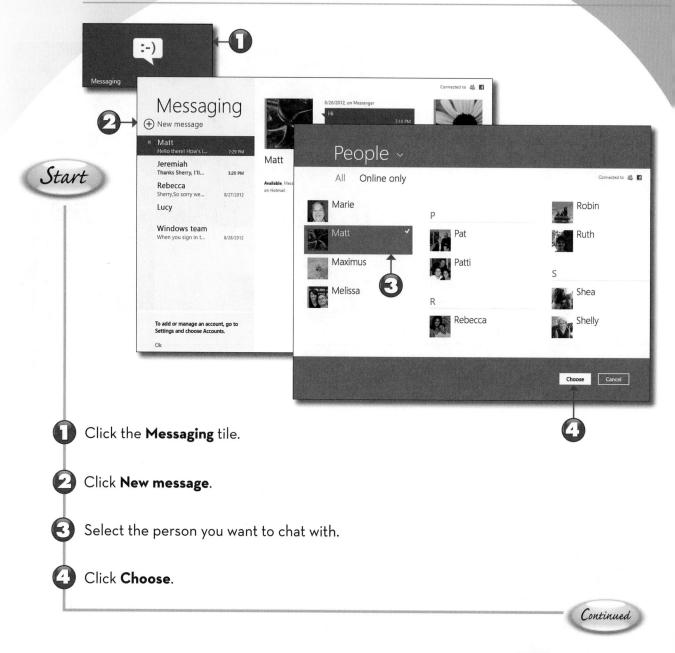

Start

1 Click the **Messaging** tile.

2 Click **New message**.

3 Select the person you want to chat with.

4 Click **Choose**.

Continued

NOTE

What Services Does Messaging Use? You can chat with people on Facebook and Microsoft Messenger at this time. Additional chat options might become available at a later date. ■

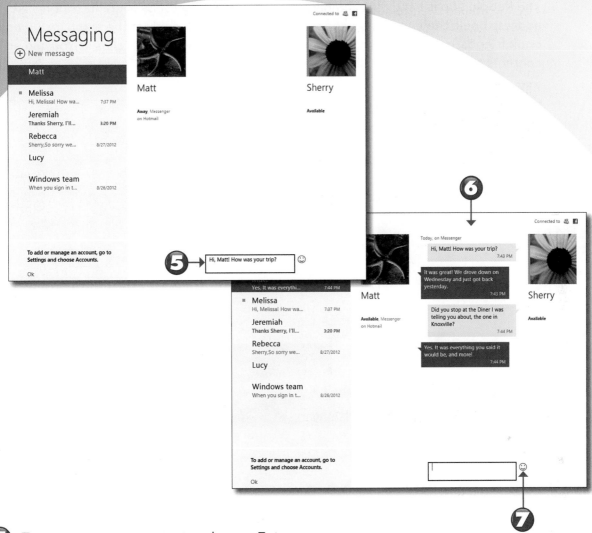

5 Type in your message text and press Enter.

6 The conversation scrolls here.

7 To add emoticons to your chat, click here and select an icon to insert.

End

TIP
Chat Options You can display the Messaging app's Apps bar to view options for inviting others to chat, a reporting feature, and a delete option for removing a conversation from your screen. To view the Apps bar, press Windows key+Z. ■

ADDING CONTACTS WITH THE PEOPLE APP

The People app is handy for compiling and maintaining a list of contacts. Acting like a digital address book, the People app keeps a list of people you contact the most, including Facebook friends, email contacts, and more. To view a contact, simply click it. You can add new contacts as needed.

1 Click or tap the **People** app.

2 Press Windows key+Z to display the Apps bar.

3 Click **New**.

4 Fill out the contact form with as many details as needed.

5 Click **Save**.

Continued

NOTE

Which Accounts Work with the People App? You can configure a variety of accounts to work with the People app, including Facebook, Google, Hotmail, Exchange, LinkedIn, and Twitter. ■

8 → ⊕ Ralph Kinkoph

Email
ralph@dogdays.com
Work

Other info
Dog Days Designs
Company

Yahoo, Facebook

Home Pin to Start Favorite Link Edit Delete

7

6 The People app creates the new contact.

7 Press Windows key+Z to view the Apps bar with additional options to set.

8 Click the **Back** button to return to the main People screen.

End

TIP

Troubleshooting If you ever find yourself stuck on a contact screen, press Windows key+Z to view the Apps bar and click Home. This takes you back to the default view of the app. ■

NOTE

Changing Views You can use the People app to view social notifications from accounts such as Facebook, favorite people, and an alphabetized listing of all your contacts. The What's New area opens the latest social account postings. ■

VIEWING YOUR CALENDAR

You can use the Calendar app to keep track of your schedule, including daily appointments, events, and other special occasions. You can switch between three different views of your calendar: Month, Week, and Day.

Start

1 Click the **Calendar** app.

2 In month view, click the arrows to move from month to month.

3 Press Windows key+Z to display the Apps bar.

4 Click **Day** to display your calendar by day.

Continued

NOTE

Calendar Views Month view is the default view when you open the Calendar app for the first time. You can switch between all the views using the Apps bar. ■

5 Click **Week** to display your calendar by week.

6 To view the current day, click **Today**.

End

TIP

Calendar Options You can change the colors displayed for birthdays and holidays on your calendar. With the Calendar app open, press Windows key+C to display the Charms bar, click Settings, and then click Options. ■

SCHEDULING APPOINTMENTS WITH CALENDAR

You can use the Calendar app to keep track of your schedule, including daily appointments, events, and other special occasions.

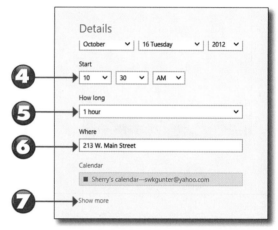

Start

1. Open the Calendar app and click the appointment date.

2. Type a title for the appointment.

3. Optionally, type any message text to be included.

4. Set a start time.

5. Set a duration.

6. Specify a location.

7. Click **Show more** to view additional options.

Continued

 8 To make the appointment a recurring appointment, click here and make a selection.

9 To add a reminder alarm, click here and set a time.

10 To show a status setting on your shared calendar, click here and make your selection.

11 Click **Save**.

12 The appointment appears on the calendar.

End

NOTE

Types of Appointments You can use the additional appointment options to specify a recurring appointment, such as a weekly staff meeting, or specify an event, such as a birthday or anniversary. Click the How Often drop-down menu and make your selection. ■

TIP

Editing Appointments To edit an appointment, simply select it on the calendar and make changes to the appointment form page. To remove an appointment, click the Delete button on the form page. ■

FINDING LOCATIONS WITH THE MAPS APP

The Maps app works with Microsoft's Bing website to help you find locations around the world or down the street. You can find directions, look up an address, or view your current location. In this task, you learn how to look up a location and find directions.

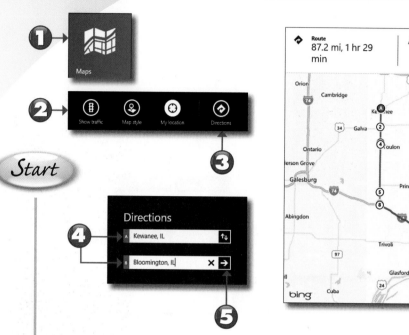

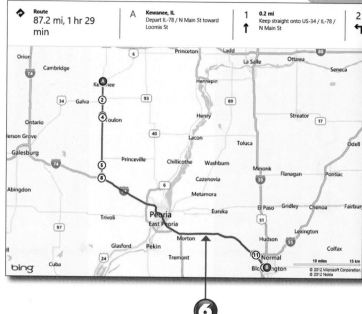

1. Click the **Maps** app.

2. Press Windows key+Z to display the Apps bar.

3. Click **Directions**.

4. Fill in the starting and destination points.

5. Click **Get Directions**.

6. Maps displays a suggested route.

Continued

NOTE

Location Services The first time you use the Maps app, you might be prompted to turn on location services to activate the app. ■

TIP

Zooming Your View You can use the Zoom buttons (the plus and minus buttons that appear when you click on the map) to zoom your map view in or out. ■

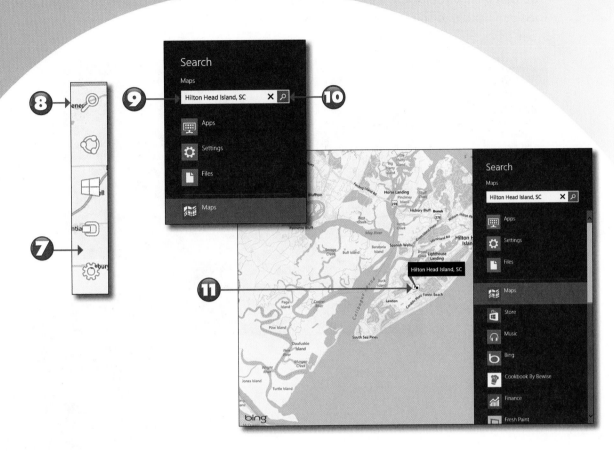

7 To look up a location, display the Charms bar.

8 Click **Search**.

9 Type a location.

10 Press **Enter** or click **Search**.

11 The location appears on the map.

End

TIP

Changing the Map View You can switch the map between Road view and Aerial view by clicking the Map style button on the Apps bar. ■

TIP

Checking Traffic To include the latest traffic information on your map, click the Show traffic button on the Apps bar. ■

CHECKING WEATHER WITH THE WEATHER APP

You can check your local weather report using the Weather app. You can specify favorite locations and see the latest forecast.

Start

① Click the **Weather** app.

② Press Windows key+Z to display the Apps bar.

③ Click **Places**.

④ Click **Add**.

Continued

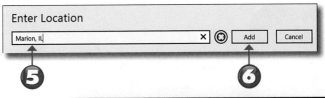

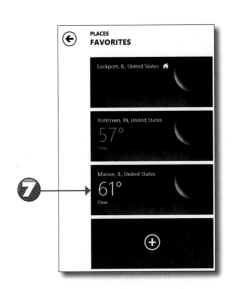

 Type a location.

 Click Add.

Click the new location.

The Weather app displays the information.

End

NOTE

Activate It The first time you use the Weather app, you might be prompted to turn on your current city to retrieve the latest data pertaining to your location. ■

TIP

Changing Default Locations To create a new default location that appears as soon as you open the Weather app, press Windows key+Z to display the Apps bar, and click the Set as default button.

Chapter 8

CUSTOMIZING THE WINDOWS 8 START SCREEN

The Windows 8 Start screen and its default appearance provide fast, easy access to the new Windows 8 apps. However, you can customize what's on the Start screen and make it your own by changing its appearance and settings. This chapter shows you how.

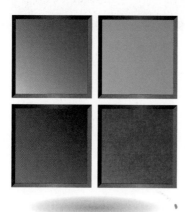

Right-Click Options for an App

Pinning a Website to the Start Screen

Some General PC Settings

Live and Static Weather Tiles

Previewing Lock Screen Options

PINNING A WEBSITE TO THE START SCREEN

If you access a particular website frequently but you don't want to make it your home page, you can add it to the Start screen. Here's how.

(1) Click **Internet Explorer**.

(2) Go to the website you want to pin.

(3) Click the **Pin site** button.

(4) Click **Pin to Start**.

Continued

5 Enter a descriptive name (optional).

6 Click **Pin to Start**.

7 The website is added to the right side of the Start screen.

End

NOTE

Desktop Apps on the Start Screen To learn how to add desktop apps to the Start screen, see Chapter 11, "Running Desktop Apps." ■

TIP

Adding Websites to the Start Screen from the Desktop If you run Internet Explorer from the Windows desktop, you can use the Tools menu to add a website to the Start screen. Open the Tools menu in IE and select Add Site to Start Screen. ■

PINNING A FOLDER TO THE START SCREEN

Just as you might want fast access to a particular website directly from the Start screen, you might also want one-click access to a folder that you use frequently. Here's how to add a folder to your Start screen.

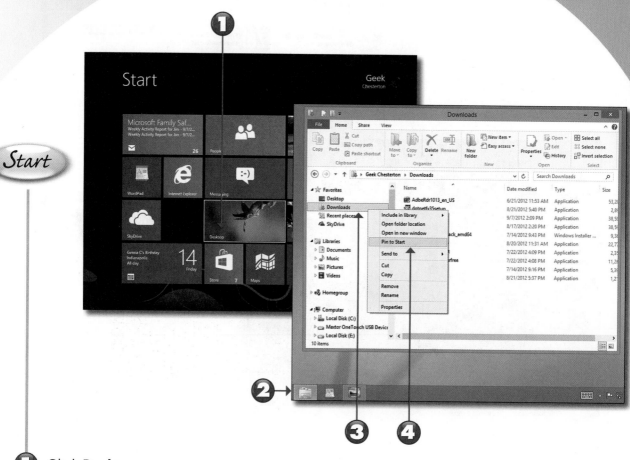

Start

① Click **Desktop**.

② Click **File Explorer**.

③ Right-click the folder to pin.

④ Select **Pin to Start**.

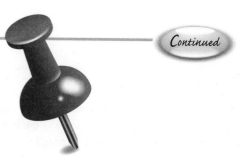

Continued

5 The folder is added to the right side of the Start screen.

End

TIP

Pin, Pin, and Pin Again You can also pin Favorites such as Downloads, Desktop, and Computer to the Windows 8 Start screen, using the same steps outlined here. ∎

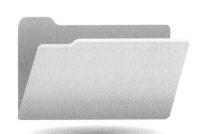

RELOCATING TILES ON THE START SCREEN

You can rearrange the tiles on the Start screen by simply dragging them to the location you want. Use this technique to place the tiles you use most on the left side of the Start screen, so they appear first.

1 Click and hold the tile you want to move.

2 Drag the tile to the preferred location.

3 Release the mouse button to drop the tile.

End

NOTE

Big Tiles for Real-Time Updates Programs that display updates in real time typically use double-width tiles for legibility, such as Photos, News, Mail, and People. ■

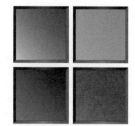

UNPINNING AN OBJECT FROM THE START SCREEN

If you decide you don't need a particular item on the Start screen, removing it is easy. Apps you unpin from the Start screen can still be started from the All Apps screen.

1 Right-click the tile you want to remove.

2 Click **Unpin from Start**.

3 The tile disappears and nearby objects realign automatically.

End

NOTE

Desktop Right-Click Options If you right-click a desktop application, you will see options such as Pin to Taskbar, Open New Window, Run as Administrator, or Open File Location. To learn more about these options, see Chapter 11. ■

NOTE

Uninstalling an App If Uninstall is listed as an option when you right-click a tile, you can remove the app from your system. Keep in mind that if you uninstall an app, you can't use it again until you reinstall it. You might not be able to use another program to open data you created with that app. ■

ADJUSTING THE SIZE OF START SCREEN TILES

Windows 8 uses square tiles for some apps and rectangular double-width tiles for apps that display live content or updates. However, if you want to change the default size settings for some tiles, here's how to do it.

1 Right-click a rectangular tile.

2 Click **Smaller**.

3 Resized Weather, Calendar, and Mail icons still display live content.

Continued

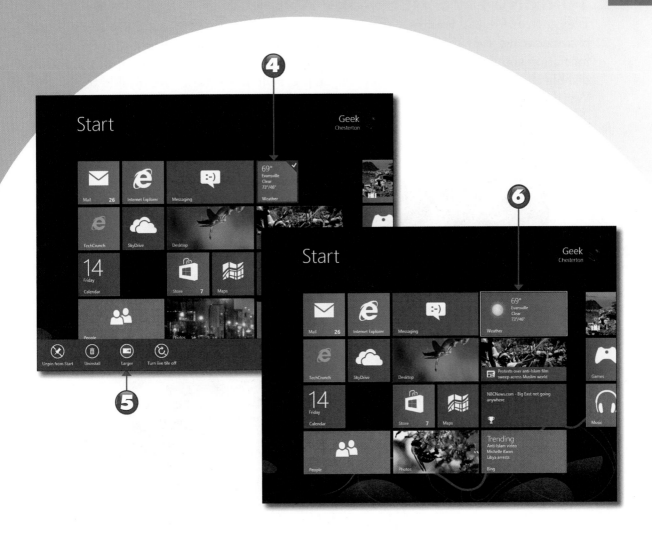

4 Right-click a square tile.

5 Click **Larger**.

6 Tile at larger (original) size.

End

NOTE

Tiles That Can't Be Resized Tiles that cannot be resized do not list Larger or Smaller as options when you right-click them. ∎

TURNING LIVE TILES OFF AND ON

Tiles such as Photos, Weather, Sports, News, Messaging, and others are live tiles—Photos provides a live slide show of your photos, while others provide real-time updates of information and social network updates. If you prefer not to see real-time updates, you can disable the live tile feature for any tiles you prefer. In this tutorial, we disable the live tile for Weather and then restore the live tile.

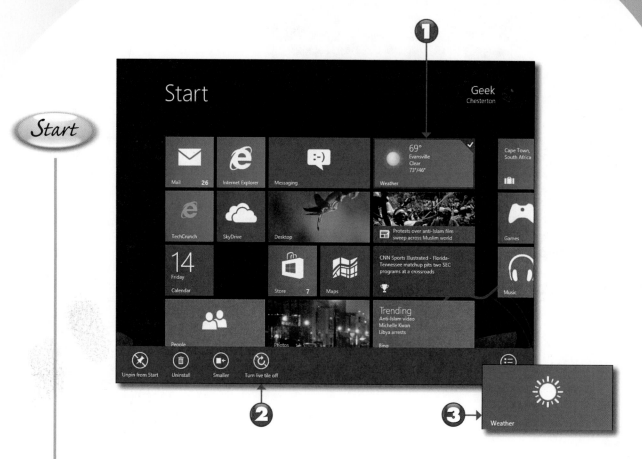

1 Right-click a live tile.

2 Click **Turn live tile off**.

3 The tile now displays static content instead of live content.

Continued

4 Right-click a tile that was previously live.

5 Click **Turn live tile on**.

6 The tile provides live content again.

End

PERSONALIZING THE LOCK SCREEN

Windows 8 enables you to give your computer a unique look through its Personalize settings. In this lesson, you learn how to select and customize the lock screen—the screen that greets you when you turn on your device or need to unlock it.

 Hover the mouse or swipe in from either right corner of the screen.

 Click **Settings**.

 Click **Change PC settings**.

Continued

NOTE

Real-Time Settings Updates The changes you make on the PC settings screen take effect immediately. ■

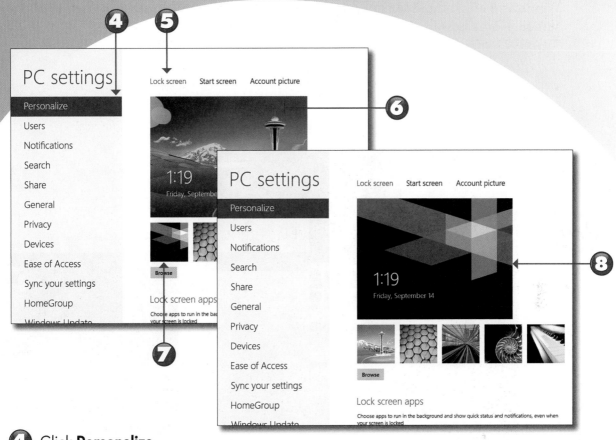

4 Click **Personalize**.

5 Click **Lock screen**.

6 Current lock screen.

7 Click a different lock screen.

8 A preview of the new lock screen.

End

TIP

Browse to Find More Choices Use the Browse button
to locate other photos or images you'd like to use as your
lock screen, such as family or personal photos. ■

PERSONALIZING THE START SCREEN

Windows 8 offers thousands of possible combinations of colors and patterns for its Start screen. Here's how to choose your favorites from the PC settings screen.

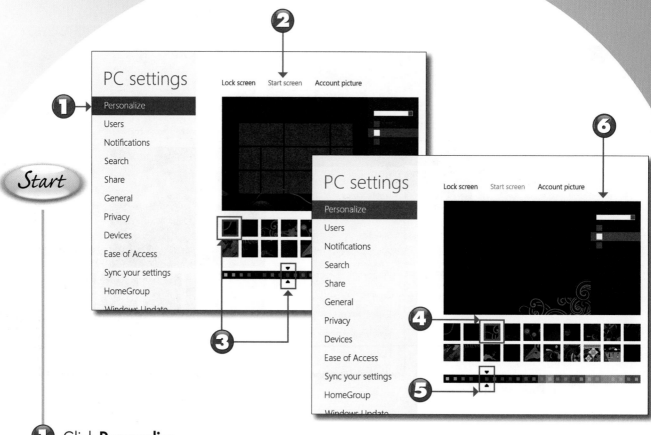

1 Click **Personalize**.

2 Click **Start screen**.

3 The current border and color settings.

4 Select a different border.

5 Select a different color setting.

6 The Start screen preview changes to reflect your new settings.

CHANGING TIME ZONE SETTINGS

If you travel with your laptop or tablet, you might need to change the current time zone. Use the General section of PC settings to make this change.

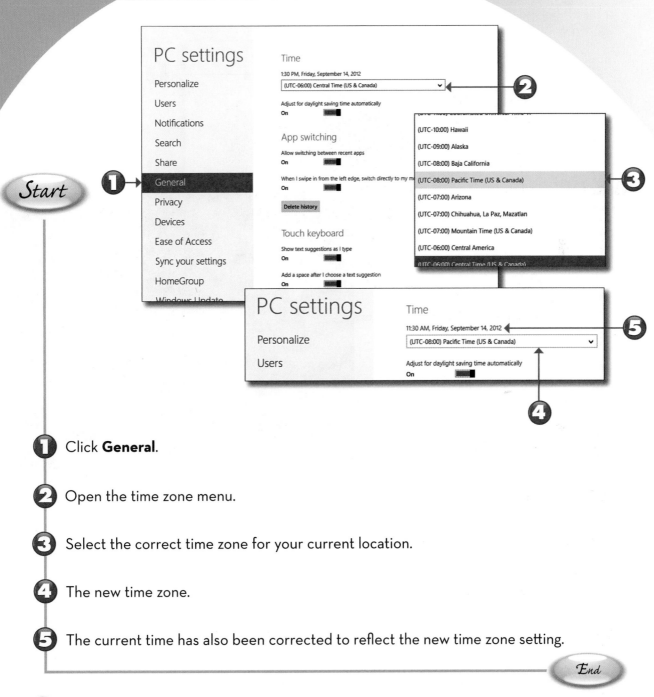

Start

1 Click **General**.

2 Open the time zone menu.

3 Select the correct time zone for your current location.

4 The new time zone.

5 The current time has also been corrected to reflect the new time zone setting.

End

NOTE

Desktop Time Zone Adjustments If you prefer, you can also make date and time adjustments from the Notification area on the Windows desktop or via the Control Panel. ■

CHOOSING A PHOTO FOR YOUR ACCOUNT PICTURE

You can select your favorite photo or use a webcam to create a picture for your account.
This picture will show up on your login screen and will also be used with social network
features. Here's how to select a photo from the Personalize screen.

Start

1. Click **Account picture**.

2. Click **Browse**.

3. Click a folder that contains the picture you want to use.

Continued

NOTE

Already Have an Account Picture? Here's Why In this example, there's already an account
picture for this account. This can happen if you sign in to your system using a Microsoft
account and set up an account picture for your Microsoft account. A Microsoft account syn-
chronizes favorites, account pictures, and other settings between computers. ■

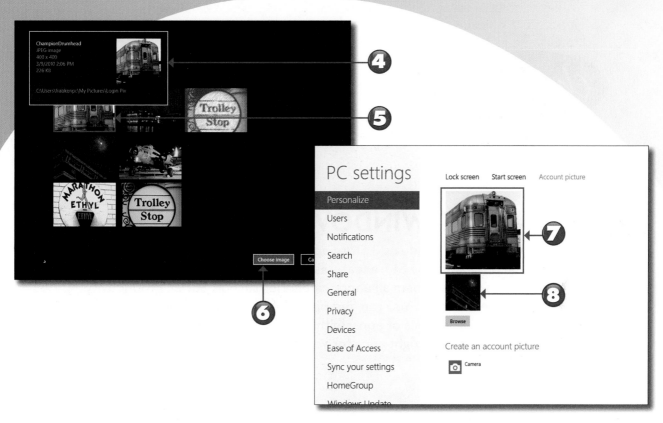

4 Hover your mouse over a photo for more information.

5 Click the picture you want to use.

6 Click **Choose image**.

7 Your new picture will be used the next time you log in to your system.

8 To revert to your previous picture, click it.

End

NOTE

Clearing Account Picture History If you don't want to see your previous account picture, right-click it and select Clear History. ■

Chapter 9

USING THE WINDOWS 8 STORE

You can use the new Windows 8 Store app to shop online for more apps and commercial programs. The Store features a wide variety of apps for a wide variety of uses and lists them all under categories such as Social, Productivity, Tools, and Entertainment. You can find plenty of free apps or paid apps in the Store, or even trial versions of apps. In this chapter, you learn how to navigate the Store to find just the right apps for your computer.

The Microsoft
Store App

Popular
Free Apps

Scroll to see additional
categories of apps.

Newly Released Apps

GOING TO THE STORE

When you first open the Store app, the Spotlight screen displays currently featured apps and links to the most popular apps and new releases. As you scroll through the Store, you can find categories of apps to explore. You can use the Store's Apps bar to navigate back to the Spotlight view or visit a list of apps you have previously installed. You can also sort the list of apps you view in any category, such as sorting by new releases or ratings.

Start

1 Click or tap the **Store** tile.

2 The default view, called the Spotlight, displays featured apps.

3 Scroll to the right to view app categories.

4 Click a category you want to view.

Continued

NOTE

More Apps Microsoft is constantly updating the Store with new apps, so be sure to shop often to see the latest releases. ■

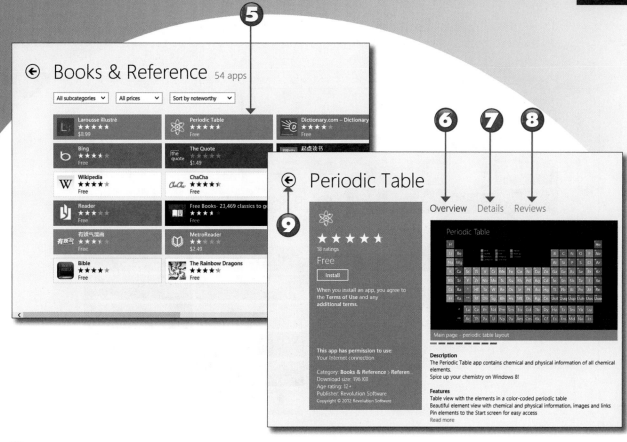

5 Click the app you want to view.

6 Click **Overview** to learn more about the app.

7 Click **Details** to view release notes, language availability, and system requirements.

8 Click **Reviews** to view user reviews about the app.

9 Click **Back** to return to the app category list.

Continued

NOTE

Sign Up If you have not yet created a Microsoft account, you will need one to buy apps. With the Store app open, press Windows key+C to display the Charms bar, and then click Settings. Click the Your Account link and click Sign Up for a Microsoft Account. Follow the onscreen prompts to establish your account. To learn more about adding payment methods to your account, see the task, "Adding a Payment Method to Your Account," at the end of this chapter. ∎

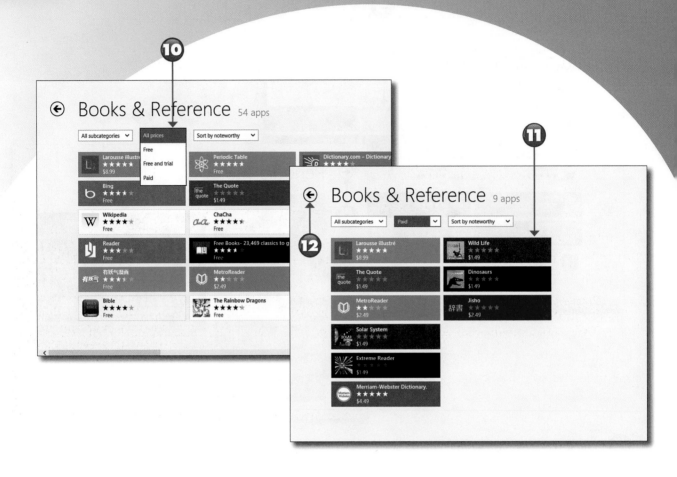

10 To sort a category, click the sort field and choose a criterion.

11 The list is immediately sorted.

12 To return to the main Store view, click the **Back** button.

Continued

NOTE

Start Screen Apps vs. Desktop Apps Some of the content available in the Microsoft Store includes desktop apps, which run exclusively on the Windows 8 desktop. This means the programs run in their own windows, not integrated with the Start screen. You can pin a desktop app to the Start screen for easy startup. Learn more about desktop apps in Chapter 11, "Running Desktop Apps." ■

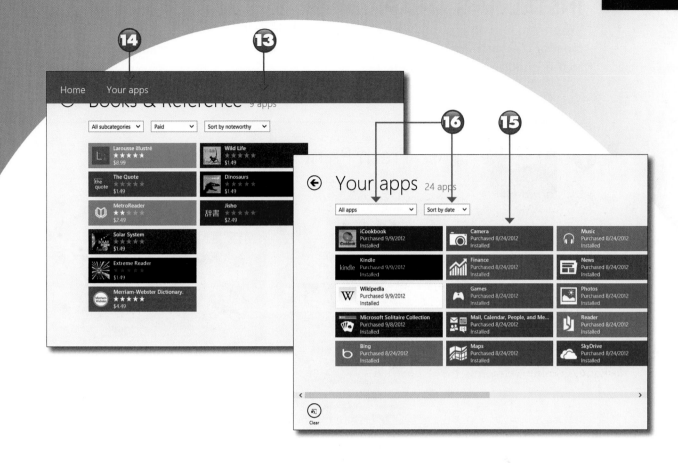

13 To view the Store's Apps bar, press Windows key+Z or right-click the screen.

14 Click **Your apps**.

15 A list of installed apps appears.

16 Click either of these fields to sort the apps.

End

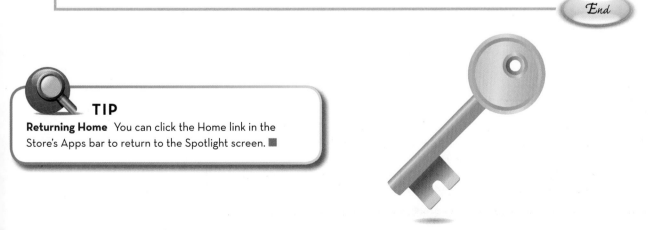

TIP
Returning Home You can click the Home link in the Store's Apps bar to return to the Spotlight screen. ■

INSTALLING AN APP

When you find an app you want, you can easily install it in just a few clicks. Windows 8 does most of the hard work for you. When you install an app, a tile representing the app is added to the Windows 8 Start screen.

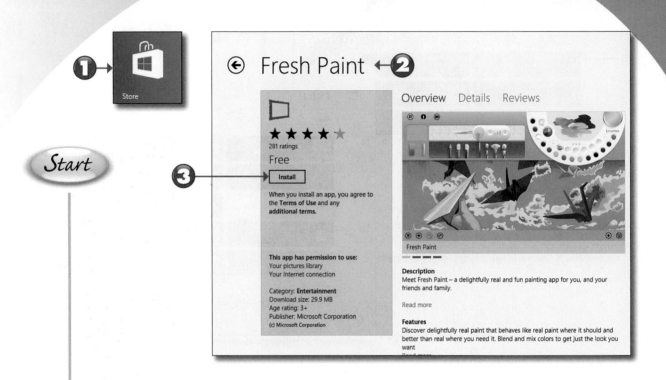

1 Click the **Store** app.

2 Display the app page for the app you want to install.

3 Click **Install**.

Continued

NOTE

Installing Paid Apps When you install a paid app, Windows directs you to a logon screen where you can log on to your Microsoft account and choose a payment method. Windows might also prompt you to log on to your Microsoft account before continuing with the download. ■

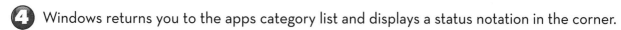

4 Windows returns you to the apps category list and displays a status notation in the corner.

5 When the download is complete, you can view the app's tile on the Start screen.

End

TIP

Using Apps Across Computers You can install your Windows 8 apps on up to five computers. To do so, right-click the app name on the installed apps page and click Install. ■

TIP

Getting Help with Apps If you run into any trouble with an app, you can revisit the app's page and click the App Support link to view the developer's support website or access contact info. ■

REMOVING AN APP

You can easily remove an app you no longer use or want. Removing an app removes it from your computer and deletes the app tile from your Start screen.

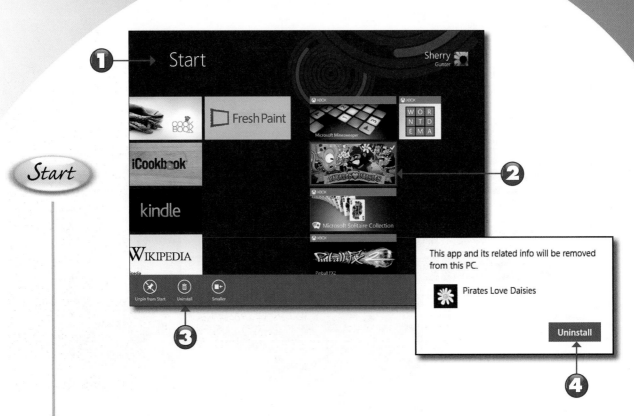

1 Display the Start screen.

2 Right-click the app you want to uninstall.

3 Click **Uninstall**.

4 A prompt box appears; click **Uninstall** and the app is removed.

End

NOTE

Reinstalling Store Apps The Your Apps page in the Microsoft Store keeps track of apps you downloaded and uninstalled. You can revisit the list and reinstall an app at any time. From the Store, press Windows key+Z, and then click Your Apps in the Apps bar. Sort the list to display Apps Not Installed on This PC, and then click the app and click the Install button. ■

SEARCHING FOR AN APP

You can use the Windows 8 Search feature to search the Store for a specific app or type of app. Using the Search charm from the Charms bar, you can conduct a search based on a keyword or words, and then choose from any matching results.

 Start

1. From the Store, display the Charms bar.

2. Click the **Search** charm.

3. Type the search text.

4. Click **Search** or press Enter.

5. Click a match from the list of results.

End

TIP

Searching Your Computer You can also use the Search feature to search for an app or program on your computer. From the Search pane, click the Apps category, and then type your search text. Windows 8 displays any matching results found on your PC. ∎

RATING AN APP

You can rate an app to let other users know about its usefulness. The Windows Store includes user reviews for all the apps. This information is helpful when deciding whether an app is right for you.

Start

① From the open app, display the Charms bar.

② Click **Settings**.

③ Click **Rate and review**.

④ Select a rating here.

⑤ Type in a title and review text.

⑥ Click **Submit**.

End

TIP

Viewing Reviews You can view all of an app's user reviews from the app's page in the Microsoft Store. Display the page and click the Reviews link. ■

UPDATING APPS

Developers frequently offer updates for their apps. You can update your apps manually from the Microsoft Store app.

1 From the Store, display the Charms bar.

2 Click **Settings**.

3 Click **App updates**.

4 Click **Check for updates**.

End

TIP

Sync Your License One of the options on the App updates page is to sync your licenses. You can activate this option if you do not see any up-to-date information about your apps. Simply click the Sync Licenses button to get started. ■

ADDING A PAYMENT METHOD TO YOUR ACCOUNT

Although there are a variety of free apps you can add to Windows 8, you might also want to buy some apps. You must specify a payment method to use along with your Microsoft account before you can buy apps through the online Store.

1. From within the Store app, display the Charms bar.

2. Click **Settings**.

3. Click **Your account**.

Continued

NOTE

Security Step One of the options found on the Your account page is a security option requiring your authorization any time an app is purchased. Leave this setting on if you share your computer with other users. If you are the only user, you can turn this setting off and bypass the account verification and sign-on procedure. ∎

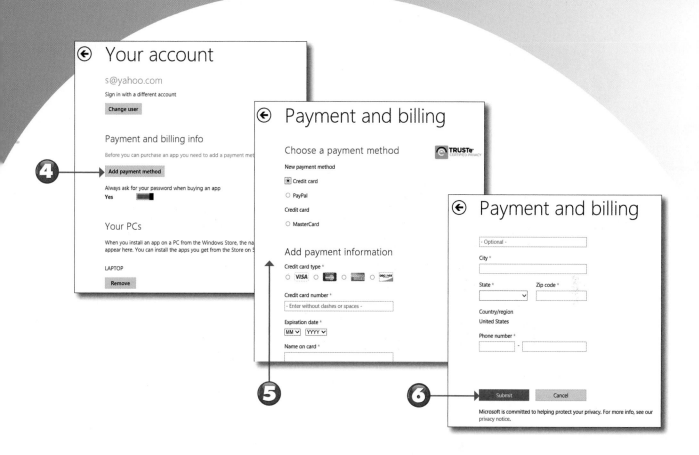

4 Click **Add payment method**.

5 Fill out your payment details, including billing address information and credit card information.

6 Click **Submit** at the bottom of the page.

End

TIP

Editing Your Account Anytime you need to make changes to your payment method, you can revisit the Your Account page and add other payment methods. ■

Chapter 10

PLAYING GAMES WITH WINDOWS 8

Computers are pretty handy for work tasks, and they are also great tools for listening to music, viewing digital photos, and watching video content. For real fun, however, computer games can offer hours of amusement. Whether you like word games, strategy games, arcade games, multi-player games, or first-person shooter games, you are sure to find some games to play among the wave of software titles available through the Xbox Games store. Windows has come a long way from the old Solitaire and Minesweeper games of yesteryear!

A free game app available
through the Windows Store.

Game details include an overview,
system requirements, and user reviews.

You can click
Install to
download and
install the app.

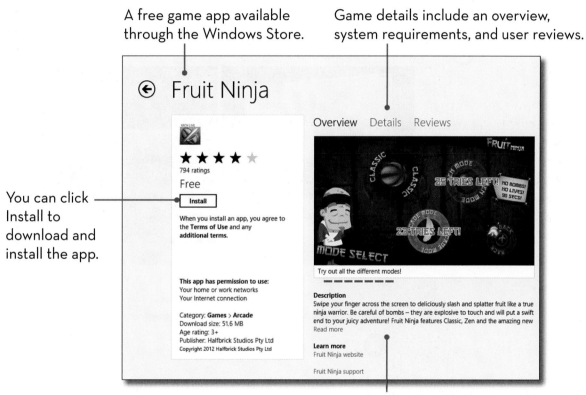

Game Description

SHOPPING FOR GAMES IN THE MICROSOFT STORE

You can shop online to access the new Xbox Games and Windows Store online offerings. You can find a wide variety of games for every kind of player of every age. Some games are available for free, and others for a price. You can use the new Store app to peruse game offerings, as demonstrated in this task.

Start

1 Click the **Store** tile.

2 Scroll to the Games category.

3 Click **Games**.

Continued

NOTE

Shop Through the Games App You can also shop for games through the Games app on the Start screen. If you are shopping for computer games, such as Windows desktop games, the Games app leads you back to the Windows Store to complete your purchase. ■

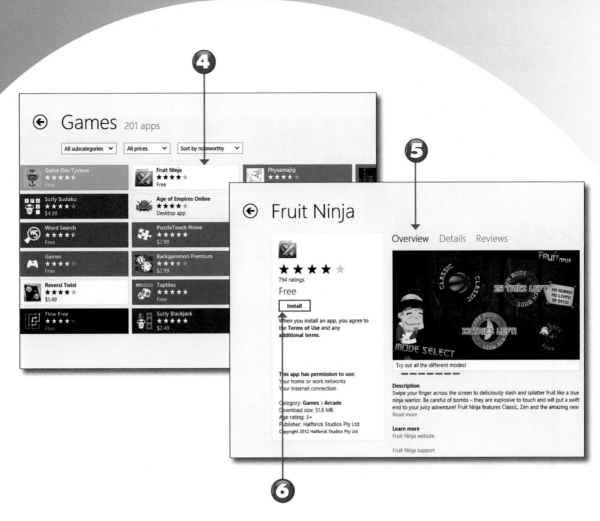

4 Click a game to view more about it.

5 Game details include an overview page, system requirement details, and user reviews.

6 You can click the **Install** button to download and install the app.

End

NOTE

Using the Windows Store To learn more about working with the Windows 8 Store app, see Chapter 9, "Using the Windows 8 Store." ∎

NOTE

Looking for Xbox Games? You can shop for Xbox games directly through the Games app. The Xbox Games store connects you directly to the Xbox site. Learn more about using the Games app next. ∎

USING THE GAMES APP

You can use the Games app on the Start screen to access the new Xbox Games and Windows Store's online offerings. You also can use the Games app to manage your Xbox avatar, view gaming friends online, see featured spotlight games, and access both the Store and the Xbox 360 Games Store.

Start

1 Click or tap the **Games** tile on the Start screen.

2 Scroll to the far left to view your gamer information. You can edit your gaming profile here, view game achievements, and customize your avatar.

Continued

NOTE

What Is Xbox Live? Xbox Live is Microsoft's online multi-player gaming delivery system. You can use the service to play games with other users, download demos and trailers, and keep a list of friends you play with the most. ■

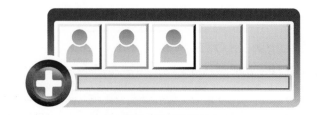

3 Scroll to the right a bit to view the friends area, which lists any online gaming friends.

4 Scroll to the right a bit more to view spotlighted games.

Continued

TIP

Xbox Games on the PC New to Windows 8, Microsoft is making a growing number of Xbox games available for the PC, laptop, or tablet. Some of these games may come preinstalled on your computer, and others are available to download. You can view many of these featured games in the Spotlight section of the Games app. ■

5 Scroll to the right some more to view your game activity. You can reopen previously played games here.

6 Scroll to the right to view the Games section of the Windows Store.

7 To view a full list of Xbox games for the PC, you can click here.

Continued

NOTE

Store Versus Store Many of the games you select in the Games app link to the Microsoft Store, where you can read more details about system requirements and user reviews before actually installing the games. ∎

8 Scroll to the far right to view the Xbox Games store.

9 To view a full list of Xbox games and categories, click here.

10 The Games app displays a list of categories and sorting criteria.

End

TIP

More About the Games App The Games app can be uninstalled just like any other app in Windows 8. If the app is not preinstalled, you can always add it from the Microsoft Store. To uninstall it, however, right-click the app on the Start screen and click Uninstall on the Apps bar. ■

ADDING AN XBOX GAME

Check the Windows Games Store through the Games app frequently to see what new Xbox games are available for PCs or laptops. When you find one you want to add, you can install it with some help from the Microsoft Store app.

1 Click or tap the **Games** app.

2 Scroll to the Windows Games Store area.

3 Click a game you want to try.

Continued

TIP

Paid Games If you choose a paid game, you must use your Microsoft account to choose a payment method before downloading the game. You can add a payment method to your account within the Games app. Display the Charms bar, click Settings, and then click Account. ∎

TIP

Free Games Many of the Xbox games for the PC are free, so you might not have to worry about choosing a payment method when downloading a game. ∎

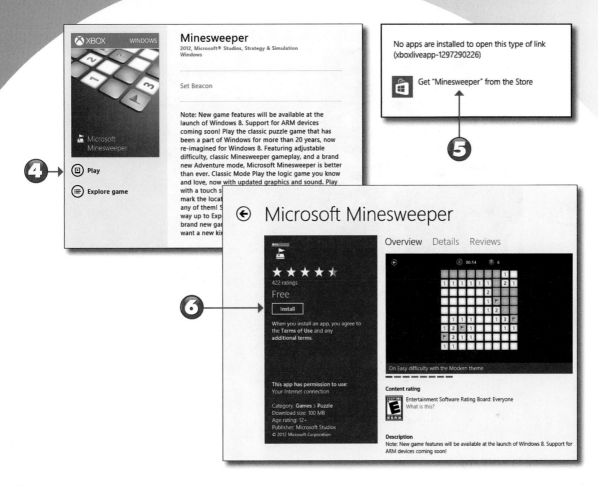

4 Click **Play**.

5 Click the link for the Store app.

6 Click **Install**.

End

TIP

Where Is My Game? When your Xbox game finishes installing, Windows 8 adds it to the Start screen. You might need to scroll to the right to find it. ■

PLAYING A GAME

Windows 8 adds tiles to the Start screen for each game you add to your computer. You can start a game from its tile or, if you have recently played the game, you can start it from within the Games app.

Start

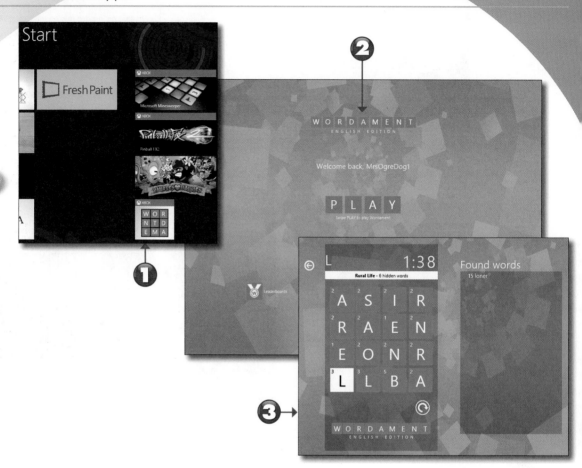

1 Click the game tile you want to open.

2 The game opens onscreen. In this example, the Wordament Xbox game opens.

3 Follow the onscreen directions and start playing.

End

 TIP
Game Help Most games offer some help with gameplay. Look for a Help link or button. ■

 NOTE
Review It You can write a review for a game to help other users determine whether the game is a good choice for them. With the game open onscreen, you can summon the review feature within the Store app and add your own rating and critique. Click Settings on the Charms bar and click Rate and Review to open the feature. ■

FINDING GAME OPTIONS

With any app in Windows 8, including games, you can display additional settings where applicable. In the case of games, you can display options for controlling settings such as sound, players, and more.

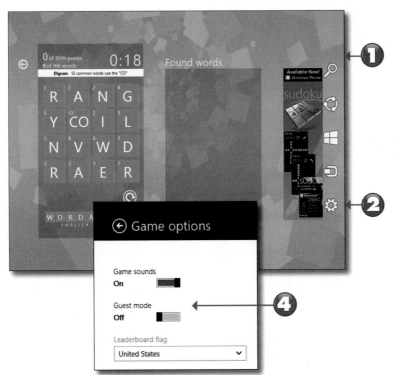

1. From the game screen, display the Charms bar.

2. Click **Settings**.

3. Click **Game options**.

4. Windows displays options for that particular game.

End

TIP

Game Help Most games offer some help with gameplay. Look for a Help link or button. You can also display the Charms bar and click Settings to find links to rules and game options. ■

Chapter 11

RUNNING DESKTOP APPS

Windows 8 includes two interfaces—the new UI tile interface that greets you when you start Windows, and the familiar Windows desktop. You'll notice, though, that the Windows 8 desktop doesn't include the Start menu used in previous versions of Windows. Every program—whether it's designed for the new Windows 8 UI or for the Windows desktop—can be started from the Start screen. In this chapter, you learn how to find desktop programs, how to add your favorite apps to the Start screen, and how to add programs to the Windows 8 desktop. You also learn how to use some of the Windows desktop apps included in Windows 8.

Use Alt+Tab to switch between apps.

Formatting a Document in WordPad

Use Win+Tab to switch between apps.

A Portion of the All Apps Screen

Using Save As with Paint

The Right-Click Menu for Desktop Apps

OPENING THE ALL APPS SCREEN

The Start screen lists mainly new Windows 8 UI apps. However, another screen in Windows 8—called the All Apps screen—displays both new UI and Windows desktop apps, including third-party apps that you have installed. Here's how to display the All Apps screen.

1 Right-click a blank area of the Start screen.

2 Click the **All apps** icon.

3 Scroll to the right to see desktop apps.

4 Desktop apps are listed in alphabetical order by vendor or category.

TIP

Can't Find an App? If you can't find the app you want to open, use the Search method described in the next section, "Searching for 'Hidden' Apps." ■

SEARCHING FOR "HIDDEN" APPS

Despite the name, the All Apps screen doesn't always show you every app on your system. You can use the Windows 8 Search tool to find other so-called "hidden" apps.

Start

① Move your mouse or pointer to the lower-right corner of the screen.

② Click **Search**.

③ Enter the search text.

④ Apps matching your search text.

⑤ Number of matching items in searched categories (Apps, Settings, and Files).

End

NOTE

Search the Same Way from the Start Screen or Desktop This tutorial shows how to perform the search from the Start screen, but the steps are the same from the Windows 8 desktop. ∎

STARTING A DESKTOP APP FROM THE ALL APPS SCREEN

When you locate the app you want to start on the All Apps screen, launching it is easy. And if it's a desktop app, the Windows desktop opens at the same time.

Start

Click the app's icon.

The app opens on the Windows 8 desktop.

Continued

3 To adjust the window size, click the lower-right corner and drag. Release the mouse button when you're done.

4 To use the entire screen for the app, click **Maximize**.

5 To go back to a window, click **Restore Down**.

6 To close the app, click **Close**.

End

TIP

"Hide" the App with Minimize To take the app off the screen but keep it running, click the Minimize button to the left of the Maximize/Restore Down button. To return a minimized app to the screen, click its icon in the taskbar. ∎

PINNING A DESKTOP APP TO THE START SCREEN

Finding an app in All Apps takes a few steps, so why not pin your favorite desktop apps to the Start screen for easier access? Here's how.

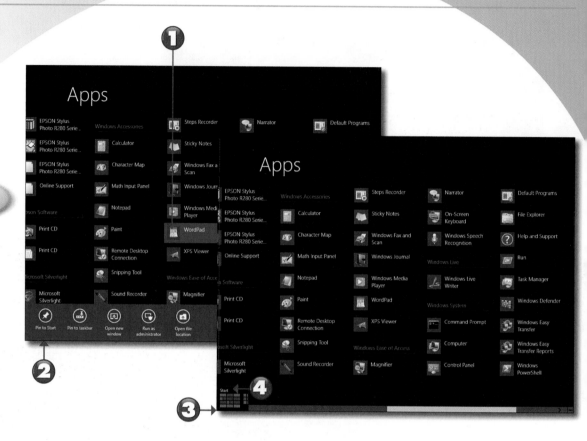

1. Right-click an app on the All Apps screen.

2. Click **Pin to Start**.

3. Hover the mouse pointer over the lower-left corner of the screen.

4. Click **Start**.

Continued

NOTE

Run as Administrator If you need to run an app as an administrator (also called "with elevated privileges"), select the Run as Administrator option from the menu shown in step 2. Some apps don't work correctly if you don't choose this option. ■

5 Click and drag the tile.

6 Drop the tile in the preferred location on the Start screen.

End

TIP

Unpinning from the Start Screen To unpin a program from the Start screen, right-click the program's tile and select Unpin from Start. ■

TIP

Locating the File If you need to work with a file represented by a tile on the Start screen or All Apps screens, right-click the tile and select Open File Location. This opens the folder that contains the file. You can rename the file or make other changes as needed. ■

SWITCHING BETWEEN THE WINDOWS 8 UI AND DESKTOP APPS

Windows 8 provides two ways to switch between apps: the new Switch List view hidden on the left edge of the Start screen, and the traditional Alt+Tab method of cycling through open apps. In this tutorial, you learn how to use each of these methods.

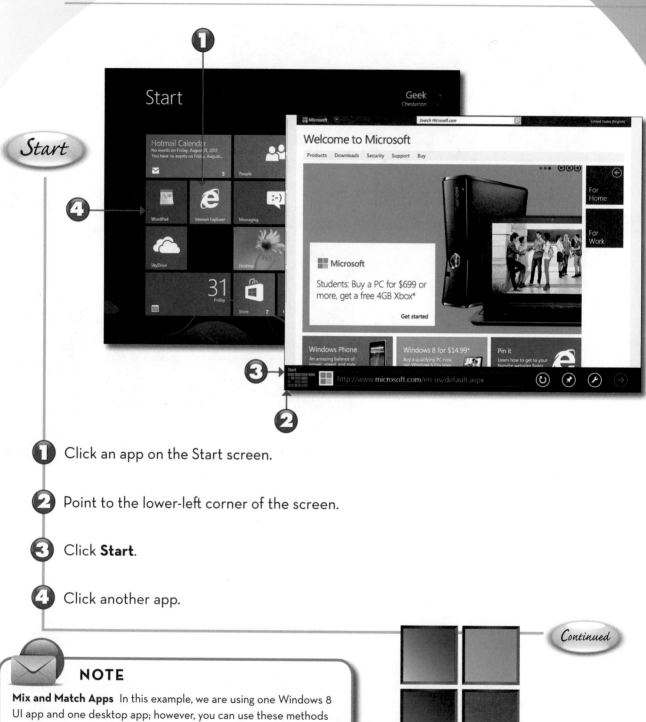

1. Click an app on the Start screen.

2. Point to the lower-left corner of the screen.

3. Click **Start**.

4. Click another app.

Continued

NOTE

Mix and Match Apps In this example, we are using one Windows 8 UI app and one desktop app; however, you can use these methods with any combination of Windows 8 UI or desktop apps. ∎

5 Point to the upper-left corner of the screen. Slide the mouse pointer down the screen until all running programs are listed.

6 Click the program thumbnail.

7 Press **Alt+Tab**.

8 Repeat (hold down **Alt** and press **Tab**) until the program you want to switch to is highlighted, and then release the keys.

End

TIP

Using Win+Tab You can also use Win+Tab in step 5 to scroll through the list of running apps. To launch an app from Win+Tab, release the keys when the app to which you want to switch is highlighted. ∎

USING WORDPAD

You can use the WordPad word processor to create new documents and view and edit several of the most common word-processing file formats. You also can add fonts and other text enhancements to documents originally created with plain-text editors, such as Notepad.

Start

1 Click **WordPad** to start the program.

2 WordPad's document-editing window after entering and formatting text.

3 To save the document, click **File**.

4 Click **Save** to continue.

Continued

TIP

Choose Save or Save As? The first time you save a new document, you can use the Save or Save As command. If you use Save to save changes after you save the document the first time, you will replace the previous version. If you want to preserve the previous version of the document, use Save As and choose a different name for the new version of the document. ■

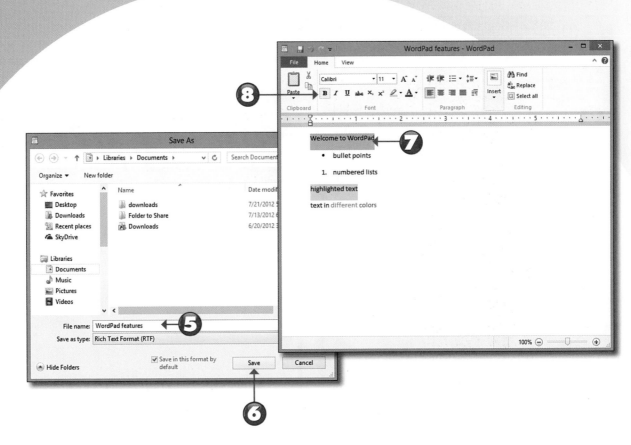

5 Enter a name for the file.

6 Click **Save**.

7 To change the font, font size, or text attributes, highlight the text: Point to the start of the text, and when the arrow changes to an I-beam pointer, click and drag to the end of the text.

8 Select the new settings from the Home tab.

Continued

NOTE

Rich Text and More By default, WordPad saves files in Rich Text Format (RTF), which can be opened by most word processors or other programs that work with text, such as photo editors, draw-type graphics programs, and publishing programs. To choose another format, open the Save As Type menu and select the format. ■

TIP

Save Wherever You Like To save a file to a different location, use the left pane in the Save As dialog box to navigate to the desired location, open it, and then click Save. ■

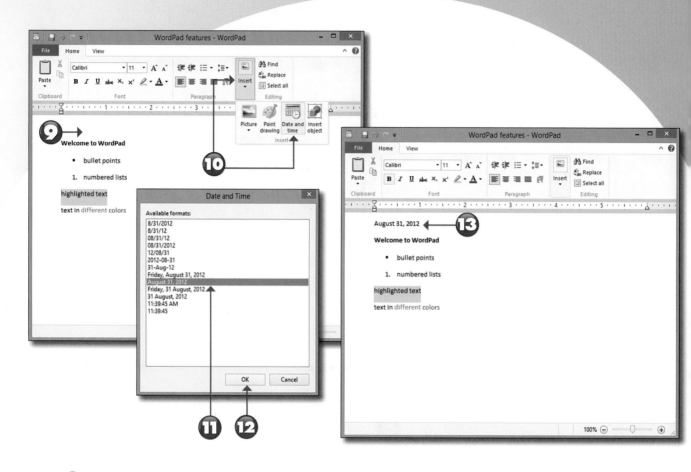

9 To add the current date to the document, place the cursor at the beginning of a blank line in the document.

10 Open the **Insert** menu and select **Date and time**.

11 Select a date/time format.

12 Click **OK**.

13 The current date or time is inserted into the document.

Continued

TIP
Click ? for Help For more help with WordPad, click the ? (Help) button near the top-right corner of the WordPad window. ■

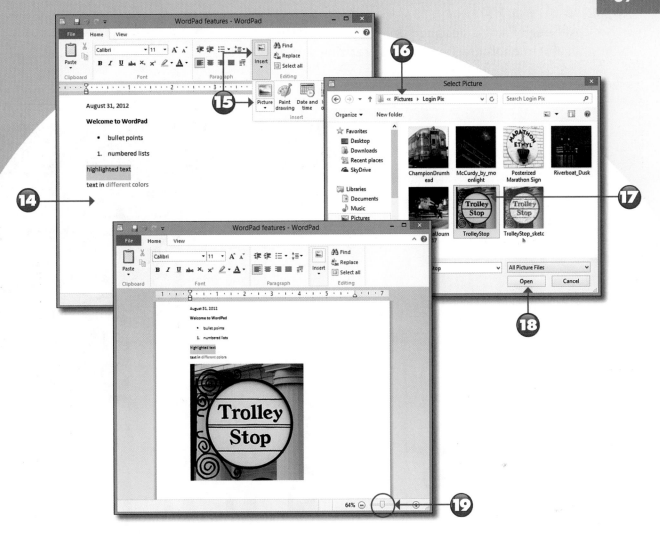

14 Click an empty line in the document.

15 Open the **Insert** menu and select **Picture**.

16 Navigate to the picture location.

17 Click the picture.

18 Click **Open**.

19 Drag the zoom control to the left to see more of the page.

End

USING PAINT

Although Paint is designed primarily as a painting program, it does include some features useful to photographers, such as resizing and skewing images.

Start

1 From the All Apps screen, click **Paint** to open the program.

2 To open an existing picture or photo, click the **File** menu and select **Open**.

3 Select a picture and click **Open**.

Continued

NOTE

Supported File Formats Paint can work with .bmp, .tif, .jpg, .gif, .dib, .ico, and .png files. If you want to use Paint with digital camera RAW files or other types of non-supported image files, convert them into maximum-quality JPEG (.jpg) or TIFF (.tif) files first, using other software. ■

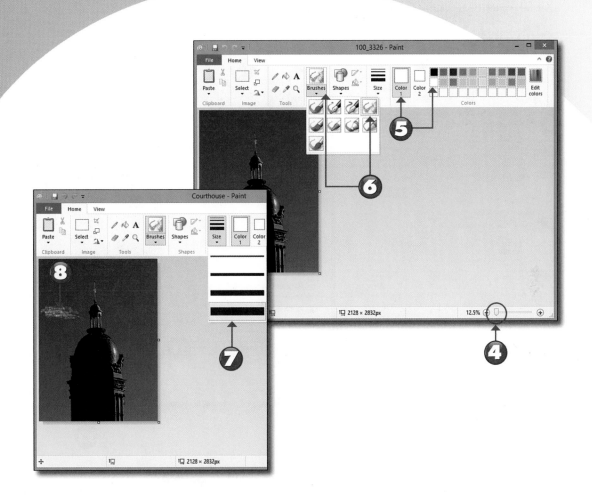

4 Adjust the zoom control until the picture fits the window.

5 To select a color for painting, select a color from the Colors palette.

6 To select a brush type for painting, open the **Brushes** menu and select a brush.

7 To select a brush size for painting, open the **Size** menu and select a line thickness.

8 To paint on the picture, use the mouse to click and drag.

Continued

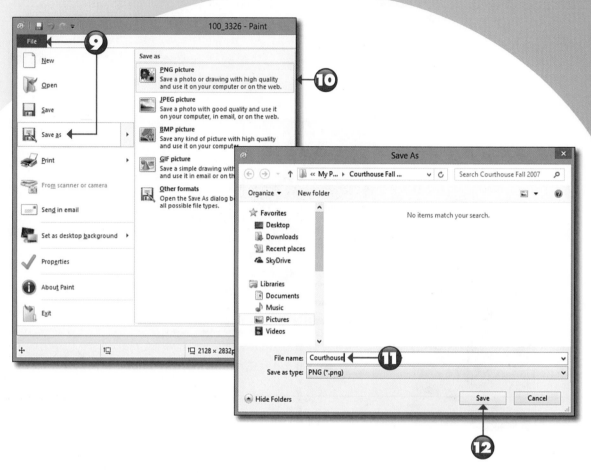

9 To save your changes, open the **File** menu and point to **Save As**.

10 Choose the desired image type.

11 Enter a new name.

12 Click **Save** to save the edited picture.

Continued

NOTE

Using Save As when Editing Pictures Be sure to use Save As (step 9) and specify a new name (step 11) for any picture you resize or otherwise edit. If you use Save, you will replace your original version with the changed version. ∎

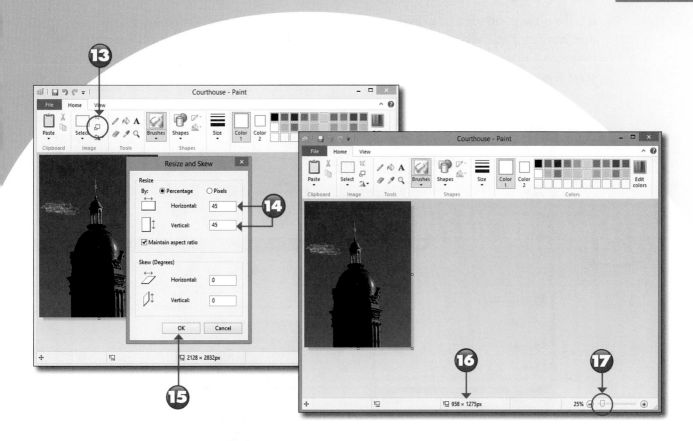

13 To resize a picture, click the **Resize and skew** button on the Home tab.

14 In the Resize and Skew dialog box, select the same percentage for Horizontal and Vertical under Resize.

15 Click **OK** to resize the picture.

16 The picture is now 958 x 1275 pixels, which will work nicely for emailing.

17 Adjust the zoom setting to the right to enlarge the onscreen view of the picture.

End

NOTE

Resizing for Email Many photos are too large to work well in email (this picture is 2128 pixels wide by 2832 pixels high). A width of no more than 1024 pixels is recommended for emailed photos. ■

NOTE

Saving Changes to a Different File Follow steps 9–12 to save your changes under a different filename. ■

PRINTING

It's always a good idea to preview your work before you print. Windows 8 desktop applications typically include a Print Preview option that you can access from the Print menu or a Print dialog box. Here's how to preview your work in the Paint application and start the print process.

Start

1. Click **File**.

2. Open the **Print** menu.

3. Click **Print preview**.

4. If your paper is not oriented properly, click **Page setup**.

Continued

TIP

Printing Quality Photos For the best print quality when printing photos or other images, print a full-size version of your photos. ■

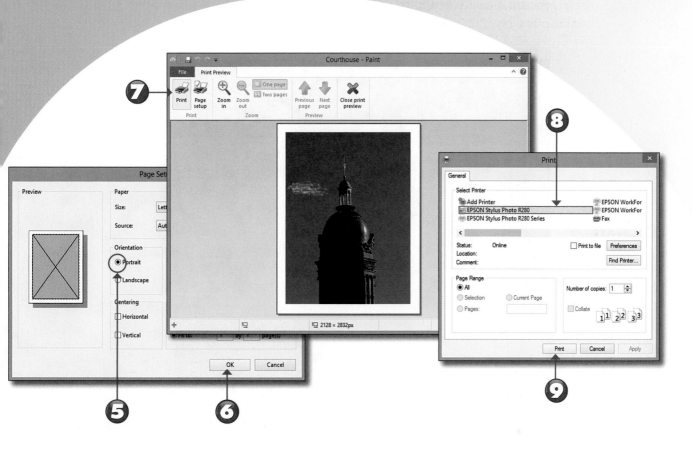

5 Select the correct orientation and other settings as needed.

6 Click **OK**.

7 Click **Print**.

8 Select your printer.

9 Click **Print**.

End

NOTE

More About Printing To learn about selecting the paper type and other printer settings, see "Managing Devices and Printers" in Chapter 18, "Advanced Configuration Options." To learn more about printing a web page, see "Printing a Web Page" in Chapter 16, "Browsing the Internet from Your Desktop." ∎

ADDING AN APP TO THE DESKTOP TASKBAR

After you add a desktop app to the Start screen, you can also add it as an icon on the Desktop taskbar.

1. Right-click a desktop app.

2. Click **Pin to taskbar**.

3. Click the **Desktop** tile.

4. The app appears on the Desktop taskbar.

End

NOTE

Pinning to the Taskbar from All Apps You can also start this process from the All Apps screen. If you start this process from the All Apps screen, you must go to the Start screen after step 2. ∎

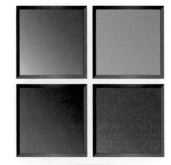

Chapter 12

MANAGING STORAGE WITH FILE EXPLORER

When it's time to work with your files in Windows 8, File Explorer (formerly called Windows Explorer) is the tool to use. In this chapter, you learn how to start File Explorer, copy and move files and folders, manage libraries, burn files to an optical disc, create a zip file archive, share folders, select the best options for viewing and grouping files, quickly access favorite locations, and view file and folder properties.

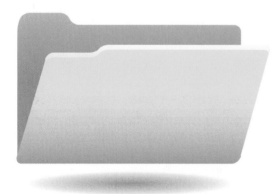

File Conflict
Dialog Box

Details Pane

Copy to
Menu

Burn a Disc
Dialog Box

Frequent
Places Menu

Managing Picture
Library Locations

Copy Details

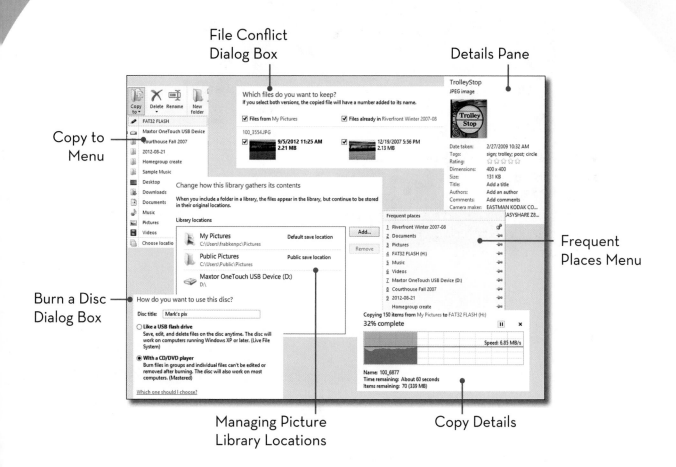

STARTING FILE EXPLORER

File Explorer is just a couple of mouse clicks away, whether you're using the new Windows 8 UI or the Windows desktop. Here's how to access and start File Explorer.

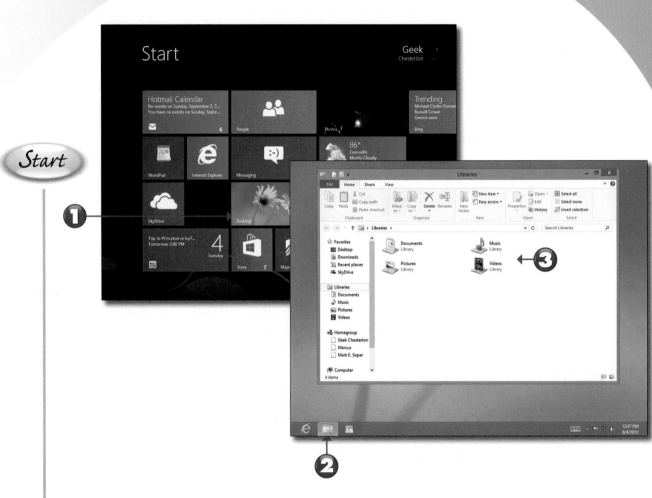

Start

End

1 Click the **Desktop** tile on the Start screen.

2 Click the **File Explorer** icon on the Desktop taskbar.

3 File Explorer displays your libraries.

INTRODUCTION TO FILE EXPLORER

File Explorer uses two panes in its default view. The left pane—called the Navigation pane—enables you to navigate to different locations, including the Windows desktop, libraries, Homegroup, and other computer and network locations. The right pane shows you details of the location selected in the left pane. Let's take a closer look at how File Explorer works.

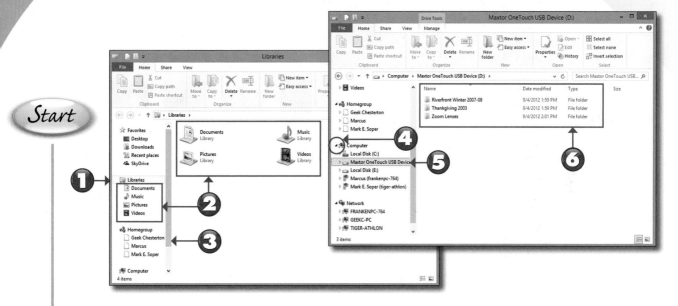

Start

1. The Libraries node is expanded by default.

2. Contents of the selected node.

3. Scroll down to view the Computer node.

4. Click the **Computer** node to see drive letters.

5. Click a drive letter to see its files and folders.

6. Contents of the selected drive.

End

NOTE

Nodes and Objects in File Explorer Each item listed in the Navigation pane of File Explorer is an object. Some objects contain other objects; these objects are called *nodes*. Click the white pointer next to a node to expand it; click the black pointer next to a node to contract it. ■

INTRODUCTION TO RIBBON MENUS

File Explorer now uses Ribbon menus that provide easier and faster access to new and improved features. Here's what they do.

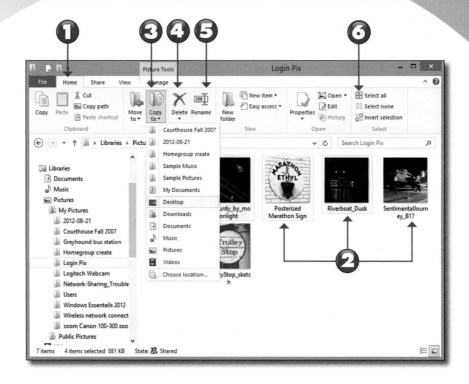

Start

1 Double-click the **Home** tab.

2 Select one or more files or folders in the right pane.

3 Open to select a destination for copying selected items.

4 Click to delete selected items.

5 Click to rename selected items.

6 Click to select all items in current view.

Continued

NOTE

Selecting Multiple Items To select more than one item, click the first item, then hold down either Ctrl key on the keyboard and click additional items. ∎

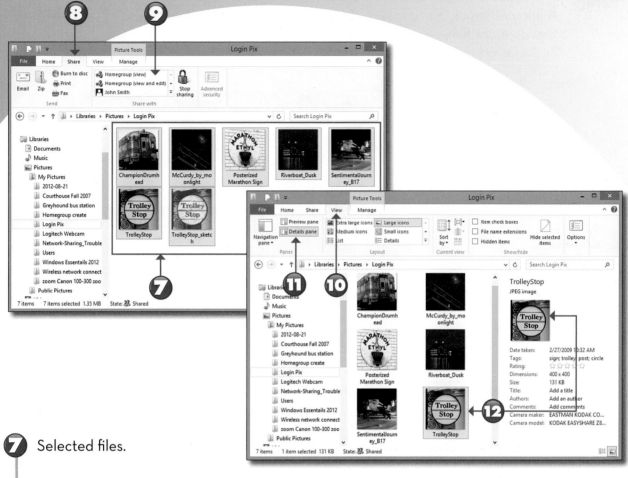

7 Selected files.

8 Click the **Share** tab.

9 Select a sharing option.

10 Click the **View** tab.

11 Click to show/hide Details pane.

12 Selected file and file details.

End

NOTE

Minimizing/Expanding the Ribbon To minimize the Ribbon menu to tab names only, click the up arrow next to the Help (question mark) button, near the upper-right corner of the File Explorer window. When the Ribbon menu is minimized, the arrow becomes a down arrow. Click it to expand the Ribbon. ■

MANAGING LIBRARIES

A library is more than a folder—it can include any folder on a local or network hard drive that contains files you want to view at the same time. In this lesson, you discover how to add a new drive or folder to a library.

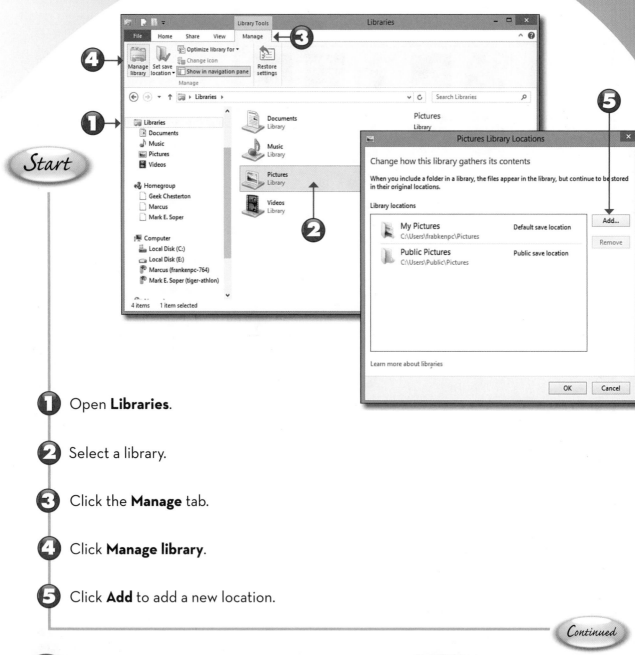

Start

1. Open **Libraries**.

2. Select a library.

3. Click the **Manage** tab.

4. Click **Manage library**.

5. Click **Add** to add a new location.

Continued

NOTE

Adding Other Drive Locations You cannot add optical or USB flash drives to a library. However, you can add external hard drives and network folders to a library. ■

6 Select the new library location.

7 Click **Include folder**.

8 The new location is listed as part of the library.

9 Click **OK**.

End

NOTE

Easy Library Backup with File History The new File History feature in Windows 8 backs up the contents of local library locations. For more information, see "Protecting Your Files with File History" in Chapter 20, "Protecting Your System." ∎

COPYING AND MOVING FILES OR FOLDERS

If you need to have a file or folder in more than one place, use the Copy To command in File Explorer. The Move To command enables you to easily move files or folders to a different location. You can select from a listed destination or choose another location with either of these commands.

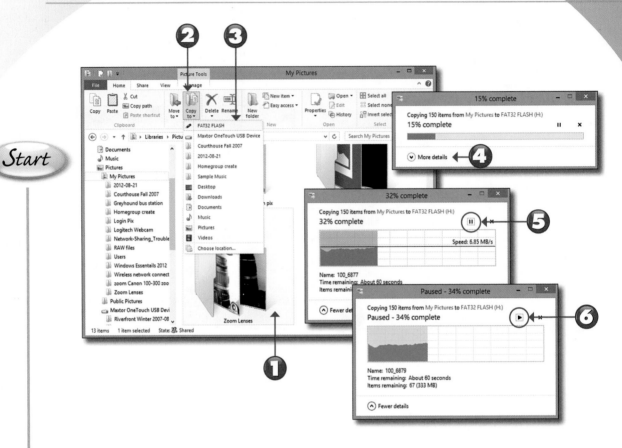

Start

Select the files or folder you want to copy.

Open the **Copy to** menu.

Click the destination.

To see more information about the process, click the down arrow next to **More details**.

To pause the process, click the **Pause** button.

To complete the process, click the **Continue** button.

Continued

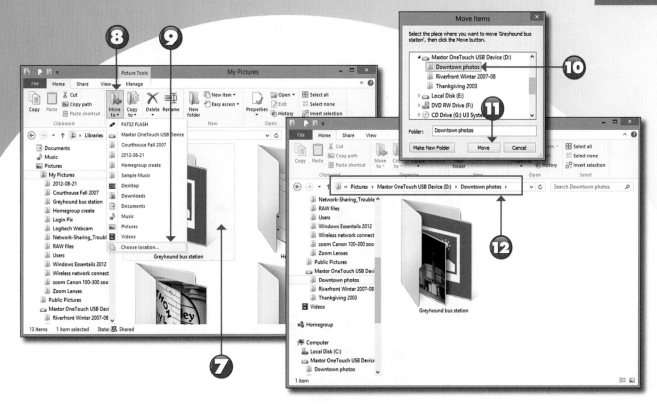

7 Select files or folders to move.

8 Open the **Move to** menu.

9 Click **Choose location**.

10 Click a location.

11 Click **Move**.

12 The folder appears in its new location.

End

NOTE

Copy Speeds When you click the More Details button shown in step 4, you can see the average copy speed, number of items left to copy, and estimated time remaining. This dialog box will not appear if the copy process takes only a few seconds, as in the case of copying a few small files. ■

NOTE

Drag and Drop You can also use drag and drop to move or copy files and folders, as explained in the next section. ■

DEALING WITH FILE/FOLDER NAME CONFLICTS

When you copy or move files with File Explorer, you might discover that some files or folders being copied or moved have the same names as files already appearing in the destination location. Here's what to do.

Start

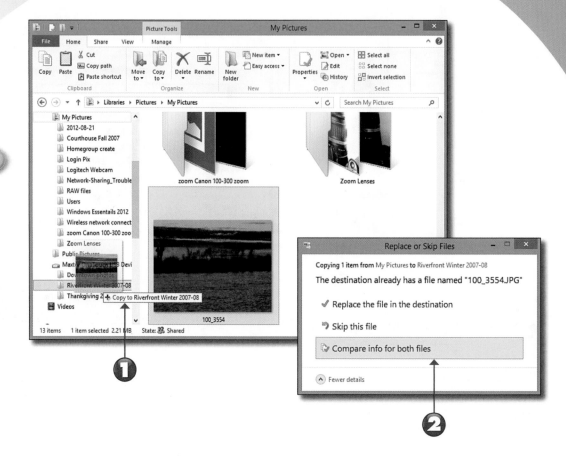

① Copy, move, or drag a file from one folder to another folder that contains a file with the same name.

② Click **Compare info for both files**.

Continued

NOTE

Using Drag and Drop You can use drag and drop to easily copy or move files. To copy a selected file, hold down the Ctrl key while you drag the file using the primary mouse button. To use drag and drop to move a file, simply drag the file to the destination location and release the mouse button. ■

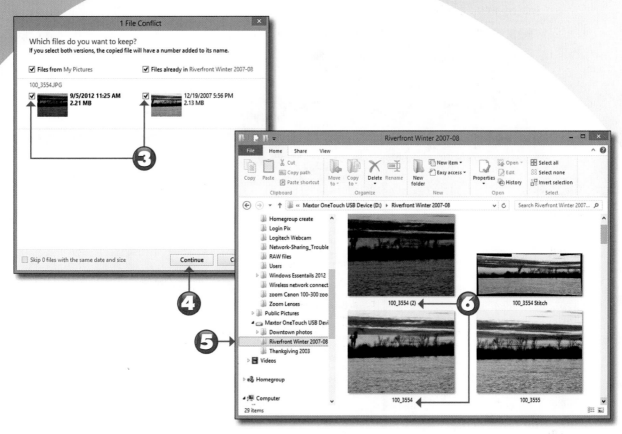

3 To keep both files, click both checkboxes.

4 Click **Continue**.

5 Open the destination folder.

6 The copied file with the name conflict is renamed to avoid replacing the original file.

End

NOTE

Free Photo Editing with Photo Gallery The photo in this example was edited with Photo Gallery, a free photo editing and organizational tool you can download from the Microsoft website. Learn more about Photo Gallery in Chapter 17, "Adding and Using Multimedia Features." ■

BURNING DATA DISCS

You can use options on the Share tab in File Explorer to easily burn CDs or DVDs of your favorite files. Here's how.

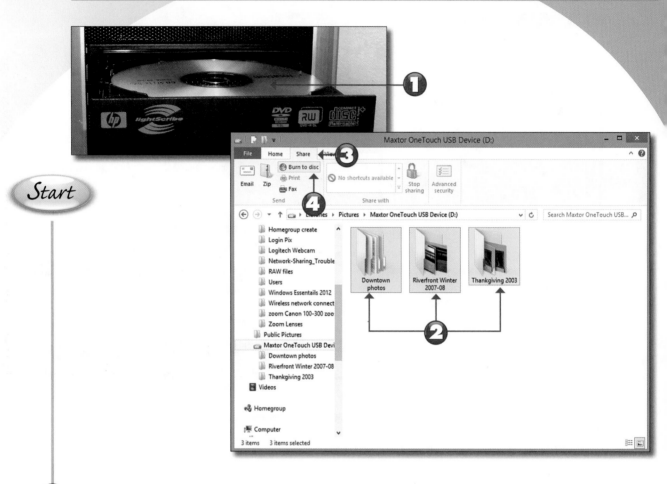

Start

1 Place a writeable disc in your optical drive and close the drive.

2 Select the files or folders you want to burn to an optical disc.

3 Click the **Share** tab.

4 Click **Burn to disc**.

Continued

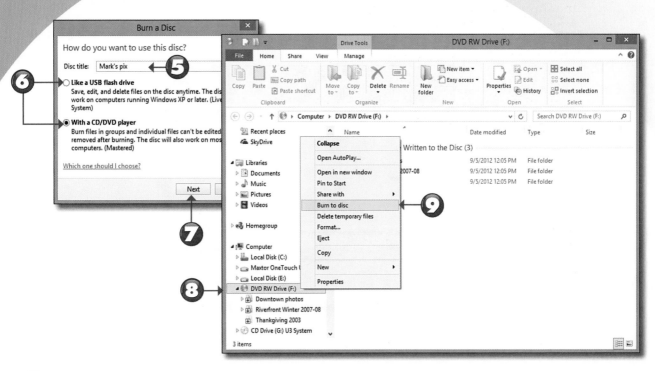

5 Enter a name for the disc.

6 Select the method to use.

7 Click **Next**.

8 Right-click the drive letter of your optical drive.

9 Select **Burn to disc**.

Continued

NOTE

Disk Formatting Options In step 6, choose the Like a USB flash drive option if you are using rewriteable (erasable) media such as a CD-RW, DVD-RW, or DVD+RW disc, and you are using the disc with Windows XP or later versions. Otherwise, choose the With a CD/DVD player option if you aren't sure what type of computer or device will be used with the media. ■

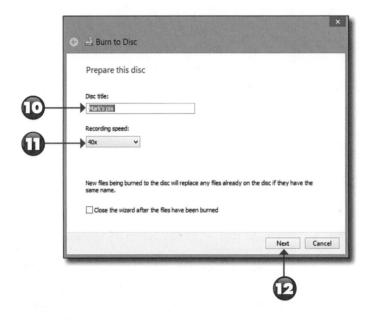

10 Confirm the disc name or type a new name.

11 Confirm the recording speed.

12 Click **Next**.

Continued

TIP

Recording Speeds Choose a slower recording speed in step 11 if you have had problems using recorded media from your computer on another device, such as a CD player. ■

13 Click the empty checkbox if you want to burn another copy of the disc.

14 Click **Finish**.

15 Remove the disc from the drive.

End

SELECTING, VIEWING, AND GROUPING OPTIONS

Windows 8 makes selecting, viewing, and grouping files easier than in previous versions of Windows. This lesson uses some folders containing photos. However, the methods described here can also be used with music files, videos, or other types of documents.

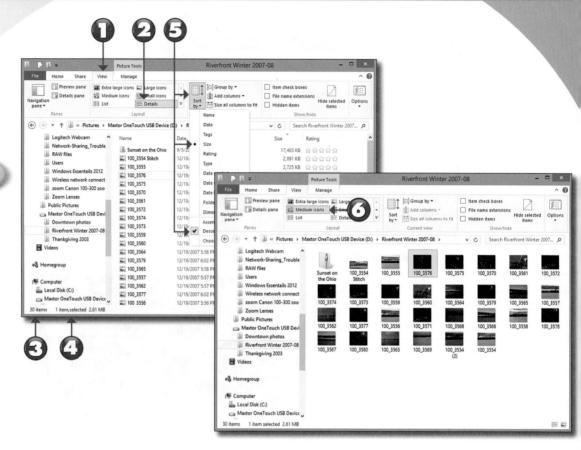

① Click the **View** tab.

② Details view displays filenames, date/time modified, file types, and file sizes.

③ The number of files in the current folder.

④ The number of files selected in the current folder.

⑤ Open **Sort by** to see the current sort option (dot) and direction (check mark).

⑥ Click **Medium icons** to see thumbnail previews.

Continued

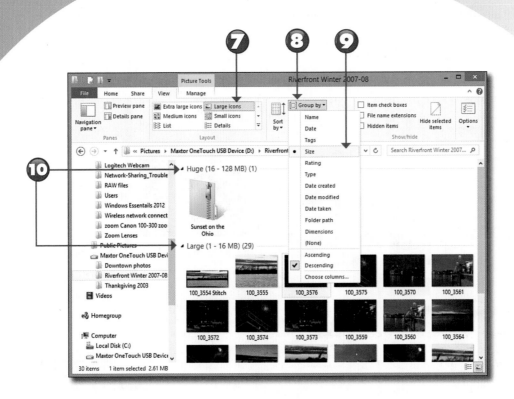

7 Click **Large icons** to display larger photo thumbnails.

8 Open the **Group by** menu.

9 Select a grouping option.

10 Groups of files arranged by size.

Continued

 TIP

Changing How Files Are Displayed Click an option in the Layout group on the View tab to see your files displayed in different views. ■

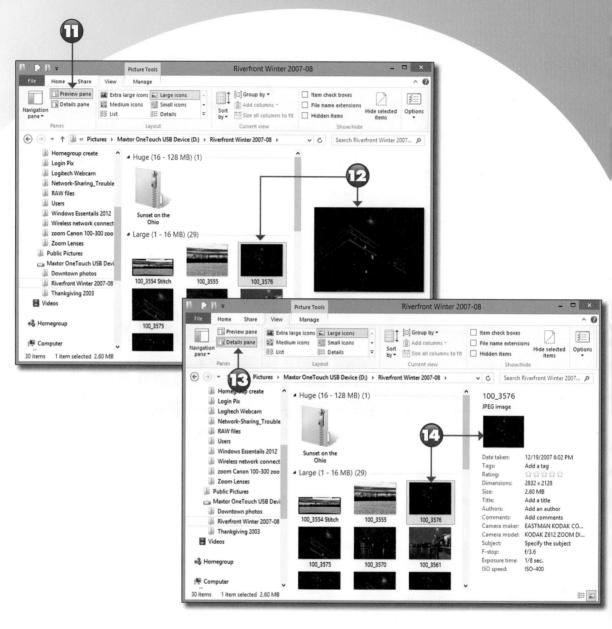

11 Click **Preview pane** in the Panes group.

12 The selected photo and preview.

13 Click **Details pane**.

14 The selected photo and details.

Continued

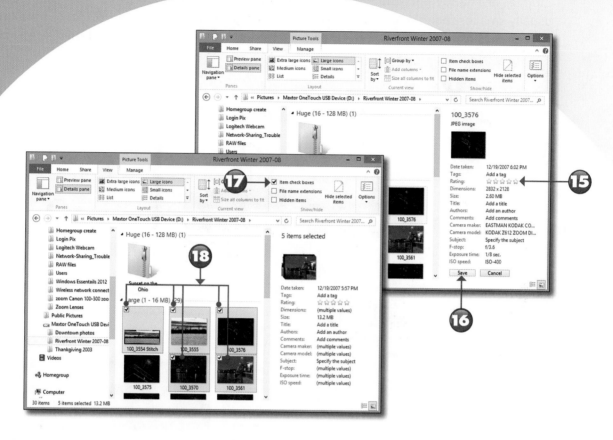

15 Click the rightmost star to select a rating.

16 Click **Save** to save the rating.

17 Click the empty box for **Item check boxes**.

18 As you click an item, a check box appears.

End

 TIP

Easier Selection of Multiple Items The Item check boxes option in step 17 makes it easier for you to select items to burn to disc, copy, move, delete, and so on. ■

CREATING ZIP FILES WITH THE SHARE TAB

Zip files are handy because you can store multiple files and folders into a single file that's usually smaller than the combined size of the original files. Microsoft Windows 8 makes this process easier than ever before by adding Zip file creation to the Share tab in File Explorer.

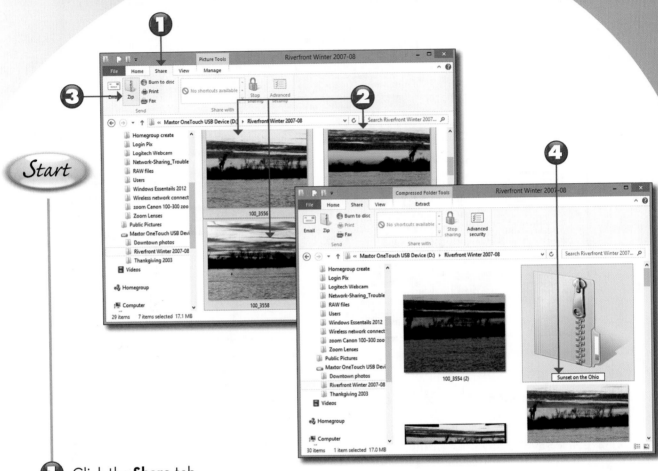

Start

1 Click the **Share** tab.

2 Select files or folders you want to include in a Zip file.

3 Click **Zip**.

4 Enter a name for the Zip file.

End

NOTE

Automatic Zip File Names If you don't change the name of the Zip file in step 4, File Explorer uses the name of the first file or folder you selected in step 2. ■

USING FREQUENT PLACES

The Frequent Places feature on the File tab makes it easy to return to locations you like to use. You can even pin places to the Frequent places menu on the right side of the File tab.

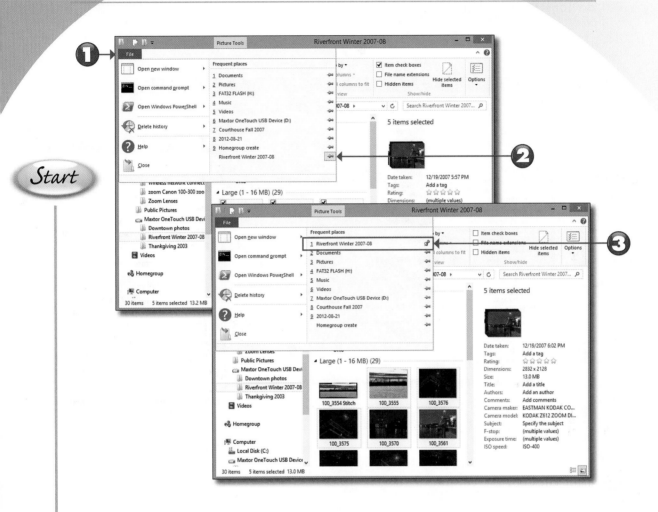

Start

1. Click the **File** tab.

2. Point to a location you want to return to.

3. Click the pin icon to keep the location on the list.

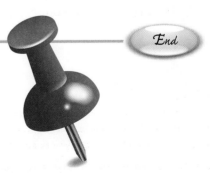

End

VIEWING FILE PROPERTIES

The Details pane in File Explorer provides some information about a selected drive, file, or folder, but you can learn much more by viewing an object's properties. You can use the context (right-click) menu or the Properties menu on the Home tab to do so. This lesson demonstrates both methods.

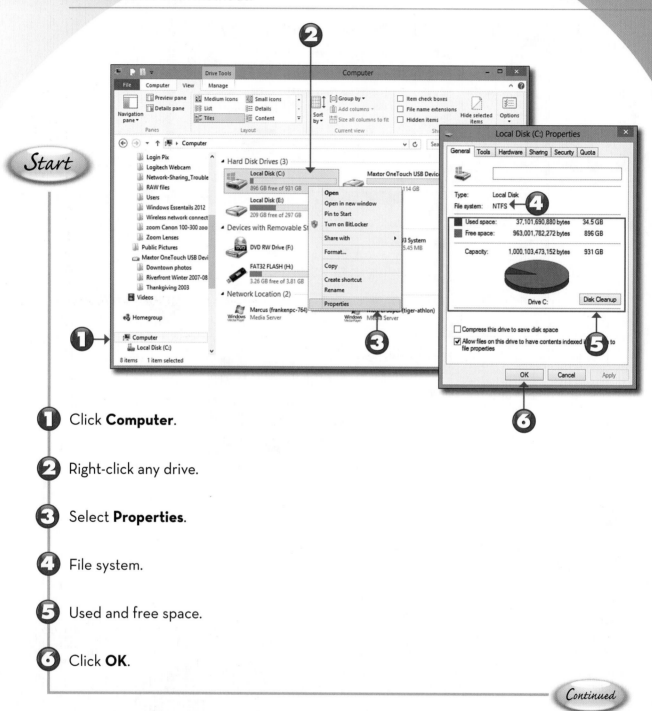

Start

1 Click **Computer**.

2 Right-click any drive.

3 Select **Properties**.

4 File system.

5 Used and free space.

6 Click **OK**.

Continued

7 Right-click a folder and select **Properties**.

8 Folder name.

9 Folder location.

10 The amount of space that the folder's contents use.

11 The number of files and folders in selected folder.

12 Click **OK**.

Continued

NOTE

The Right File System's NTFS You must use an external hard disk formatted with NTFS for file protection options. See Chapter 20 for details on how to protect your system. ∎

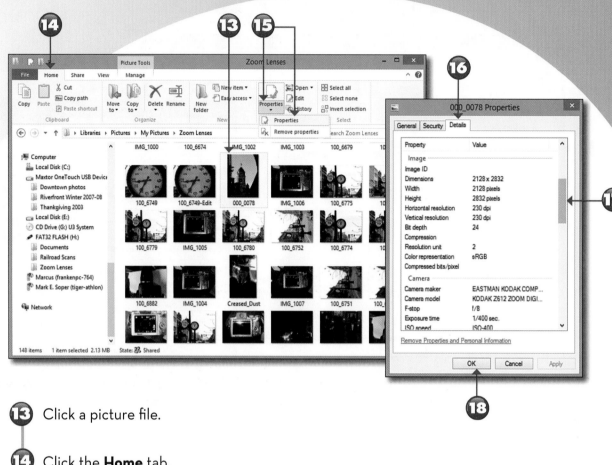

13 Click a picture file.

14 Click the **Home** tab.

15 Open the **Properties** menu and select **Properties**.

16 Click **Details**.

17 Scroll down to view image, camera, exposure, and other image properties.

18 Click **OK**.

Continued

NOTE

Metadata 101 Information about the camera and camera settings used to capture an image is often referred to as *metadata*. Digital cameras store metadata along with each picture taken. ■

19 Select a music track.

20 Open the **Properties** menu and select **Properties**.

21 Click **Details**.

22 Note the track length and bit rate.

23 Scroll down to see the track name and file type.

24 Click **OK**.

End

NOTE

Removing Properties from Files If you don't want to share information about ratings, name, or location tags, or other personal information listed as part of a file's properties, click the Remove Properties and Personal Information link at the bottom of the Properties dialog box. ■

Chapter 13

NETWORKING YOUR HOME WITH HOMEGROUP

Windows 8 provides two interfaces for connecting to and managing network connections with the Internet and with other users on your home or small-business network. These interfaces are the Start screen and its PC settings screen for basic network settings using HomeGroup, and the desktop's Control Panel for fine-tuning HomeGroup networking. This chapter shows you how to work with the HomeGroup settings in each of these interfaces.

Setting Sharing and
Connection Options for a
New Network Connection

Configuring Sharing
for a HomeGroup
Network

A Typical
HomeGroup
Password

Connecting
to a Hidden
Network

Editing
Streaming
Media Settings

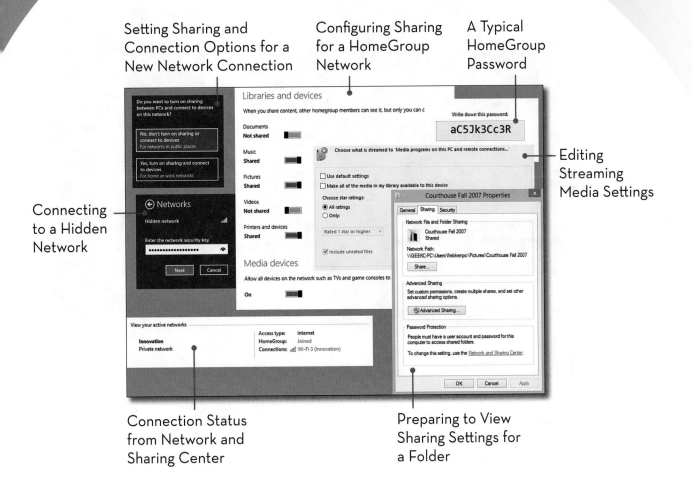

Connection Status
from Network and
Sharing Center

Preparing to View
Sharing Settings for
a Folder

CONNECTING TO AN UNSECURED PUBLIC WIRELESS NETWORK

Your home and office networks should be secure networks; however, wireless networks found in locations such as coffee shops, restaurants, and hotels are often unsecured. Here's how to connect to these networks with Windows 8.

Start

1 Hover the mouse over the upper- or lower-right corner of the display.

2 Click **Settings**.

3 Click **Available**.

4 Secured networks (user must provide encryption key).

5 Unsecured networks.

6 Click an SSID.

Continued

7 If you plan to connect to the network again, click the empty **Connect automatically** box.

8 Click **Connect**.

9 Click **No, don't turn on sharing or connect to devices**.

10 Your network connection is listed first.

End

NOTE

The Windows Security Shield and Wireless Networks
Unsecured networks—networks that do not use an encryption key—are marked with the Windows security shield to remind you that they are not secure. Some of these networks, typically business networks, use a login for security rather than an encryption key. ■

NOTE

Starting the Connection Process from the Windows Desktop You can also start this process from the Windows desktop by clicking the wireless network icon in the notification area of the taskbar. ■

CONNECTING TO A SECURED PRIVATE NETWORK

If you want to connect to a secured network, such as a home or office network, you must enter a network security key. Windows 8 can remember your network security key and the rest of your connection details for you. Here's how this process works.

1 From the Networks screen, click a secure network.

2 Enter the network security key.

3 To see the characters, click the eye icon.

4 Click **Next**.

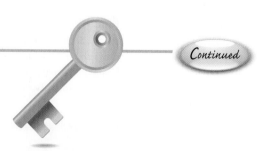

Continued

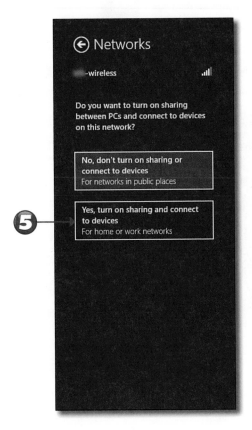

5 Click **Yes, turn on sharing and connect to devices**.

6 Your network connection is listed first.

End

DISCONNECTING AND OTHER NETWORK OPTIONS

Concerned about how much data you're sending through your wireless connection? Need to get more information about your connection? Is it time to disconnect, grab your laptop, and get back to the office? You can do all of this and more with a couple of mouse clicks in Windows 8.

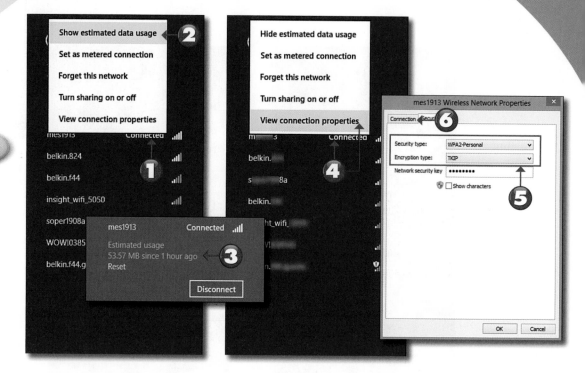

Start

1. Right-click your connection.

2. Select **Show estimated data usage**.

3. Estimated data usage in the last hour.

4. Right-click your connection and select **View connection properties**.

5. The security type and encryption type used by this connection.

6. Click to view connection properties.

Continued

7 Click to connect even if the SSID isn't broadcast.

8 Click **OK**.

9 Hover the mouse over the lower-right corner, and then click **Settings**.

10 Click the wireless icon.

11 Click the active connection.

12 Click **Disconnect**.

End

NOTE

Metered Connection? Windows 8 Can Handle It You can also specify that you have a metered connection. This is useful if you're using a cellular broadband connection. ■

NOTE

Fixing a "Broken" Connection You can change the encryption information shown in step 5 if the wireless connection you use changes its settings, or you can right-click the connection and select Forget This Connection to discard the connection and stored settings. You can then set up a new connection. ■

CONNECTING TO A HIDDEN NETWORK

Most wireless networks broadcast their names (SSIDs). However, some are set up so that you must know the name of the network if you want to connect to it. This tutorial shows you how to connect to a hidden network.

1 Click **Hidden network**.

2 Click **Connect**.

Continued

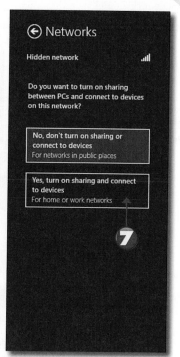

3 Type the name of the network (SSID).

4 Click **Next**.

5 Enter the network security key (if prompted).

6 Click **Next**.

7 Click **Yes, turn on sharing and connect to devices**.

End

CREATING A HOMEGROUP FROM THE START SCREEN

Windows 8 supports an easy-to-use, yet secure, type of home and small-business networking feature called a HomeGroup. HomeGroup networking enables home network users to share libraries and printers—you can specify which libraries to share and whether to share printers and devices on a particular system. All users of a HomeGroup use the same password but don't need to worry about specifying particular folders to share. You can create a new HomeGroup from the Start screen.

1 Hover over the upper- or lower-right corner of the Start screen.

2 Select **Settings**.

3 Click **Change PC settings**.

Continued

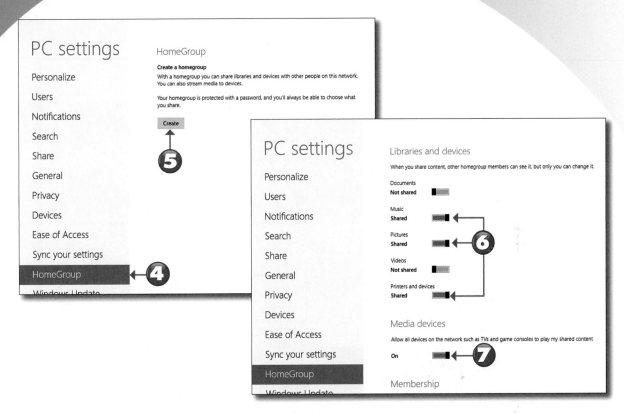

4 Click **HomeGroup**.

5 Click **Create**.

6 Move sliders to the right to share content in libraries and printers.

7 Move the Media devices slider to the right to enable access to streaming media for playback.

End

NOTE

Your HomeGroup, Your Choice In steps 6 and 7, you can select any or all of the items listed to share. Sharing Documents, Music, Pictures, and Videos with Home-Group members provides them with read-only access to all the items in each library. You can use File Explorer to adjust access levels for folders you select. To learn more about libraries, see Chapter 12, "Managing Storage with File Explorer." ■

VIEWING THE PASSWORD FOR YOUR HOMEGROUP

A HomeGroup needs at least two computers. You can add any Windows 8 computer—or a Windows 7 computer with its network location set as Home—to your HomeGroup. They'll need the HomeGroup password, which you can display directly from the HomeGroup menu in PC settings.

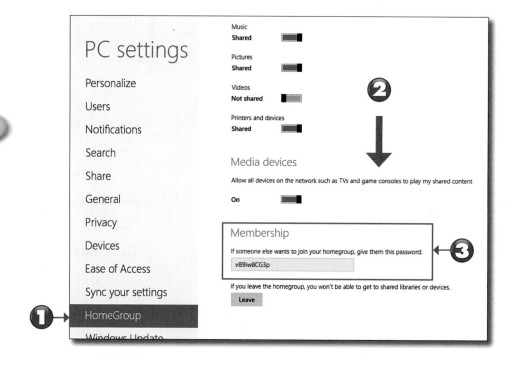

1 From the PC settings screen, click **HomeGroup**.

2 Scroll down to **Membership**.

3 Write down the password and use it on other computers you want to add to the HomeGroup.

End

NOTE

How to Print the HomeGroup Password If you want to print the HomeGroup password and instructions for joining a HomeGroup, see "Setting Up a HomeGroup from Network and Internet." ∎

JOINING A HOMEGROUP FROM THE START SCREEN

Microsoft introduced HomeGroups in Windows 7, so if you have one or more Windows 7 computers in your home or small office, you might already have a HomeGroup. Here's how to add your Windows 8 computer to an existing HomeGroup from the PC settings screen.

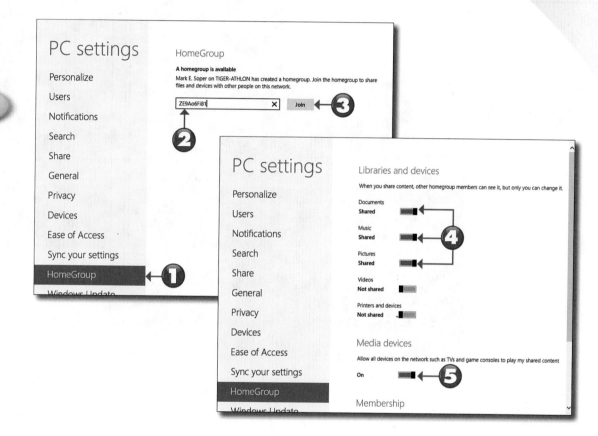

1 From the PC Settings screen, click **HomeGroup**.

2 Enter the HomeGroup password.

3 Click **Join**.

4 Move sliders to the right to share content in libraries and printers.

5 Move the Media devices slider to the right to enable access to streaming media for playback.

End

OPENING THE NETWORK AND INTERNET WINDOW IN CONTROL PANEL

If you want more control over HomeGroup and streaming media settings, you must start with the Network and Internet window in Control Panel. Here's how to open it.

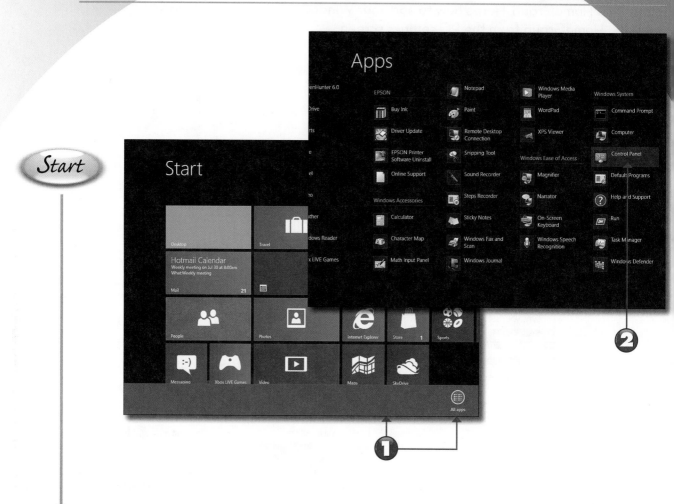

Right-click the bottom of the Start screen and select **All apps**.

Click **Control Panel**.

Continued

TIP

Instant Search from the Start Screen You can also type control panel from the Start screen to quickly locate Control Panel in step 1. ■

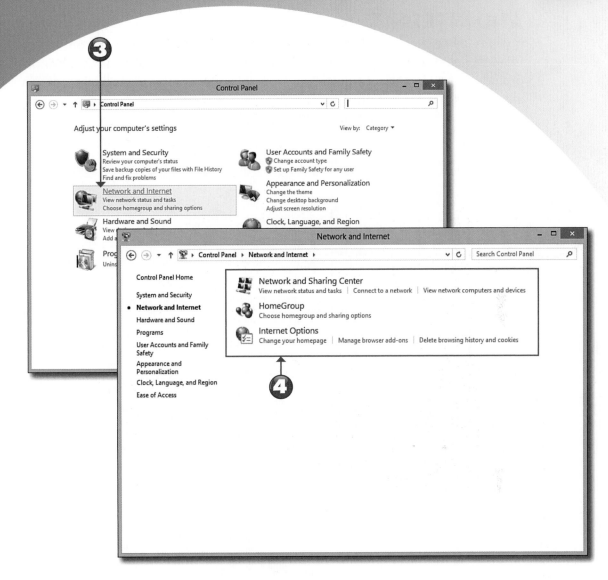

3 Click **Network and Internet**.

4 The settings available in Network and Internet.

End

NOTE

How to Use the Network and Internet Window Use the Network and Sharing Center to set up and view connections. Use HomeGroup to set up or connect to a HomeGroup, an easy-to-manage, secure network of Windows 7 and/or Windows 8 computers. Use Internet Options to configure the Internet Explorer browser. ■

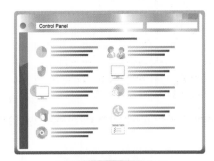

SETTING UP A HOMEGROUP FROM NETWORK AND INTERNET

If you're more comfortable setting up and managing a HomeGroup from the Windows Control Panel, Windows 8 provides the same HomeGroup options that Windows 7 provides. The HomeGroup setting in Control Panel's Network and Internet window also provides more options than the Windows 8 Start screen. Here's how to set up a HomeGroup from the Windows desktop.

From the Network and Internet window, click **HomeGroup**.

Click **Create a homegroup**.

Click **Next**.

Continued

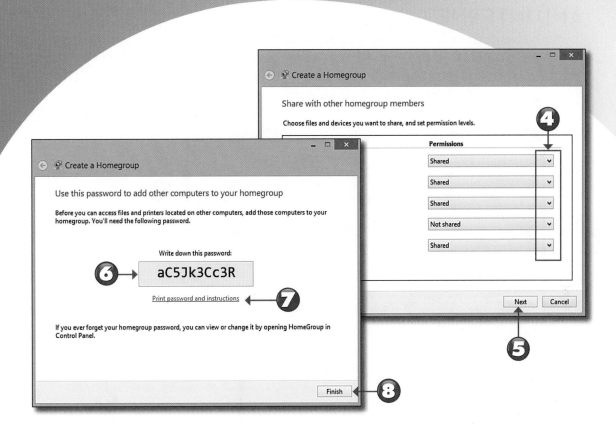

4 Select the items you want to share.

5 Click **Next**.

6 Write down the HomeGroup password.

7 Click to print the password and instructions for other computers.

8 Click **Finish.**

End

NOTE

HomeGroups Are Lonely with Just One Member Before a HomeGroup can be used to share information and printers, other users must join it, or you must join an existing HomeGroup. ■

JOINING A HOMEGROUP FROM NETWORK AND INTERNET

If your network already has a HomeGroup, you should connect to it rather than create a new one. If you created the HomeGroup, other users on your network must connect to it. This tutorial covers the steps for connecting a Windows 8 computer to a HomeGroup, but the steps are similar for Windows 7 computers.

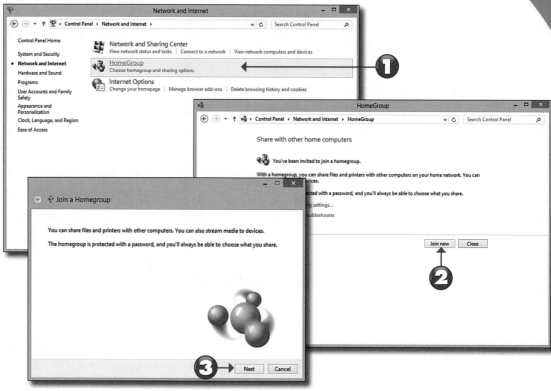

 Start

1 From the Network and Internet window, click **HomeGroup**.

2 Click **Join now**.

3 Click **Next**.

Continued

NOTE

Adding Windows 7 Computers to Your HomeGroup A computer running Windows 7 can join a HomeGroup only if its network location is set as Home. To change the network location, use the Network and Sharing Center. A computer running Windows 8 can join a HomeGroup only if you select the Yes, Turn on Sharing and Connect to Devices option when you connect to the network. ■

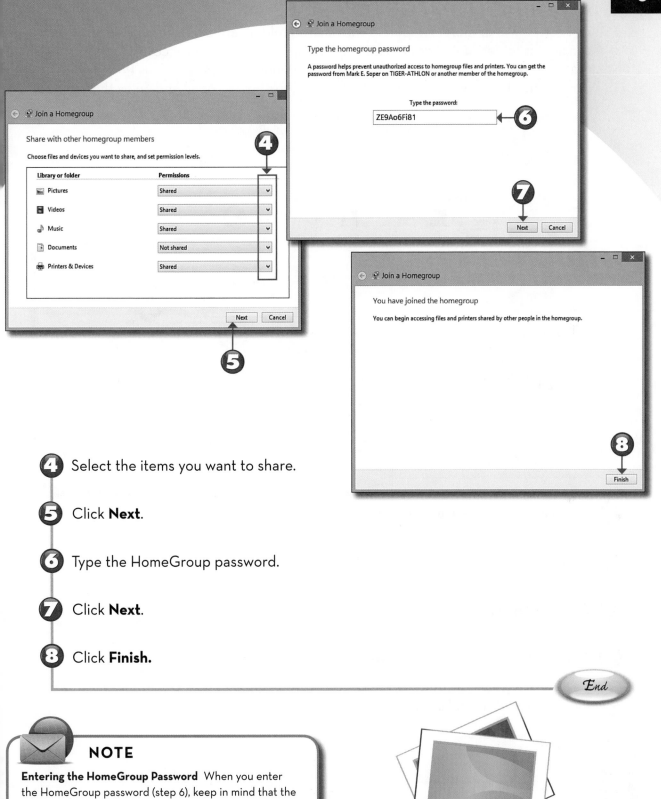

4 Select the items you want to share.

5 Click **Next**.

6 Type the HomeGroup password.

7 Click **Next**.

8 Click **Finish.**

End

NOTE

Entering the HomeGroup Password When you enter the HomeGroup password (step 6), keep in mind that the password is case-sensitive; you must use uppercase and lowercase letters as listed. ■

OPENING HOMEGROUP FILES

As soon as two or more computers with shared folders are part of your HomeGroup, you can access folders and files on the HomeGroup as easily as you access your own files from the Windows desktop. Keep in mind that new Windows 8 apps, such as Photos and Music, can't be used to play files on shared folders. Here's how to open and enjoy those files.

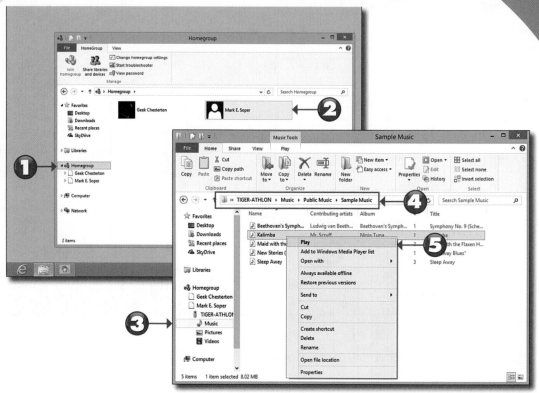

1 In File Explorer, click **Homegroup**.

2 Click a user's name.

3 Click a category.

4 Navigate to the folder that includes the file you want to use.

5 Right-click an item and select what you want to do with it.

Start

End

TIP

Double-Clicking to Open an Item You can also double-click an item to open it in its native application. ■

CUSTOMIZED SHARING FOR FOLDERS YOU CHOOSE

The normal setting for a HomeGroup permits read-only access to files in shared libraries. However, if you need to share files that might need to be changed by other HomeGroup members, you must specify this on a folder-by-folder basis. Here's how it works.

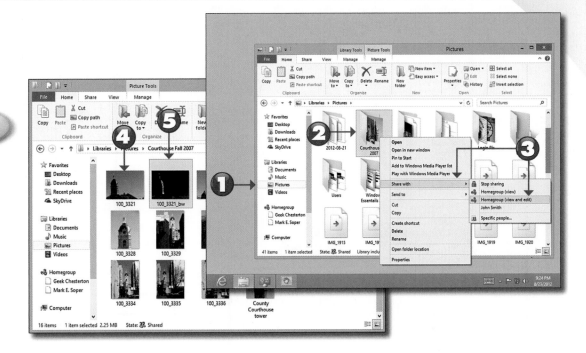

1 In File Explorer, locate a folder or library you want other users to be able to edit.

2 Right-click the folder or library.

3 Point to **Share with** and select **Homegroup (view and edit)**.

4 The original photo.

5 The version of the photo edited by another user on the HomeGroup.

End

NOTE

Sharing with Specific Users on the Network If you want to share with a specific user on the network, you can select the name and click Add in step 4. ∎

VIEWING A FOLDER'S SHARING SETTINGS

If you customize sharing for individual folders, it might sometimes be difficult to remember exactly which folders are shared in a particular way. Use the folder's Properties dialog box to see how a folder is shared.

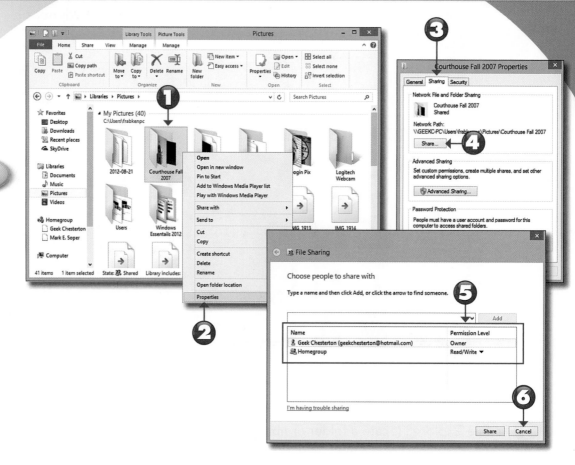

Right-click a folder in File Explorer.

Click **Properties**.

Click the **Sharing** tab.

Click **Share**.

Note the sharing settings.

Click **Cancel**.

End

LEAVING A HOMEGROUP FROM THE PC SETTINGS SCREEN

A HomeGroup is an easy way to share files and devices, but if you need to leave a HomeGroup, you can do so from either the PC settings screen or from the Home-Group window in Control Panel. This lesson covers leaving a HomeGroup from the PC settings screen.

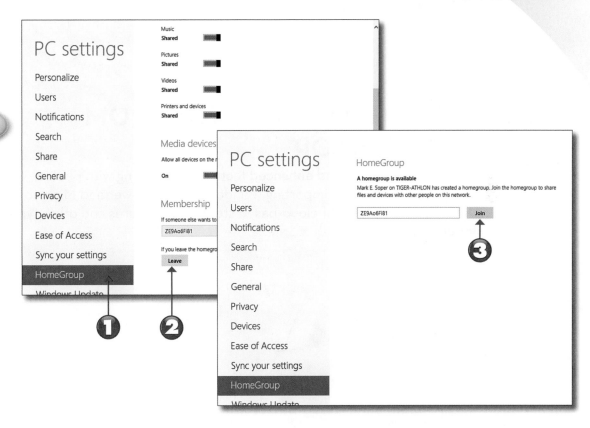

1 Click **HomeGroup**.

2 Click **Leave**.

3 You can later rejoin the HomeGroup by clicking **Join**.

End

NOTE

Persistent Passwords Unless the HomeGroup password has been changed, Windows 8 remembers the password and supplies it for you, as shown in step 3. ■

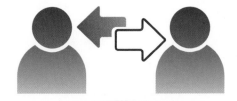

Chapter 14

WORKING WITH PHOTOS FROM YOUR DESKTOP

Windows 8 includes new and enhanced features for working with photos, including improved picture importing. Windows Photo Viewer and Microsoft SkyDrive place the power of cloud-based storage for pictures and other types of files on your desktop.

Importing Photos
and Videos

Adjusting Zoom Controls in
Windows Photo Viewer

Sharing Files
on SkyDrive

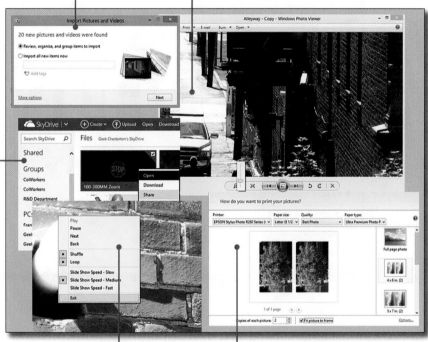

Slide Show
Playback Controls

Printing Photos with the
Print Pictures Wizard

ADDING PICTURES TO YOUR PICTURES LIBRARY

If you upgraded to Windows 8, your Pictures library includes the contents of the Pictures or My Pictures folders from your previous version of Windows. However, if you have a preinstalled version of Windows 8 on a new computer, your Pictures library doesn't include any of your photos. Here's how to copy photos from another location into your Pictures library.

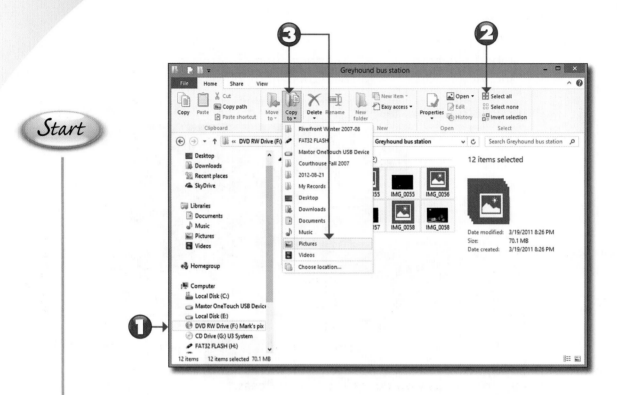

 In File Explorer, open a location that contains pictures.

 Click **Select all** to select all photos.

 Open the **Copy to** menu and select **Pictures**.

Continued

TIP

Choosing Only Your Favorite Photos In step 2, you can select individual photos by clicking the first photo, and then holding down the Ctrl key and clicking other photos. You also can use the Item check boxes option available from the View tab to select photos. These options work with all file types in Windows. ■

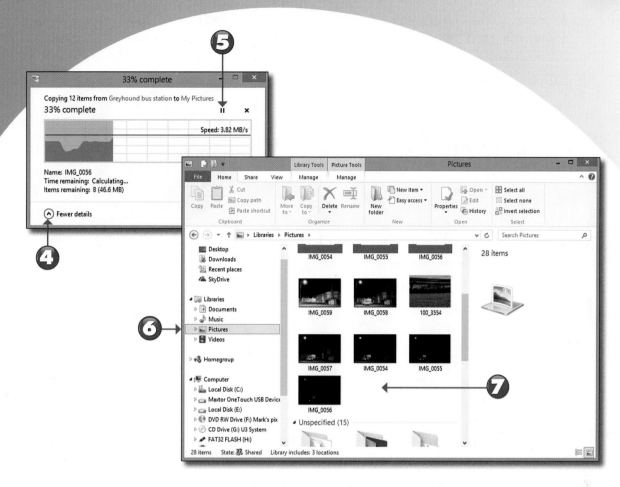

4 Click to change the details view during the copy process.

5 Click to pause or resume the copy process.

6 Click **Pictures**.

7 You see pictures copied from the other location.

End

IMPORTING PICTURES

When you take photos with your digital camera, the next logical stop for them is your Pictures library. Here's how to import your photos from your camera.

Start

① Connect the USB cable for your digital camera to your camera and to a USB port on your computer.

② Turn on the camera.

③ Press the **Playback** key if the camera is not recognized.

④ Right-click the camera icon in File Explorer.

⑤ Select **Import pictures and videos**.

⑥ Click **Next**.

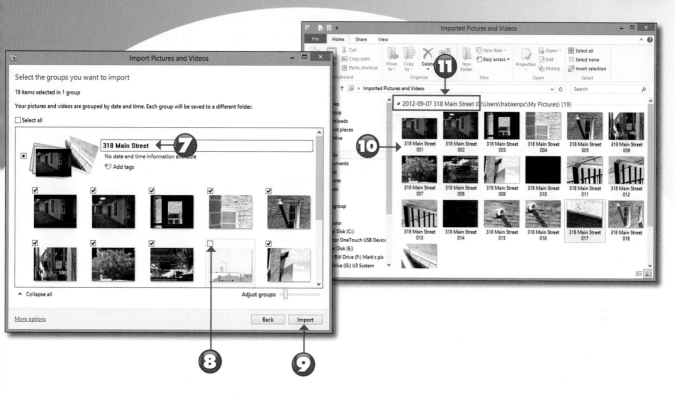

7 Enter a name for the group of photos.

8 Clear the check boxes from photos you don't want to import.

9 Click **Import**.

10 Photos are imported and renamed to include the group name.

11 The folder name is the date followed by the group name.

End

TIP

Finding Your Digital Camera in File Explorer You can view your Pictures library (like all other libraries) in File Explorer. Your digital camera or camcorder displays in the Computer section of the left pane of File Explorer—just after the drive letters on your computer system. ■

TIP

RAW Photos Displayed as Icons Windows 8 displays preview icons for JPEG photos, but RAW photos, which are proprietary to different camera models, are displayed as icons. To solve this problem, install Microsoft Digital Camera Codec Pack from Windows Update when available, or contact the digital camera vendor for a RAW image codec made for Windows 8. ■

SELECTING IMPORT OPTIONS

The standard import options in File Explorer change the name of your pictures and create a folder that includes the date and the group name. If you prefer other import options, you can change these settings.

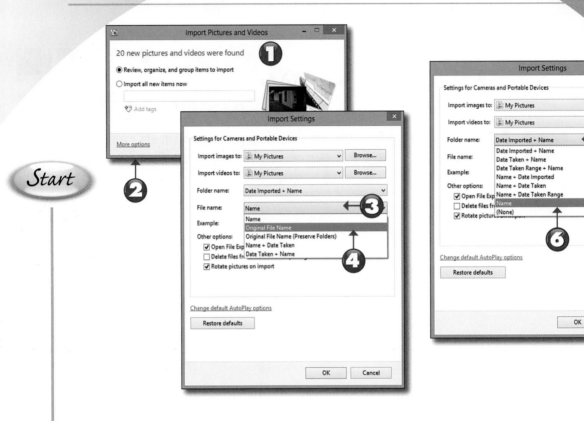

Start

1 Start the import process as listed in steps 1-5 of the previous lesson.

2 Click **More options**.

3 The default setting for the picture name.

4 Select to keep the original filename.

5 The default setting for the folder name.

6 Select to use group name only for folder name.

Continued

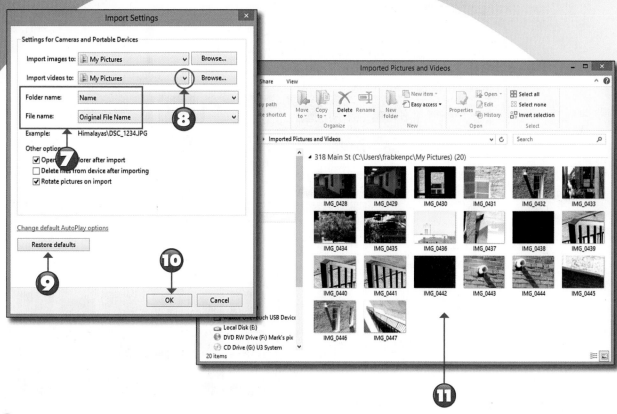

7 New folder and filename settings.

8 Open to choose a new default folder for video imports (such as Videos).

9 Click to restore the defaults.

10 Click **OK** to return to the Imported Pictures and Videos window.

11 The imported photos and folder using the new import settings.

End

NOTE

Why Use the Original File Name for Photos? If you need to use photos for evidence in a civil or criminal case, the filenames should not be changed. Another benefit of using the original filenames for photos is to make it easier to determine which camera you used—different camera brands use different numbering schemes for their photos. ■

CHANGING PICTURE SETTINGS

You can rotate and rename your photos in the Pictures library.

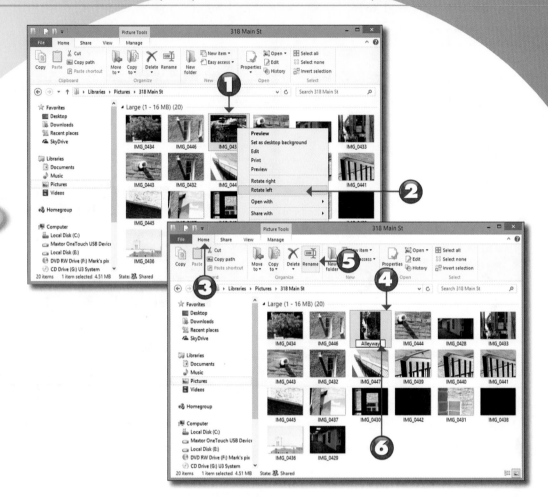

Start

1 Right-click a photo.

2 Select **Rotate left** (or Rotate right).

3 Click the **Home** tab, if it isn't already selected.

4 Click a photo you want to rename.

5 Click **Rename**.

6 Enter a new name for the selected photo.

End

MAKING A COPY OF A PHOTO

If you need to edit a photo, you should make a copy of it and edit the copy. This keeps your original image intact. Here's how to make a copy.

Start

1 Click a photo.

2 Click **Copy**.

3 Click **Paste**.

4 A copy of the photo is created next to the original version.

End

USING WINDOWS PHOTO VIEWER

Do you want to see your photos in full-screen view? Or, maybe you'd like to view your photos as a slide show. You can use Windows Photo Viewer for each of these tasks. Here's how to start and use this application.

Start

1 Right-click a photo.

2 Click **Preview**.

3 Move to the previous or next photo.

4 Rotate the photo to the left.

5 Rotate the photo to the right.

6 Delete the current photo.

Continued

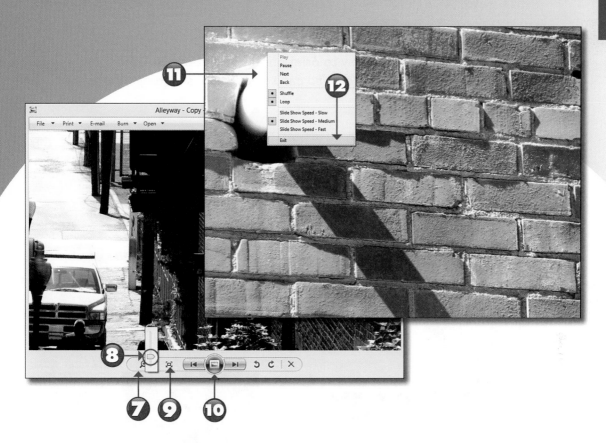

7 Click to open zoom control.

8 Click and drag up to make the image larger; click and drag down to make the image smaller.

9 Toggle between Actual size and Fit to window.

10 Click **Play slide show**.

11 Right-click the image in the slide show to view or change the slide show settings.

12 Click **Exit** to end the slide show.

End

NOTE

Slide Show Playback Options The dots shown to the left of the menu options in step 12 indicate the current settings for playback and slide show speed. You can also pause or resume the slide show, move to the previous or next photo, and enable or disable shuffle and loop playback modes. ■

PRINTING PHOTOS WITH WINDOWS PHOTO VIEWER

Windows Photo Viewer makes it easy to print photos in different sizes and place multiple photos on a single sheet of paper. You also can select the best settings for printing your photos.

Start

1 Open the **Print** menu and select **Print**.

2 Select the correct paper size.

3 Choose the desired print quality.

4 Select the paper type.

Continued

NOTE

Solving Limited Photo Printing Options If you are using a printer driver included with Windows 8, you might not be able to adjust settings for print quality or paper type. Download a Windows 8 printer driver (or a Windows 7 driver, if a Windows 8 driver is not available) from your printer vendor. Install the new driver so you can use your printer's advanced settings. ■

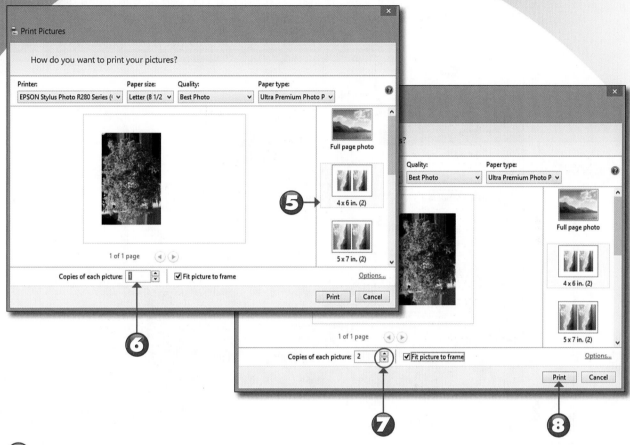

5 Click the desired print size.

6 The normal setting prints one copy per sheet, even if you select a smaller print size.

7 Adjust the number of copies to fill the sheet.

8 Click **Print**.

End

TIP

Printing with Plain Paper Some vendor-supplied printer drivers might not include Plain Paper as an option in Windows Photo Viewer's Print utility. Select the original driver provided with Windows 8 or open your photos in a different program, such as Paint, and use its Print menu to choose your printer and its print options. ■

INSTALLING MICROSOFT SKYDRIVE

Microsoft SkyDrive provides cloud-based (online) storage for photos and other types of files. Anyone with a Microsoft email ID—ending in @hotmail or @live—can use Microsoft SkyDrive. If you want to share photos or files with several people, SkyDrive makes it easy. SkyDrive is built in to the Windows 8 Start screen, but you can also install a desktop version of SkyDrive to make synchronizing photos and other files even easier.

Start

1. Click to open Internet Explorer.

2. Type **https://apps.live.com/skydrive** and press **Enter**.

3. Click to download the app.

4. Click **Run** to install the app.

5. Click **Get started**.

6. Click **Next**.

Continued

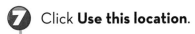

7 Click **Use this location**.

8 If you want files on this PC available to you on your other devices, make sure this box is checked.

9 Click **Done** to start using SkyDrive on your Windows desktop.

10 Your Skydrive folder opens.

End

NOTE

Local Versus Microsoft Accounts and SkyDrive If you log in to Windows 8 using a local account, you will be prompted to log in to SkyDrive with your Microsoft ID and password during the setup process. The user shown in this chapter logs in to Windows 8 with a Microsoft account, so a separate login is not required. ■

COPYING FILES TO SKYDRIVE

After you install SkyDrive, you can use it to gain easy access to cloud-based files on your desktop and send files from your desktop to the cloud.

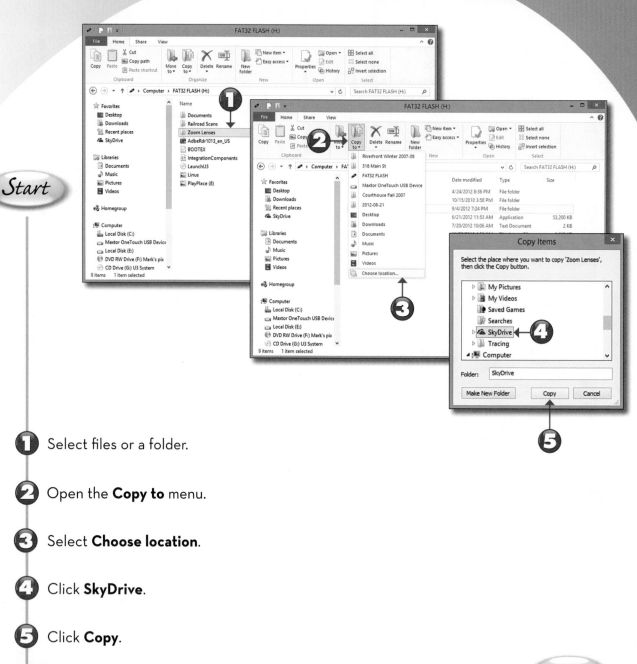

Start

1. Select files or a folder.

2. Open the **Copy to** menu.

3. Select **Choose location**.

4. Click **SkyDrive**.

5. Click **Copy**.

Continued

NOTE

Copying Speed The dialog box shown in steps 6 and 7 on the following page displays only if the copy process takes longer than a second or two. ∎

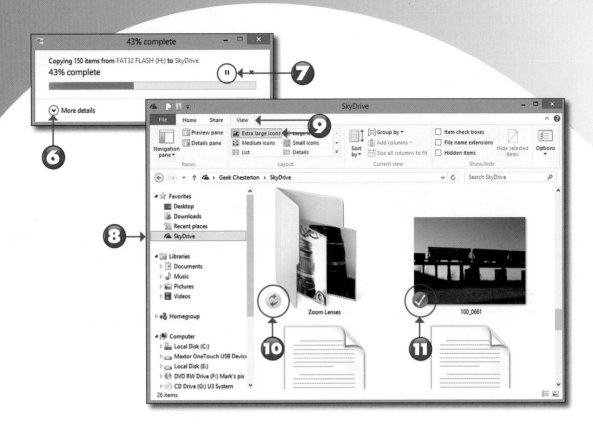

6. Click to show more or fewer details.

7. Click to pause or continue copy process.

8. Click **SkyDrive**.

9. On the **View** tab, click **Extra large icons**.

10. The copied folder being synced to SkyDrive.

11. The folder already synced to SkyDrive.

End

NOTE

Viewing SkyDrive Sync Status Regardless of the view you choose in step 9, the icons visible in steps 10 and 11 are shown. The Extra large icons view was selected to make them easier to see. ■

SHARING PHOTOS ON SKYDRIVE

In this lesson, you learn how to view your photos on SkyDrive's cloud-based storage. You also learn how to use email to share photos with other users.

1 Click the **Internet Explorer** icon.

2 Type **https://skydrive.live.com** and press **Enter**.

3 Right-click a file or folder and select **Share**.

4 Select a sharing method (in this example, email).

5 Start typing the name of a contact.

6 Click the correct match.

Continued

7 Enter a personal message (optional).

8 Change the default settings as needed.

9 Click **Share**.

End

NOTE

SkyDrive Logins with a Local Account If you log in to Windows 8 using a local account, you will be prompted to log in to SkyDrive with your Microsoft ID and password after you enter the SkyDrive URL. ∎

TIP

Sharing via Facebook, Twitter, and LinkedIn You can also share photos with Facebook, Twitter, and LinkedIn. Before you can share photos with social media services, you must connect your Microsoft account with those services. Use your Microsoft Account Profile page to make these connections. To get started, click your name in the upper-right corner of the SkyDrive window. For more details about sharing, click the Help me choose how to share link. ∎

Chapter 15

WORKING WITH MUSIC FROM YOUR DESKTOP

Windows Media Player includes familiar ways to organize, play, and burn music CDs. You also can synchronize your music to media players. With Windows Media Player, you can enjoy music on your system, from your network, or from around the world.

Burning a
Music CD

Preparing to Sync to a
Media Player

A Visualization
of the Current
Music Track

Using Drag and
Drop to Create
a Playlist

Ripping an
Album

Viewing Music
By Artist

AutoPlay Dialog Box
for an Audio CD

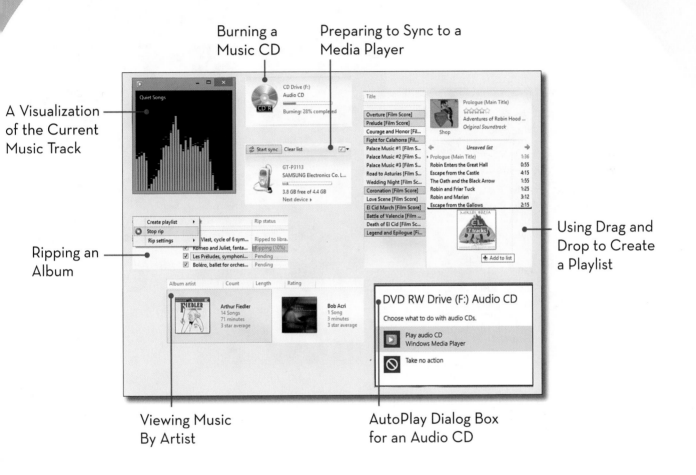

STARTING WINDOWS MEDIA PLAYER

Windows Media Player enables you to play and create digital music tracks from CDs, watch video clips, and share media with other users. In this lesson, you discover how to launch Windows Media Player and add it to the Windows taskbar.

1 Right-click an empty area of the Start screen and click **All apps**.

2 Click **Windows Media Player**.

Continued

NOTE

DVD Playback Now in Windows Media Center Only In Windows 8, Windows Media Player is no longer designed to play back DVDs. However, Windows Media Center (available as an optional feature for Windows 8) can be used to play back DVDs. ■

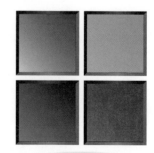

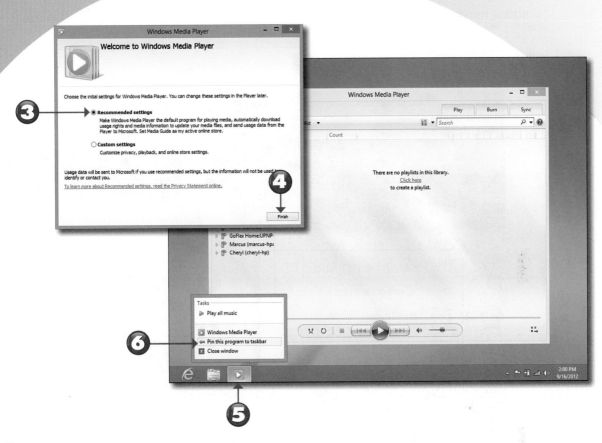

3 Click **Recommended Settings**.

4 Click **Finish**.

5 Right-click the Windows Media Player icon on the taskbar.

6 Select **Pin this program to taskbar**.

End

PLAYING AN AUDIO CD

If you're not interested in downloading music, you can use Windows Media Player to play audio CDs. And, playing audio CDs puts you just a couple of clicks away from ripping them to digital music tracks.

Start

1. Insert an audio CD into your computer's optical drive.

2. Click the AutoPlay notification.

3. Click **Play audio CD - Windows Media Player**.

4. The current album.

5. The current track playing.

6. Point to the playback window and click the **Switch to Library** button.

Continued

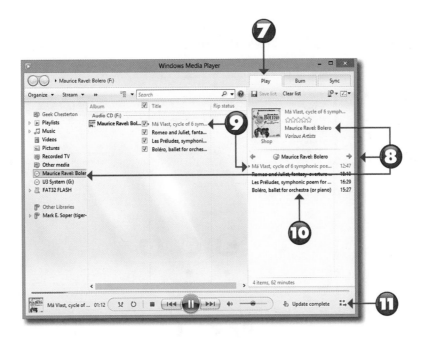

7 Click the **Play** tab.

8 The current album.

9 The current track.

10 The current playlist.

11 Click to switch back to **Now Playing** mode.

End

USING PLAYBACK CONTROLS IN WINDOWS MEDIA PLAYER

Windows Media Player makes it easy to play your media in any order you choose, or to pause it when it's time to grab a phone call. Here's an explanation of these and other playback controls in Windows Media Player.

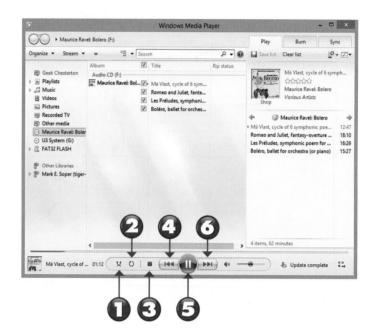

1 Shuffle playback.

2 Repeat current playlist.

3 Stop playback or recording.

4 Go to previous track.

5 Pause playback.

6 Go to next track.

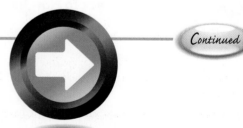

Continued

7 Click and drag to desired position in current track (Seek).

8 Click to resume playback.

9 Click to mute volume; click again to restore volume.

10 Drag to adjust playback volume.

End

NOTE

Controls in Now Playing Mode The Now Playing view also includes stop, previous/next track, pause/play, and volume controls. ■

RIPPING (COPYING) AN AUDIO CD

Tired of shuffling CDs in and out of a boom box? If you haven't yet discovered how easy it is to convert your CDs into audio tracks, let Windows Media Player do the work for you. In this example, you learn how to rip a CD that has already been inserted into your computer's optical drive.

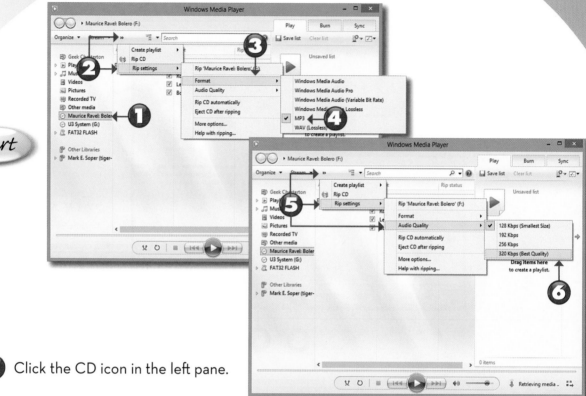

Start

1. Click the CD icon in the left pane.

2. Expand the menu (if necessary) and point to **Rip settings**.

3. Point to **Format**.

4. Click **MP3**.

5. Select **Rip settings** again, and then point to **Audio Quality**.

6. Click **320 Kbps (Best Quality)**.

Continued

NOTE

MP3 Versus WMA MP3 files can be played by all digital media players. Windows Media Audio formats work well with Windows-based players but don't work with Apple iPods, iPhones, or iPads. ■

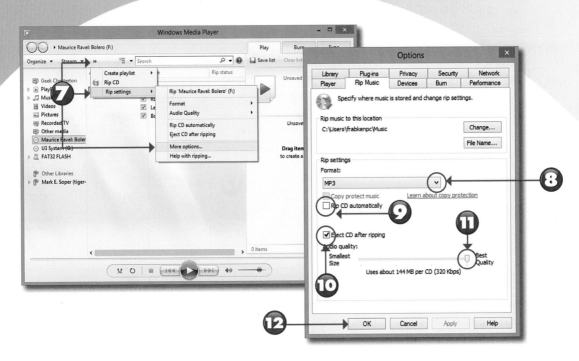

7 Select **Rip settings**, and then click **More options**.

8 Click to select a different file format.

9 Click the empty checkbox if you want to rip CDs automatically when you insert them.

10 Click the empty checkbox to eject a CD after ripping it.

11 Drag to adjust quality/size settings for ripping.

12 Click **OK**.

Continued

NOTE

Full-Screen View and WMP Menus If you run Windows Media Player in full-screen view and all menu items are visible, you will not see the >> symbol. This symbol is displayed if some menu items are hidden due to space limitations. ■

NOTE

Quality Settings By ripping files at the highest quality, you create files that can be copied to lower-quality versions for playback on portable devices. ■

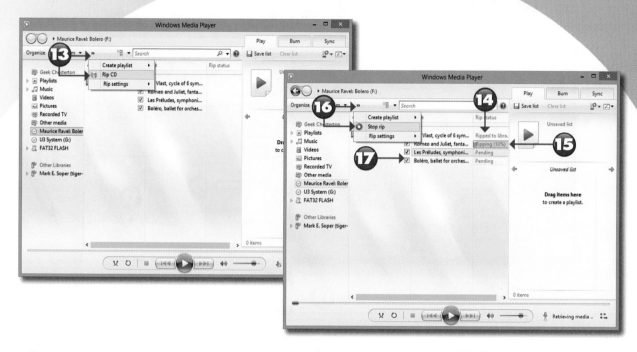

13 Expand the menu and click **Rip CD**.

14 A ripped track.

15 A track being ripped.

16 Expand the menu and click to stop rip.

17 Tracks waiting to be ripped.

Continued

NOTE

Toggling the Playlist Pane On and Off The Playlist pane shown in this section can be toggled off and on. To learn how, see the section "Setting Up Playlists," later in this chapter. ■

18 All tracks ripped.

19 Expand the **Music** category.

20 Click **Album**.

21 The album is listed in the Music library.

End

TIP

Ripping Another CD Windows Media Player sometimes has difficulty figuring out whether you're finished with a CD. To get ready to rip another CD, right-click the CD in Windows Media Player and select Eject. After the disc is ejected, remove it and close the drive. If the track list is still on-screen, open File Manager, open Computer, and double-click the optical drive icon. When it changes from the disc icon to the drive icon, Windows knows the drive is empty. Return to Windows Media Player, and the track list should be empty. You can now insert another disc and rip it. ■

SELECTING AND PLAYING ALBUMS AND INDIVIDUAL TRACKS

Downloaded music, music ripped from CDs, and audio you record yourself are all digital music tracks, as far as Windows Media Player is concerned. You can view and play albums or individual tracks in a variety of ways.

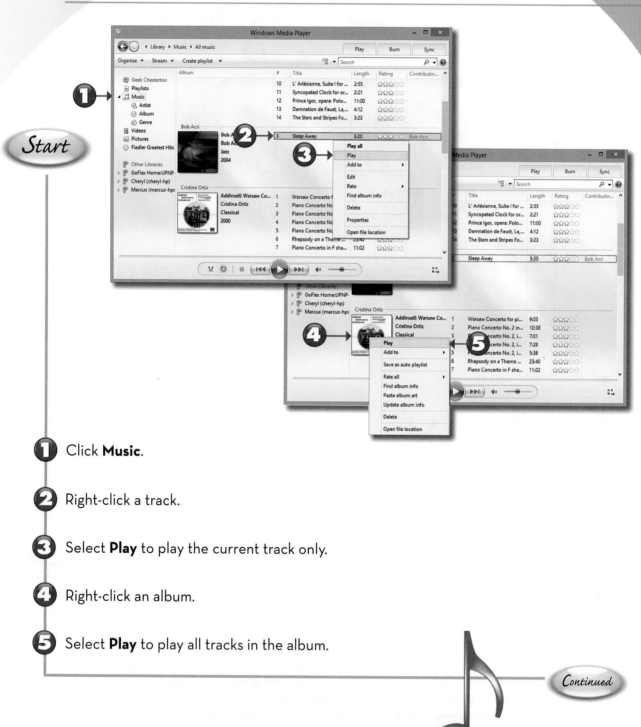

Start

1 Click **Music**.

2 Right-click a track.

3 Select **Play** to play the current track only.

4 Right-click an album.

5 Select **Play** to play all tracks in the album.

Continued

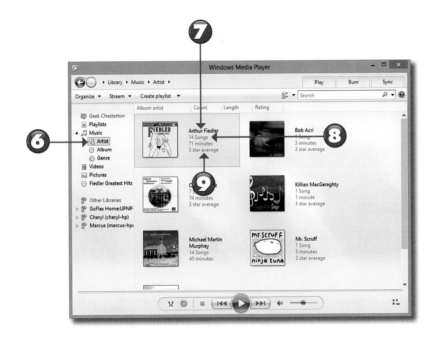

6 Click **Artist**.

7 Click an artist.

8 The number of tracks (songs) by artist.

9 The total time and current rating.

Continued

TIP

How to Rate Albums and Songs To change the rating for an album, right-click it, select Rate All (Songs), and select the rating desired (1–5 stars or Unrated). Windows Media Player also assigns ratings based on how often you play a song; all songs (and hence all albums) start out with a three-star rating. To rate a song, open the Album view and highlight the stars in the Rating column. ∎

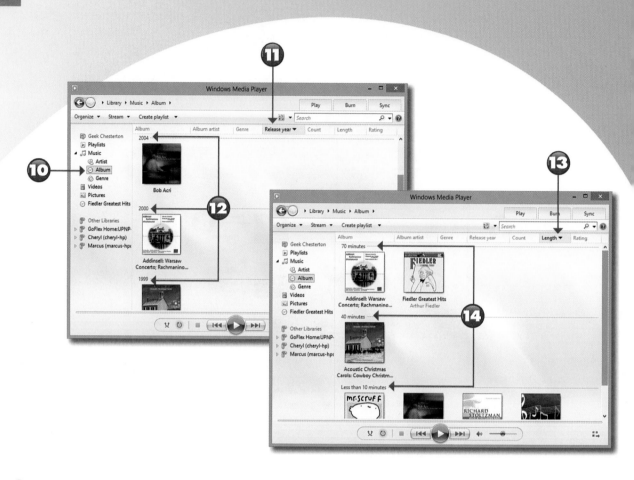

10 Click **Album**.

11 Click **Release year**.

12 The albums listed from most recent to oldest.

13 Click **Length**.

14 The albums listed from longest to shortest playing time.

Continued

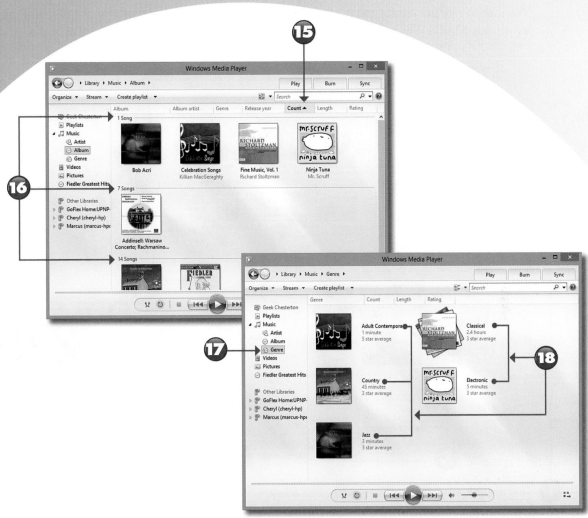

15 Click **Count**.

16 The albums are grouped by number of songs (tracks).

17 Click **Genre**.

18 The songs are stacked by genre.

End

USING VISUALIZATIONS

Want some visual excitement while you listen to music? You can choose a visualization in Windows Media Player to see shapes and colors move in time with the music. Here's how.

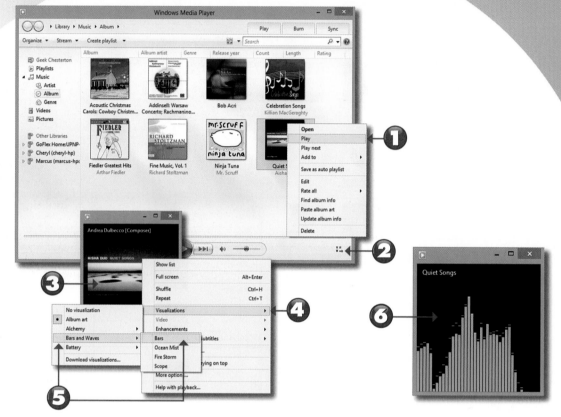

Start

1 Right-click a song or album and click **Play**.

2 Click **Now Playing**.

3 Right-click the album cover.

4 Point to **Visualizations**.

5 Point to a visualization category, and then select an option.

6 The visualization plays in the window.

Continued

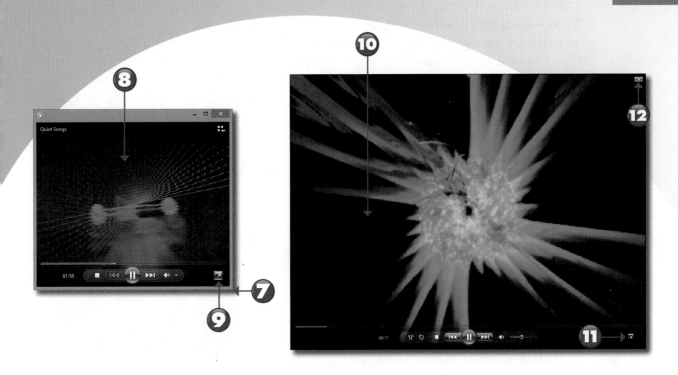

7 Drag the lower-right corner of the window to make the visualization larger or smaller.

8 Hover the mouse over the playback window to display the playback and full-screen controls.

9 Click the **View full screen** button.

10 Hover the mouse over the screen to display the playback and other controls.

11 Click to return to windowed playback.

12 Click to close Windows Media Player (and stop playback).

End

NOTE

Album Art and Visualizations Album art (see step 3) is the standard visualization in Windows Media Player. In steps 5 and 6, the Bars and Waves—Bars variation was used. In step 7, the Alchemy visualization was selected. ■

SETTING UP PLAYLISTS

With Windows Media Player, you can create a mix of tracks just for playback on your PC, sync music with a digital media player, or burn a CD of your personal "greatest hits." First, you need to set up a playlist. Here's how to make one.

Start

1 Click **Organize**.

2 Point to **Layout**.

3 Select **Show list**.

4 Click **Music**.

5 Right-click a track and point to **Add to**.

6 Select **Play list**.

Continued

TIP

Selecting by Artist, Album, or Genre Selecting Music in step 4 enables you to scroll through all the albums in your collection; however, if you prefer to select by other categories, choose Artist, Album, or Genre in step 4 after clicking Music (if necessary). ■

NOTE

Hiding/Displaying the Playlist Pane If the Playlist pane is already visible on the right side of the Windows Media Player window, skip steps 1–3. To hide the Playlist pane, uncheck Show List in step 3. ■

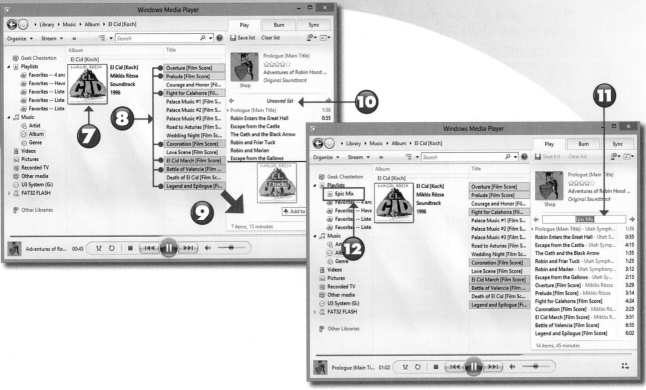

7 Select another album.

8 Click the first track; then hold down the **Ctrl** key and click additional tracks.

9 Drag them into the list window.

10 Click **Unsaved list**.

11 Enter a name for the list.

12 The new playlist is now available.

End

TIP

Editing a Playlist To edit a playlist, click it. Then, click a song and drag it to a new position, or right-click the song in the playlist and select Remove from List, Move Up, or Move Down. ■

SYNCING FILES TO A MEDIA PLAYER

You can sync files from a list you create on the spot in Windows Media Player or from a playlist you have already created. In this tutorial, we use the playlist we created in the previous tutorial.

Start

1. Connect a media player to your computer.

2. Click the **Sync** tab.

3. Click **Playlists** if the list is not expanded.

4. Click a playlist.

5. Verify that the correct device is listed on the Sync tab.

6. Click to start the sync process.

Continued

7 The available space on the device.

8 Click **Start sync**.

9 After the sync process is over, click to see sync results.

10 The sync results.

End

TIP

What Else Is On the Media Player? Click the Music, Videos, or Pictures categories listed under the media player in the left pane to see other media content. ■

BURNING (CREATING) A MUSIC CD

In Windows Media Player, you can select music and burn it to a CD that will play in most CD players. You can use a playlist you have already created or use drag and drop to create a new list specifically for the CD. We use the second method in this tutorial.

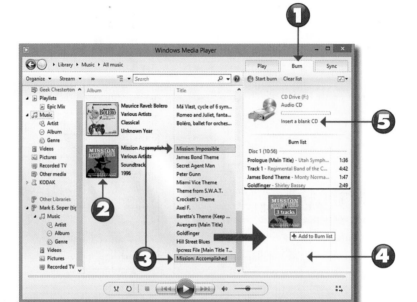

Start

1 Click the **Burn** tab.

2 Select an album.

3 Select music tracks. Use the Ctrl key to select more than one track from an album or other category.

4 Drag the tracks to the Burn list window.

5 Insert a blank CD.

Continued

6 The space available on the CD.

7 Click **Start burn**.

8 Click the **Blank Disc** icon.

9 The burn process indicator.

10 Click here if you choose to cancel the burn.

11 The track being burned.

End

NOTE

Finishing Up Your Disc At the end of the burn process, the CD is ejected and you can label the disc. ∎

Chapter 16

BROWSING THE INTERNET FROM YOUR DESKTOP

Windows 8 includes Internet Explorer 10 (IE10), the latest version of Microsoft's web browser. When you launch IE10 from the Start screen, you are using a touch-optimized version of the browser that doesn't fully support Adobe Flash and has limited support for plug-ins. If you use IE10 from the Windows desktop, however, you have a full-featured web browser that fully supports Adobe Flash, other plug-ins, favorites, and other familiar Internet Explorer features.

IE10 offers features similar to IE9, such as its built-in download manager, a searchable address bar, and the capability to pin individual websites to the taskbar. IE10 is even faster than IE9 and renders pages better than IE9. This chapter shows you how to use IE10's most important features when you run it from the Windows desktop.

Bing Mapping Web
Accelerator

InPrivate Browsing

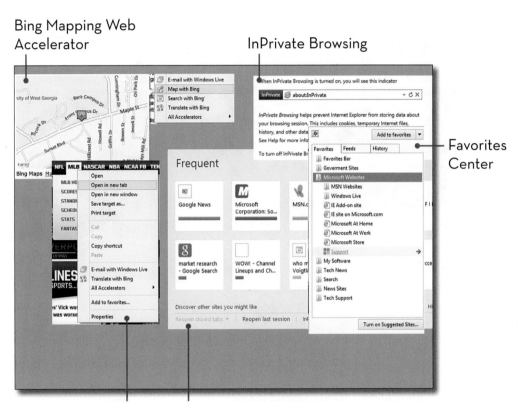

Favorites
Center

Right-Click Menu

Frequently Visited Websites

STARTING IE10 FROM THE DESKTOP

There are two methods of starting Internet Explorer 10: directly from the Start screen or from the Windows desktop. When you run IE10 from the Windows desktop, you have full support for plug-ins, working with tabs is easier, and you have full access to settings you might want to change. Here's how to start IE10 from the Windows desktop.

1. Click the Desktop tile on the Start screen.

2. Click the IE icon on the Windows desktop.

3. The IE10 address bar.

4. A blank tab.

5. The IE10 Home, Favorites, and Tools icons.

End

NOTE

Browsing the Web in the New UI Refer to Chapter 5, "Browsing the Web in the New UI," for details on how to browse the web using the new Windows 8 user interface. ■

ENTERING A WEBSITE ADDRESS (URL)

Internet Explorer 10 now displays more information about website addresses you've previously visited when you enter an address (URL). It's now easier to go back to an address you've previously visited, even if you have visited several pages in the same domain.

Start

1 Begin typing the name of a website. You do not need to add the "www."

2 If you have already visited a web page with the text in either the website name (URL) or the web page title, these appear in the History list.

3 To choose the first match, press **Shift+Enter**.

4 Point to a website in the list with your mouse or stylus, and click it.

5 To go to the exact match for what you typed, press **Enter**.

6 Click to turn on suggestions from Bing search.

End

TIP

Keyboard Navigation In step 4, you can also use the down arrow to highlight the page you want to load, and then press Enter. ■

WORKING WITH TABS

Internet Explorer 10 includes tabbed browsing. In this tutorial, you learn how to open and work with new tabs in IE10.

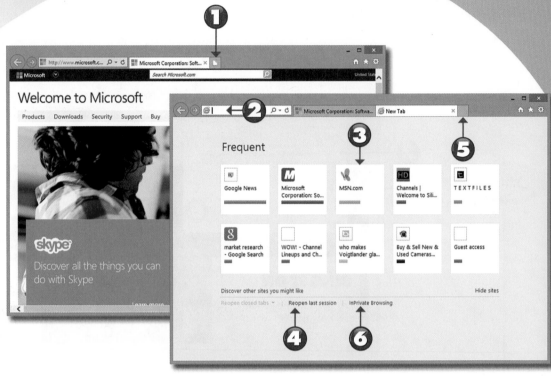

Start

1. Click to open a new tab.

2. Click to enter a website address (URL).

3. Click to reopen a website.

4. Click to reopen the last browsing session.

5. Click to open another new tab.

6. Click to open an InPrivate Browsing window.

End

NOTE

InPrivate Browsing For information about opening a window in IE10 for InPrivate Browsing, see "Using InPrivate Browsing from the Desktop," later in this chapter. ∎

SETTING YOUR HOME PAGE

You can change your home page whenever you want with Internet Explorer 10, and you also can use a tab group as a home page. Here's how to do it.

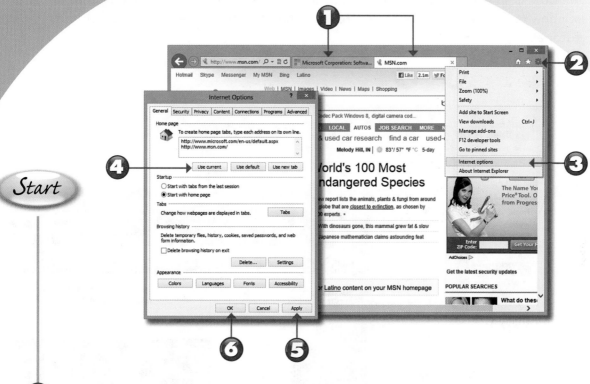

Start

1. Open the page(s) you want to use as your home page.

2. Open the **Tools** menu.

3. Click **Internet options**.

4. Click **Use current**.

5. Click **Apply**.

6. Click **OK**.

End

NOTE

Selecting a Single Tab When Multiple Tabs Are Open If you have opened multiple tabs in IE10 but want to use only one tab for your home page, make sure you click that tab before you open the Internet Options dialog box. Skip step 4, and only the current tab will be set as your home tab. ■

OPENING A LINK

Because Internet Explorer 10 supports tabbed browsing, you can open a link to another website in three ways—as a replacement for the current page, as a new tab in the same window, or in a new window. When you click on a link, the link might open in the same window or in a new window. To control how the link opens, use the method shown in this tutorial.

1 Right-click a link.

2 To open the link in the current tab, select **Open**.

3 Right-click a link in the new window.

4 Select **Open in new tab**.

Continued

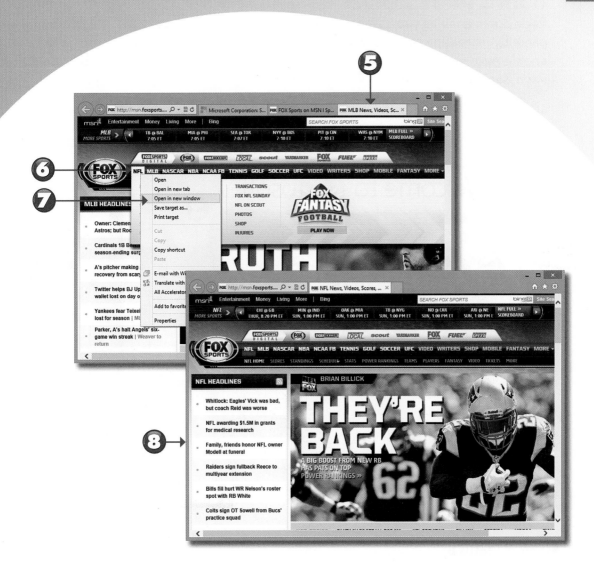

5 To view the contents of the new tab, click it.

6 Right-click a link on the new tab.

7 Select **Open in new window**.

8 A new window opens to display the link.

End

USING PAGE ZOOM

Page Zoom enables you to increase or decrease the size of text and graphics on a web page. By increasing the size, you make pages easier to read, and by reducing the size, you enable page viewing without horizontal scrolling. By enabling the status bar, you can make Page Zoom easier to use.

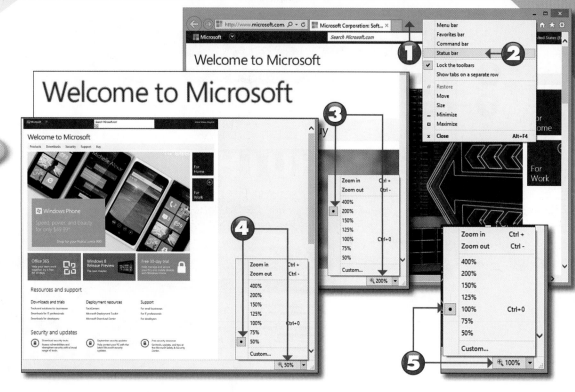

 Start

1 Right-click the browser window's top border.

2 Select **Status bar**.

3 Click the page zoom control and select **200%**.

4 Click the page zoom control and select **50%**.

5 Click the page zoom control and select **100%**.

End

NOTE

Enabling More Bars in IE10 You can also enable the Menu bar (displays File, View, Tools, and other menus), Favorites bar (quick access to favorite websites), and Command bar (quick access to printing and other features) in step 2. ■

PREVIEWING AND PRINTING A WEB PAGE

Internet Explorer 10 enables you to preview and print web pages intelligently. Whether you want to save paper or make full-size page printouts, IE10 does the job the way you want it.

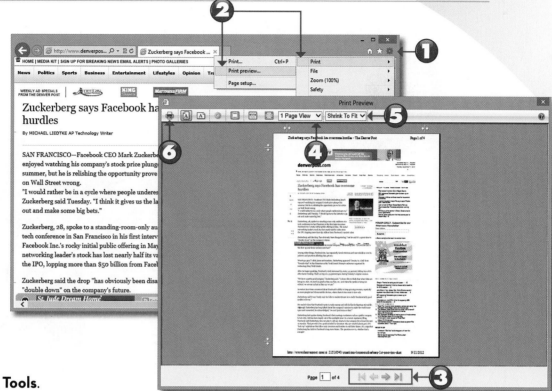

Start

1 Click **Tools**.

2 Point to **Print**, and select **Print preview**.

3 Click to move through pages.

4 Select viewing options.

5 Select print size options.

6 Open the Print dialog box.

End

TIP

See More Pages in Page View To see more pages of a multi-page document at the same time, choose a different view from the Page View menu (step 4). ■

OPENING THE FAVORITES CENTER

The Favorites Center "remembers" your favorite websites so you can go to them with just a couple of mouse clicks whenever you want. Here's how to open it.

Start

1 Click the **Favorites** button to view favorite websites or categories.

2 Click the **Favorites** tab to make it active.

3 Click a folder to view the website links it contains.

4 Click the right-arrow icon to open all the links as a tab group.

5 Click to pin the Favorites Center to the left of the browser window and keep it open at all times.

6 Click **Close** to close the Favorites Center.

End

ADDING FAVORITES TO THE FAVORITES BAR

Internet Explorer 10 makes it even easier to get to your favorite websites with the Favorites Bar. The Favorites Bar sits just below the address bar, providing one-click access to the sites you use most often. Here's how to add sites to the Favorites Bar.

Start

1. Navigate to a website you want to add to the Favorites Bar.

2. Click the **Favorites** button.

3. Open the **Add to favorites** menu.

4. Click the **Add to Favorites bar** menu option.

5. The website is added to the Favorites Bar.

6. To close the Favorites Center, press **Esc** or click any part of the web page that does not have a link.

End

ADDING FAVORITES TO THE FAVORITES CENTER

If you want to revisit some websites—but don't need one-click access to them in the Favorites Bar—add them to the Favorites Center.

Start

1 Right-click a link on a web page.

2 Select **Add to favorites**.

3 To add the link to the Favorites folder, click **Add**.

4 To add the link to a new folder, click **New Folder**.

5 Enter a folder name.

6 Click **Create**.

Continued

TIP

Saving the Current Tab as a Favorite If the website is the only tab in use, you can also save it by clicking Favorites, Add to Favorites and specifying where to save the favorite. For more details, see "Saving a Tab Group as a Favorite," later in this chapter. ■

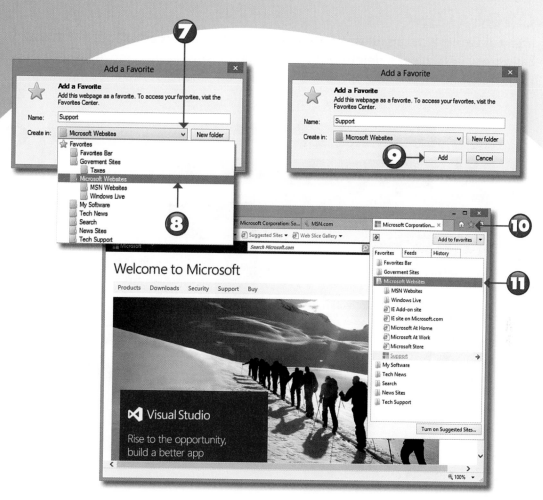

7 To add the link to an existing folder, click the **Create in** arrow.

8 Select the folder.

9 Click **Add**.

10 To see the new favorite, click **Favorites**.

11 Click the folder to expand the category.

End

ORGANIZING FAVORITES

Internet Explorer 10 enables you to organize your favorites even after you create them. You can create new folders, delete favorites you no longer use, and move favorites as desired. In this tutorial, you learn how to move a favorite from one folder to another.

1 Click **Favorites**.

2 Open the **Add to favorites** menu.

3 Click **Organize favorites**.

4 The root Favorites folder opens. To organize a different folder, click it.

5 Select the favorite to move.

6 Click **Move**.

Continued

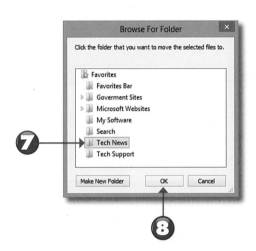

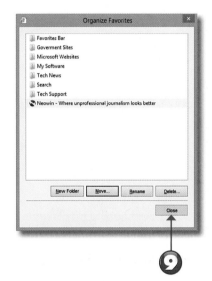

7 Select the folder where you want to move the favorite.

8 Click **OK**.

9 Click **Close**.

End

NOTE

Favorites, Feeds, and History You can also use the Favorites Center to subscribe to RSS feeds (Feeds tab) and to view websites visited by date (History tab). ■

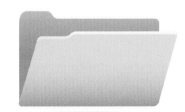

SAVING A TAB GROUP AS A FAVORITE

If you have several websites you rely on throughout the day, such as a web-based email client, news, and sports sites, you can save time by opening them in separate tabs and then saving the tab group as a favorite. In this tutorial, you learn how to set up three tabs and save them as a tab group.

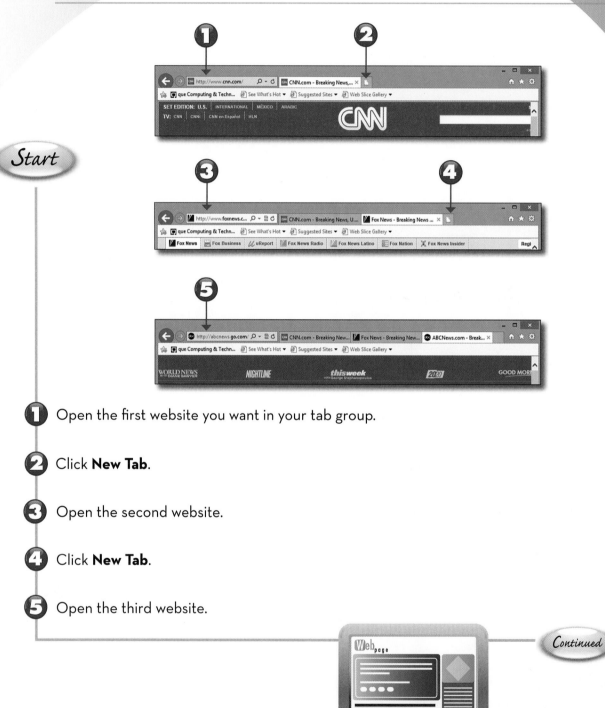

Start

1. Open the first website you want in your tab group.

2. Click **New Tab**.

3. Open the second website.

4. Click **New Tab**.

5. Open the third website.

Continued

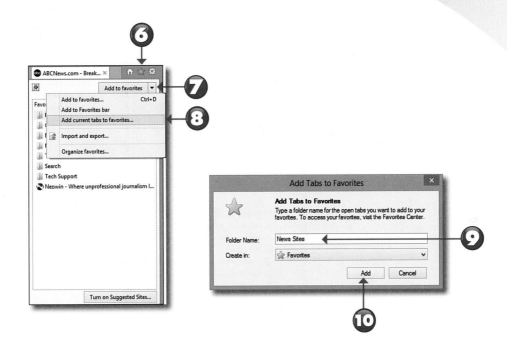

6 Click **Favorites**.

7 Open the **Add to favorites** menu.

8 Click **Add current tabs to favorites**.

9 Enter a name for the folder used to store the tab group.

10 Click **Add**.

End

TIP

Storing Your Tab Group in a Subfolder If you want to store your tab group in a different folder, open the Create In menu and select the folder you prefer. ■

OPENING A FAVORITE WEBSITE OR TAB GROUP

The Favorites Center enables you to open either individual favorites or tab groups whenever you want.

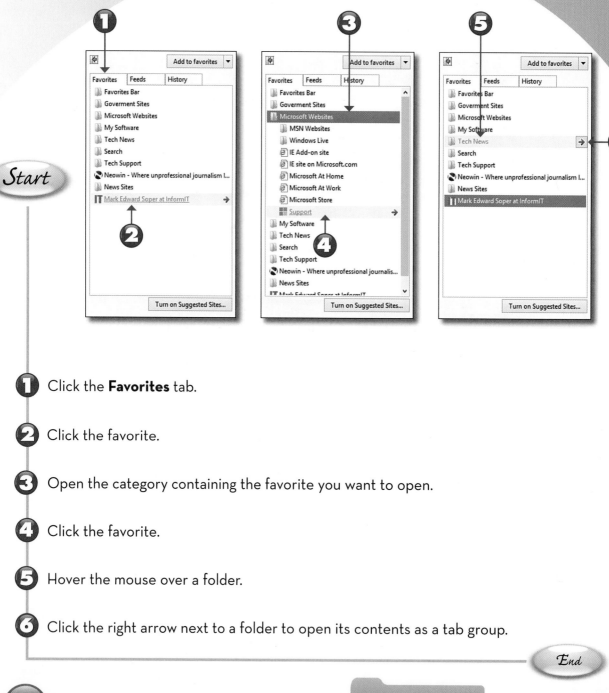

Start

1 Click the **Favorites** tab.

2 Click the favorite.

3 Open the category containing the favorite you want to open.

4 Click the favorite.

5 Hover the mouse over a folder.

6 Click the right arrow next to a folder to open its contents as a tab group.

End

NOTE

Tab Groups and Tab Colors Tabs in a tab group use matching colors for their tabs. ■

USING ACCELERATORS

The Accelerators feature in Internet Explorer 10 makes it easier than ever to research names, places, or other information in any web page. Here's how to use the accelerators built in to IE10.

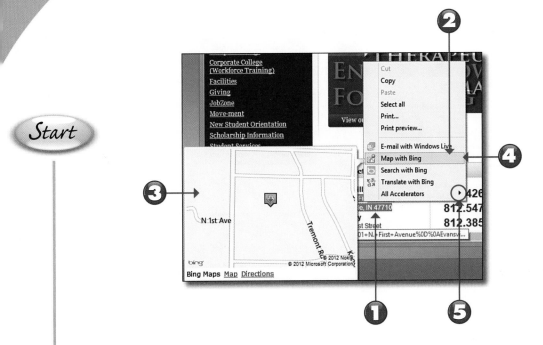

Start

Highlight text in a web page and right-click it.

Hover the mouse over an accelerator.

Some accelerators display results in a popup window when you point to them.

To open the results of the accelerator in a new page, click the accelerator link.

Point to **All Accelerators** to see more accelerators.

End

TIP

In Search of More Accelerators To get more accelerators, open the All Accelerators menu and click Find More Accelerators. ■

USING INPRIVATE BROWSING FROM THE DESKTOP

Worried about leaving traces of where you've been online on a public computer, such as in a library or Internet cafe? The InPrivate Browsing feature in Internet Explorer 10 covers your tracks. When InPrivate Browsing is enabled, your browsing history, temporary Internet files, form data, cookies, usernames, and passwords are not retained. What happens in the InPrivate Browser window is forgotten as soon as you close it. As you learn in this section, you can use InPrivate Browsing from the desktop as well as from the Start screen.

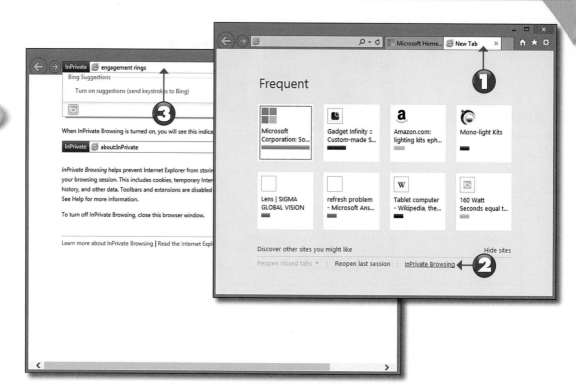

Start

1 Click **New Tab**.

2 Click **InPrivate Browsing**.

3 A new InPrivate window opens. Enter the URL or search terms.

Continued

NOTE

Blocking Access to InPrivate Browsing To block access to InPrivate browsing for other accounts, enable parental controls for those accounts. Refer to Chapter 19, "User Accounts and System Security," for details on how to enable parental controls. ■

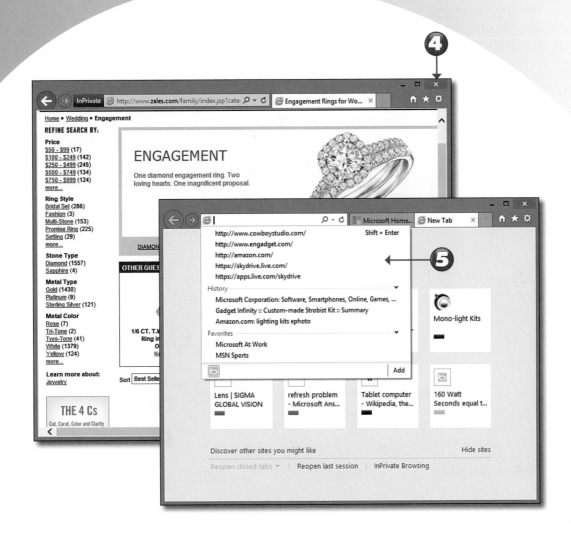

4 When you're finished browsing, close the InPrivate window.

5 Your browser history does not list any sites you visited while using InPrivate Browsing.

End

NOTE

Cookies and InPrivate Browsing InPrivate Browsing automatically blocks third-party cookies by default. To adjust how cookie blocking works in InPrivate, enable the status bar and click InPrivate: Blocking in the status bar at the bottom of the InPrivate window. ■

MANAGING POPUPS

By default, Internet Explorer 10 blocks popups. However, if you need to use a site that relies on popups, you can disable the popup blocker temporarily, turn it off for the site, or disable popup blocking entirely. The Popuptest.com website provides a convenient way to try these methods.

Start

1 Open a website that uses popups.

2 IE10 blocks the popup. Open the **Options for this site** menu to set options.

3 Click to always allow popups from the current site.

4 Click **Refresh** to see popups if the page doesn't display them automatically.

5 To view allowed sites or adjust settings, click **More settings.**

Continued

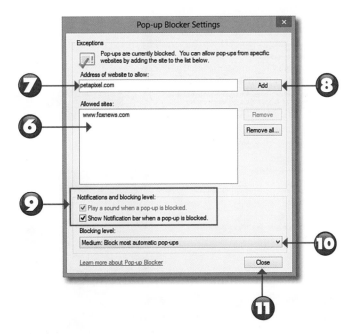

6 Sites on the Allowed sites list.

7 Enter a URL to allow.

8 Click **Add**.

9 Set notification options, as desired.

10 Adjust the blocking level.

11 Click **Close**.

End

NOTE

Removing Allowed Sites To remove a site from the Allowed sites list, select it and then click Remove. To remove all listed sites, click Remove all. ■

SETTING INTERNET PRIVACY FEATURES

The Internet Options settings are used to configure many features of Internet Explorer 10, including privacy features. Here's how to protect your privacy.

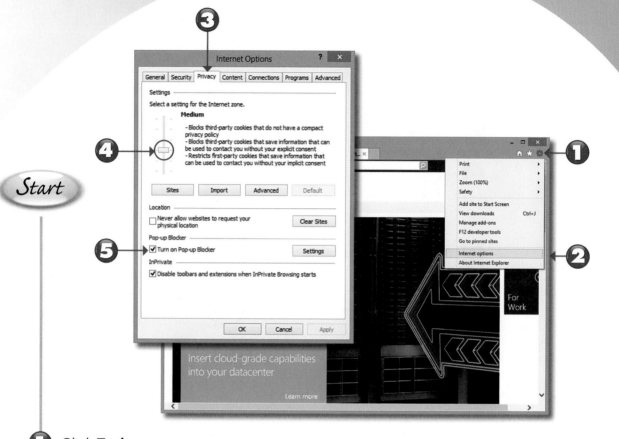

Start

1 Click **Tools**.

2 Click **Internet options**.

3 Click the **Privacy** tab.

4 Select **Medium** or higher to restrict cookies.

5 Make sure the Pop-up Blocker is enabled.

Continued

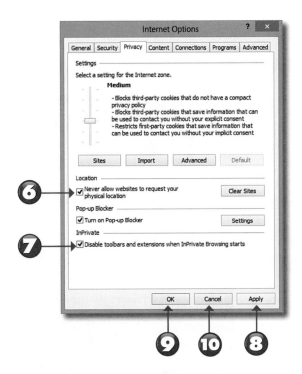

6 Click the **Never allow websites to request your physical location** box to enable this option.

7 Make sure the **Disable toolbars...** box is checked.

8 Click **Apply** to apply your changes.

9 Click **OK** to close the dialog box after making changes.

10 Click **Cancel** if you want to cancel any changes.

End

NOTE

Privacy Tradeoffs If you select the Never allow websites... option (step 6), websites that use your physical location to provide localized searches or information might not work correctly. ■

DELETING SELECTED ITEMS FROM YOUR HISTORY LIST

Internet Explorer 10 enables you to delete specified listings from your website history. Here's how to delete these sites.

1 Open the **History** menu in the address bar.

2 Point to the entry you want to remove.

3 Click the **X** beside the entry.

4 The entry is removed.

Start

End

TIP

Removing History Items from the Favorites Center You also can remove an entry from the History tab in the Favorites Center. Select the date, right-click the entry, click Delete, and click Yes to confirm the deletion. ■

DELETING ALL ITEMS FROM YOUR HISTORY LIST

In addition to deleting selected items from your History list, Internet Explorer 10 also enables you to clear all items from your History list. You also can delete other files created during web surfing.

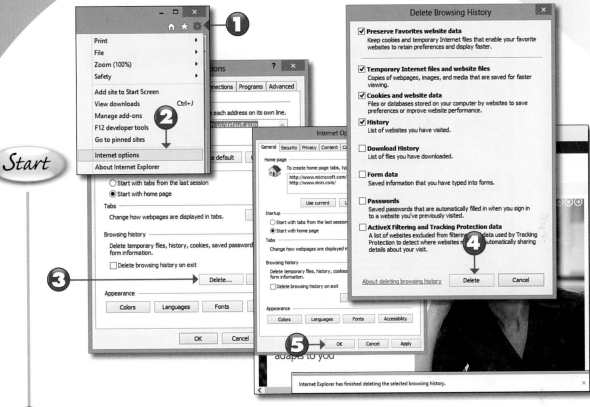

Click Tools.

Click Internet options.

Click Delete.

Click Delete to delete History, Cookies, and Temporary Internet files.

Click OK.

NOTE

You're In Charge of What Is Removed In step 4, you can check and uncheck the options you want to delete from your browsing history. ■

NOTE

No History, If That's What You Prefer The Internet Options General tab (step 3) also has a checkbox you can select that will delete your browsing history each time you exit the browser. ■

SAVING A WEB PAGE

Internet Explorer 10 can save web pages as a single MHTML (also known as a web archive) file for easy retrieval or emailing to other users. You can also save pages in other formats. Here's how to build a library of web pages.

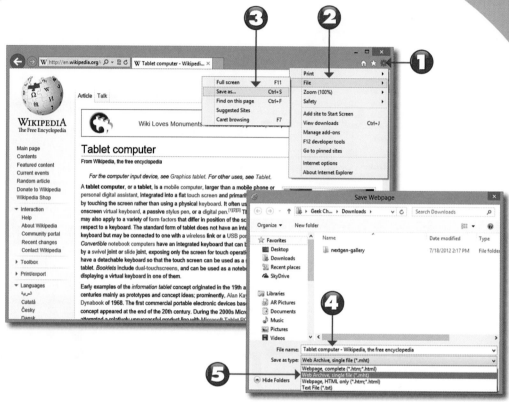

Start

1 Click **Tools**.

2 Point to **File**.

3 Select **Save as**.

4 Enter a different filename if desired.

5 Select **Web Archive, single file (*.mht)**.

Continued

6 Select where to save the file.

7 Click **Save**.

8 The saved web page as it appears in File Explorer.

End

NOTE

Lots of File Types to Choose From Other file format options include Webpage, complete (saves images and other components to a folder below the target folder); Web Page, HTML only (*.htm, *.html; saves HTML code only); and Text File (.txt; plain text only). ■

Chapter 17

ADDING AND USING MULTIMEDIA FEATURES

Windows 8 includes basic features for viewing photos, watching videos, and listening to music from either the new Windows 8 UI or the Windows desktop. However, if you want to edit photos, create videos, or enjoy media from the comfort of your media cave, Windows 8 needs a few add-ons. In this chapter, you learn how to add multimedia pizzazz by installing and using Windows Essentials 2012's Photo Gallery and Movie Maker, as well as Windows Media Center.

Selecting Windows Essentials
2012 Components to Install

Watching a DVD with
Windows Media Center

Viewing Photos
by Date with
Photo Gallery

The Sports Menu Strip in
Windows Media Center

Preparing to Add Music to
a Video in Movie Maker

ADDING WINDOWS ESSENTIALS 2012

Windows Essentials 2012 provides photo organization and editing, video editing and creation, photo and video sharing, and other services. It's a great addition to Windows 8, and it's free. If it wasn't preinstalled on your computer, here's how to download and install it.

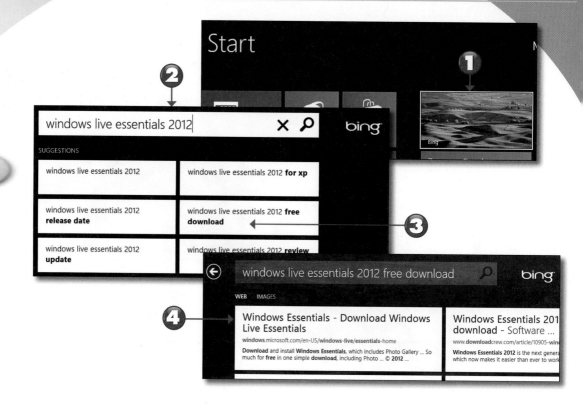

 Start

1 From the Start screen, click **Bing**.

2 Type **windows live essentials 2012** in the search box.

3 Click the **free download** link.

4 Click the **Windows Essentials – Download Windows Live Essentials** link.

Continued

NOTE

You Might Already Have Windows Essentials 2012 To learn whether Windows Essentials 2012 is already installed, check the right side of the Start screen. If you see Photo Gallery or other Windows Essentials 2012 components listed, the collection has already been installed. ■

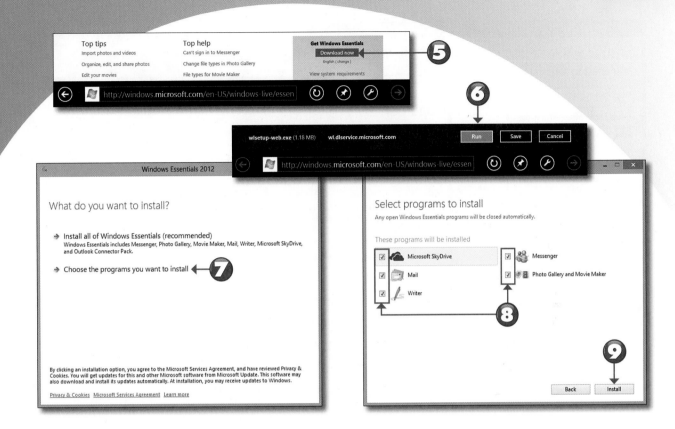

5 Click **Download now**.

6 Click **Run**. A User Account Control dialog box appears—click through it or provide a supervisor password, if prompted.

7 Click **Choose the programs you want to install**.

8 Click to clear checkboxes for features you don't want to install.

9 Click **Install**.

Continued

TIP
Take All or Some, It's Up to You In step 7, you can click Install All of Windows Essentials (Recommended) if you don't want the opportunity to skip some components. ■

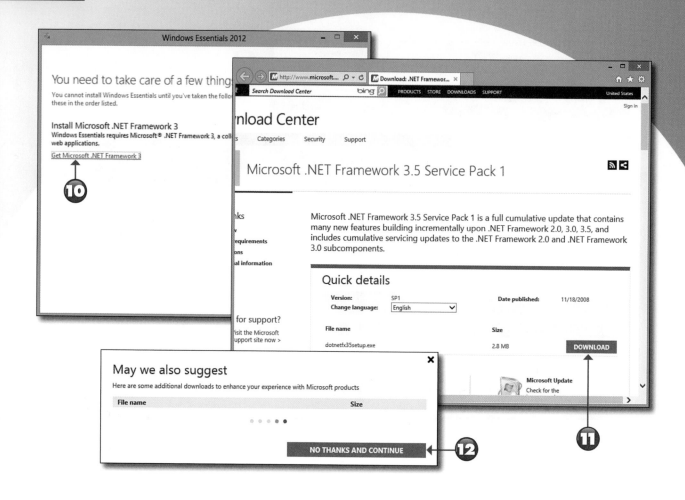

10 Click **Get Microsoft .NET Framework 3**. If you don't see this link, the program might already be installed; skip to step 17.

11 Click **Download**.

12 Click **No Thanks and Continue**.

Continued

CAUTION

.NET Framework—Essential to Essentials The link in step 10 takes you to the download page for .NET Framework 3.5 SP1, which contains .NET Framework 3. Do not close the installation window for Windows Essentials 2012. The installation will continue after you download and install .NET Framework. ■

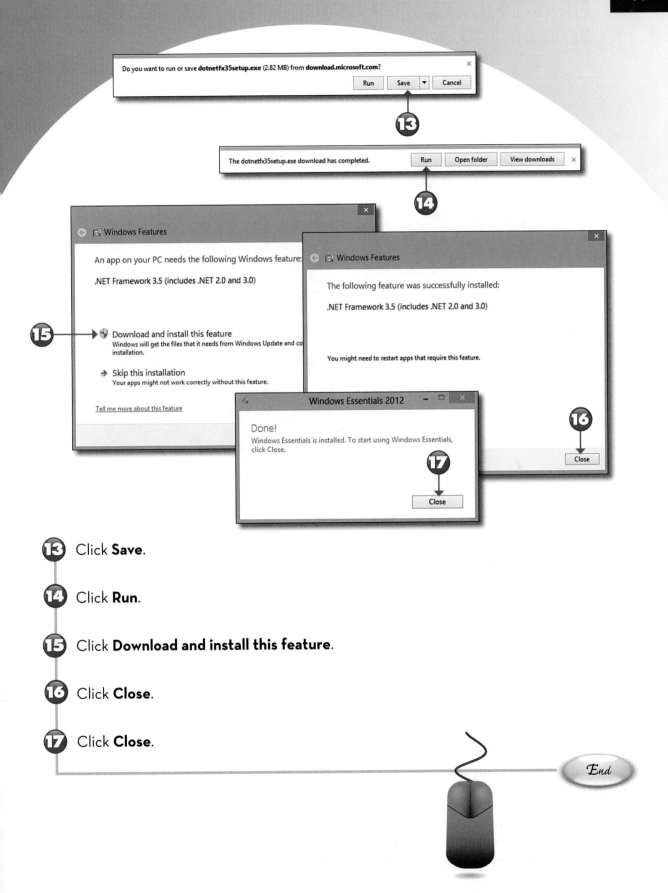

13 Click **Save**.

14 Click **Run**.

15 Click **Download and install this feature**.

16 Click **Close**.

17 Click **Close**.

End

FIRST-TIME STARTUP OF WINDOWS ESSENTIALS 2012 PROGRAMS

The programs included in Windows Essentials 2012 are installed to the Start screen. Here's what happens when you run one of the programs for the first time.

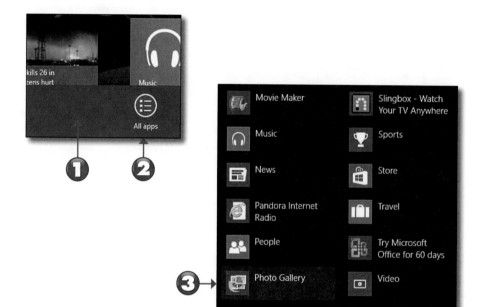

 Start

1 From the Start screen, right-click an empty area of the screen.

2 Click **All apps**.

3 Click **Photo Gallery**.

Continued

NOTE

Do It Once, and That's All, Folks! The first time you run a Windows Essentials 2012 program, you are prompted to accept the license agreement (step 4). The license agreement covers all components of Windows Essentials 2012, so you will not be prompted again. ■

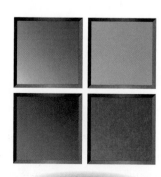

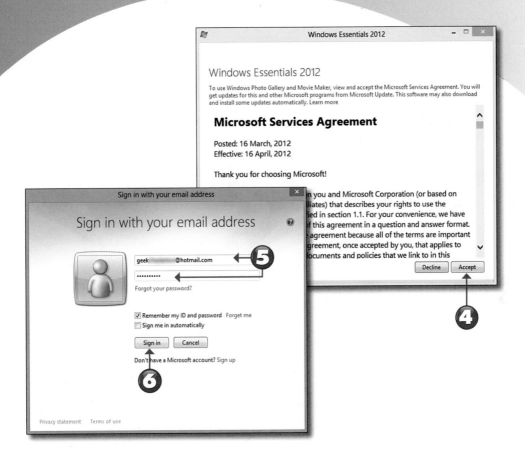

4 Click **Accept** (first-time use only).

5 Enter your email address and password.

6 Click **Sign in**.

End

NOTE

Save Time with Auto Sign In If you are the only one who uses your account, consider clicking the Sign Me in Automatically checkbox shown in steps 5–6. This will make the process of sharing files via your Microsoft account quicker and easier. ■

DISPLAYING YOUR PHOTOS BY FOLDER AND DATE

When you start Photo Gallery, you see the photos in your Pictures library by folder, but it's easy to view them by date. Here's how.

Continued

1 Open the Pictures and My Pictures folders.

2 Scroll down to a particular folder and click it.

3 Adjust the zoom setting as desired.

4 Click **File**.

5 Click **Options**.

TIP

Fixing the "Disappearing" Folder View Problem If you don't see the folders shown in step 1, move or point to just inside the left edge of the Photo Gallery window. A right-arrow pointer appears. Click it to display the Navigation pane. ■

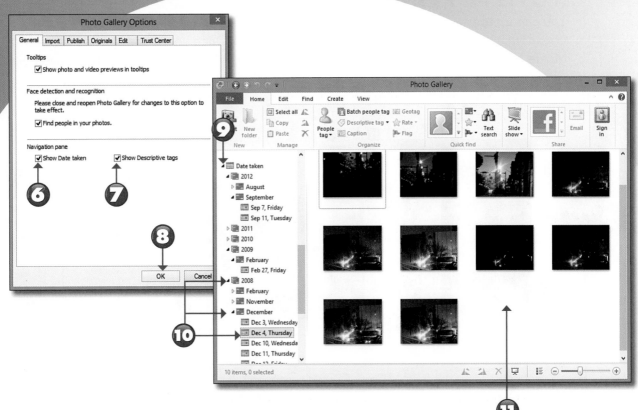

6 Click the empty **Show Date taken** box.

7 Click the empty **Show Descriptive tags** box.

8 Click **OK**.

9 Click the arrow next to **Date Taken**.

10 Expand the year, month, and day, as desired. Select a date.

11 Photo Gallery displays photos taken during the selected time period.

End

NOTE

Bad Pics? Pics to Share? Photo Gallery to the Rescue! Photo Gallery can also repair color, exposure, and other problems with your photos, tag your photos, automatically recognize faces in photos, and share photos online. To learn more, see Appendix A, "Windows Essentials 2012." ■

CREATING A MOVIE FROM YOUR SLIDE SHOW WITH MOVIE MAKER

You can create a slide show in Photo Gallery, and once the slide show is playing, it takes just one mouse click to create a movie from a slide show. Once your slide show is loaded into Movie Maker, the rest is up to you. You can also start Movie Maker from the Start screen.

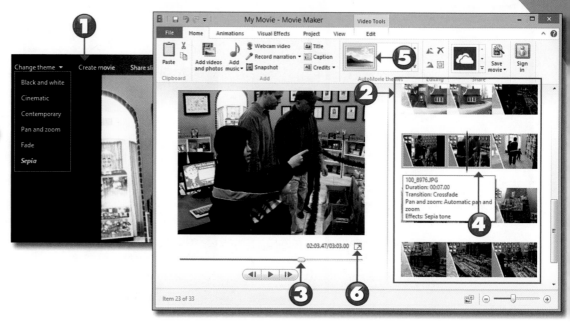

1 While playing a slide show in Photo Gallery, click **Create movie**.

2 The photos are imported in the order played.

3 Move the slider to advance or rewind the show.

4 Hover the mouse over a photo to see its current settings.

5 The current AutoMovie setting is the one selected in the slide show.

6 Click to play in full-screen view.

NOTE

Slow Motion, Fixes for Shaky Video, and More Movie Maker can be used with video from standard and HD camcorders, narration, and audio tracks. The program can balance audio sources and fix shaky video. To learn more about Movie Maker, see Appendix A, "Windows Essentials 2012." ∎

ADDING AUDIO TO YOUR VIDEO OR SLIDE SHOW

You can add audio to a Movie Maker video or slide show by adding recorded music (as in this example) or narration. You can download music that is royalty-free, which is recommended if you are creating a video for public viewing or commercial purposes. Once you download the music, you can select it from your PC.

Start

1. Open the **Add music** menu and click **Add music**.

2. Navigate to the music location.

3. Click the music track.

4. Click **Open**.

5. The selected music track is added to the movie.

End

TIP

Music and Movie Timings If the music is longer than the video or slide show's running time, it fades out automatically. If the music is shorter than the run time, move the slider to the end of the audio you added, select Add Music at the Current Point in step 2, and continue to add another track after the first one. ■

ADDING WINDOWS MEDIA CENTER

Windows Media Center makes it easy to enjoy videos, photos, music, and DVD movies from the comfort of your living room on an HDTV or projector connected to a PC running Windows. Its "10-foot UI" works well with either a wireless keyboard and mouse or a Windows Media Center remote to make media playback easy.

Depending on how and when you purchased Windows 8, Windows Media Center might be an extra-cost item (around $15 US in local currency) or it might be included as part of your purchase. In either case, you can't use it unless you add it to your Windows 8 installation. This example assumes that you already have a product key.

1 Display the Start screen.

2 Type **add fea**.

3 Click **Settings**.

4 Click **Add features to Windows 8**. Click through the UAC dialog box or provide an administrator's password, if prompted.

Continued

NOTE

No Key? Buy One! If you do not have a product key, click I Want to Buy a Product Key Online in step 5 and follow the on-screen instructions. ■

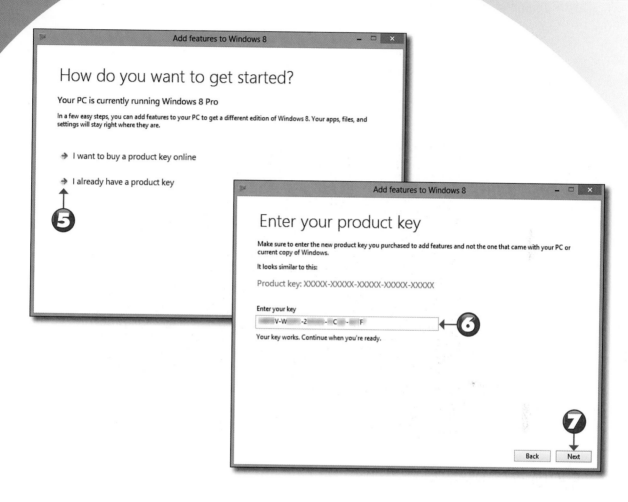

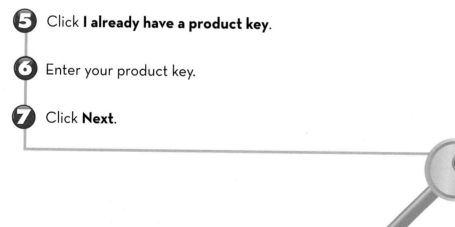

5 Click **I already have a product key**.

6 Enter your product key.

7 Click **Next**.

Continued

8 Click the empty **I accept the license terms** checkbox.

9 Click **Add features**.

Continued

NOTE

How Long Will Installation Take? If the installation process needs to download Windows Media Center, the speed of the installation depends on your Internet connection speed. ■

Thanks, you're all done and your PC is ready to go.

Close

10 Click **Close**.

11 Hover your mouse over the lower-left corner of the screen, and click **Start**.

12 Windows Media Center is added to the Windows 8 Start screen.

End

NOTE

First-Time Startup of Windows Media Center The first time you start Windows Media Center, click Continue, and then select the Express Setup option. Other changes can be made through the Tasks menu. ■

AN OVERVIEW OF WINDOWS MEDIA CENTER

Windows Media Center uses strip menus for each of its features. In this section, you learn about each of the major features in Windows Media Center.

Start

1. Scroll up and down until the menu you want is highlighted.

2. Scroll left and right until the selection you want is highlighted.

3. The current menu.

4. The current selection.

5. Select to play back recorded TV.

6. Select to set up a TV tuner for live TV watching and recording.

Continued

NOTE

Program Guide After you set up live TV, a program guide is also provided so you can choose what to watch or what to record. ■

7 Select to view sports scores and see upcoming game information for pro and college leagues.

8 Select to add players to your fantasy team and track their statistics.

9 Select to configure the Sports menu band.

10 Select to configure Netflix to play back through Windows Media Center.

11 Select to watch your movie library.

12 Select to play a DVD.

Continued

NOTE

Full Screen or Windowed, Your Choice You can enjoy Windows Media Center in a window or display it in full-screen view. ■

13 Point to the playback window to display playback and menu controls while watching or listening to your favorite media.

14 Click to go to the previous menu.

15 Click to open the main menu of Windows Media Center.

16 The Pictures and Videos menu.

17 Play the slide show.

18 Select sorting options.

19 Point to a picture to see more information.

Continued

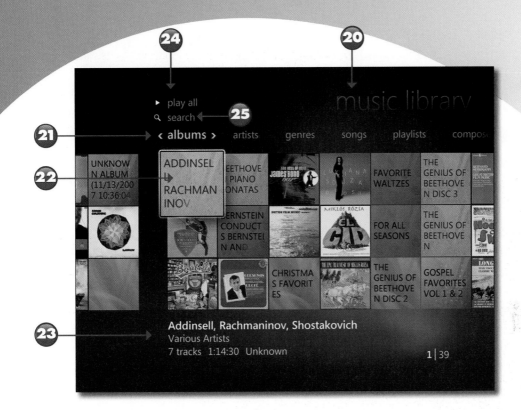

20 Select **music library**.

21 Select the **albums** category.

22 Select an album.

23 Information on the selected album appears here.

24 Click **play all** to play the album.

25 Click **search** to find a specific item in the music library.

End

NOTE

More About Windows Media Center To learn more about Windows
Media Center, see Appendix B, "Windows Media Center." ■

Chapter 18

ADVANCED CONFIGURATION OPTIONS

Windows 8's standard configuration provides settings that many users like. However, you might want to change some of these settings. In this chapter, you learn how to connect and use an additional display, customize your desktop background and borders, run both a Windows 8 application and your desktop on a single display, manage your hardware, change default settings for media and media files, and add features to Windows.

Configuring Devices
and Printers

Selecting a
Screen Saver

Snapping Apps
Feature

Turning
Windows
Features On
and Off

Selecting Pictures for
the Windows Desktop
Background

Configuring an
Additional Display

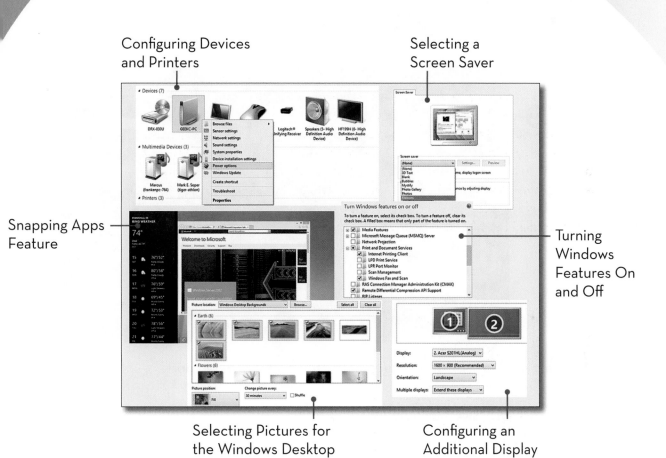

314

ADDING AND USING AN ADDITIONAL DISPLAY

You can add an additional display by using a laptop's video port or a second video port on a desktop computer that already has a display connected to it. You can use the additional display to duplicate the first display, but for normal use, you might prefer to set it up as an extended desktop. With an extended desktop, you can run different programs on each display. Here's how to make it happen.

1 Connect a video cable from your monitor to an unused video port.

2 Display the Windows Start screen.

3 Type **displ**.

4 Click **Settings**.

5 Click **Change display settings**.

Continued

NOTE

Instant Search Made Simple As soon as you begin typing in step 3, Windows 8 opens the Search box and displays the text you type. ■

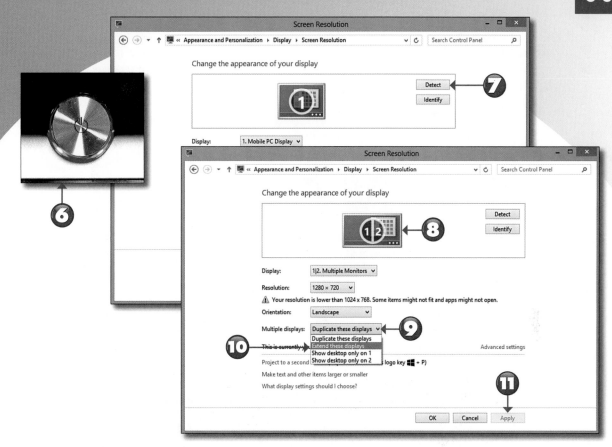

 6 Turn on the display.

7 Click **Detect**.

8 The second display is detected.

9 Open the **Multiple displays** menu.

10 Click **Extend these displays**.

11 Click **Apply**.

Continued

NOTE

Laptops Versus Desktops in Display Setup This example shows how to add a second display to a laptop. On a desktop, the second display icon might be displayed with a black frame (indicating it is inactive) as soon as you turn it on in step 6. ■

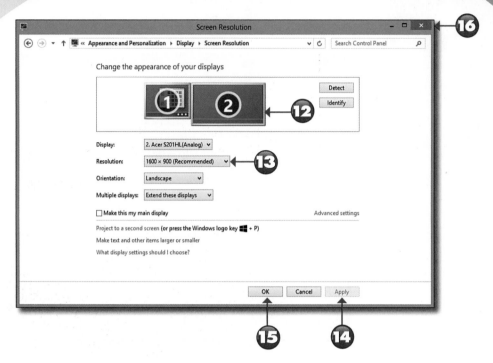

12 Click the second display icon.

13 Select the recommended resolution.

14 Click **Apply**.

15 Click **OK**.

16 Click **Close**.

Continued

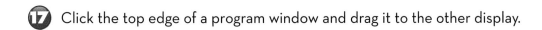

17 Click the top edge of a program window and drag it to the other display.

18 Release the mouse button to place the window.

End

NOTE

Windows 8 Remembers Which Display to Use When you close a program after dragging it to an additional display, Windows remembers which display was last used for the program. When you open the program again, Windows uses the additional display to run the program. ■

PERSONALIZING YOUR DESKTOP BACKGROUND

Windows 8 normally uses a photo background for the Windows desktop. If you want to change to a different background, a plain background, or select multiple pictures for your desktop background, this tutorial shows you how.

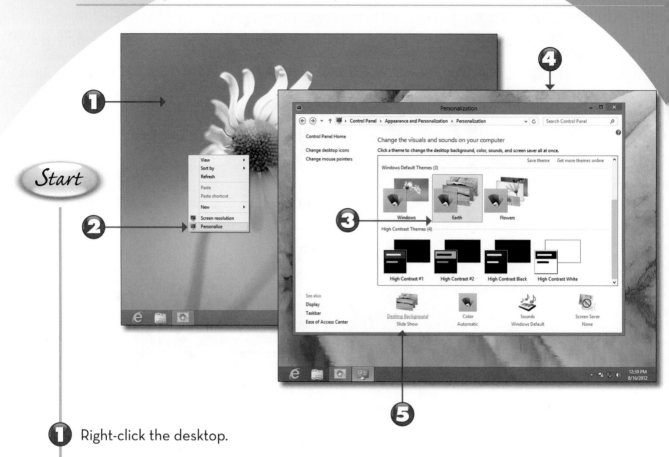

Start

1 Right-click the desktop.

2 Select **Personalize**.

3 Choose a theme.

4 The preview of the current theme.

5 Click **Desktop Background** to select images or background colors.

Continued

NOTE

Desktop Background = Wallpaper If you're a longtime user of Windows, you might remember that desktop backgrounds were once called *wallpaper*. ■

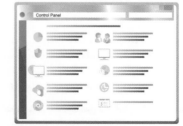

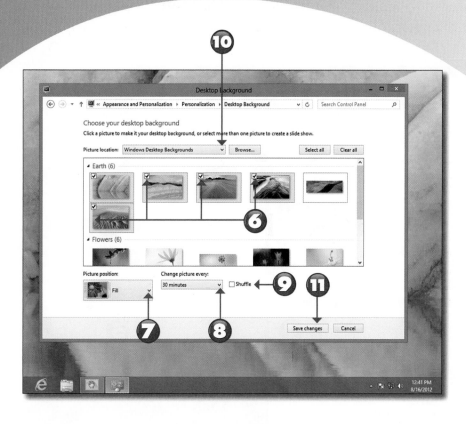

6 Click empty checkboxes to select images.

7 Open to select the picture position.

8 Open to select how often to change the picture.

9 Click to shuffle pictures.

10 Open to select other backgrounds (your photos, solid colors, and so on).

11 Click **Save changes**.

End

TIP

Need More Background Choices? If you are not satisfied with the standard desktop backgrounds, use the Browse button to locate a picture folder as a background source. You also can select a solid color for the desktop. ■

SELECTING A STANDARD WINDOW COLOR

The Personalization window also includes options for selecting your preferred window and taskbar color. Here's how to choose your favorite.

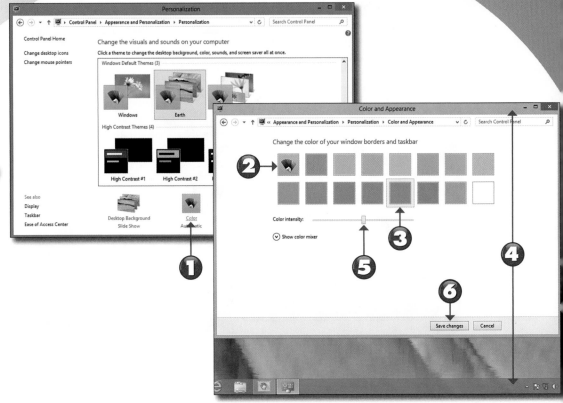

Start

1 Click **Color**.

2 Automatic is the default selection.

3 Click a different color.

4 A preview of the current window and taskbar color.

5 Adjust the slider to lessen (left) or increase (right) color intensity.

6 Click **Save changes**.

End

CREATING A CUSTOMIZED WINDOW COLOR

The Color and Appearance window also includes a color mixer. Here's how to create and select a custom window and taskbar color.

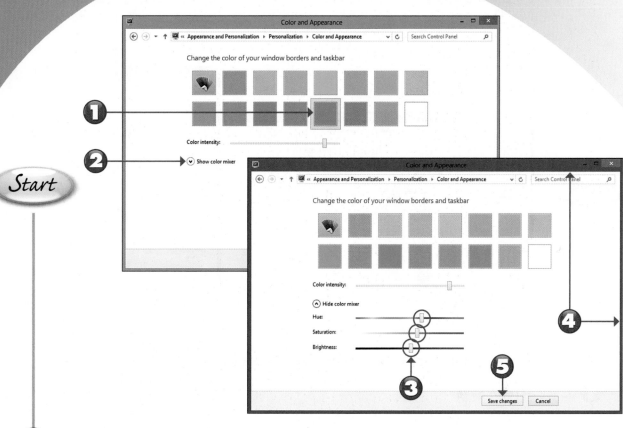

Start

1 Select a standard color.

2 Click **Show color mixer**.

3 Adjust the **Hue**, **Saturation**, and **Brightness** sliders.

4 The window (and taskbar) color changes in real time as you adjust sliders.

5 Click **Save changes**.

End

TIP
Starting Over with Another Color To abandon your changes, click Cancel in step 5. To use a different color, click any color desired and continue from step 1. ■

SELECTING A SCREEN SAVER

The Windows 8 screen saver function helps to protect the privacy of your display when you're away from your computer. This feature also helps to prevent an image being permanently burned into your screen—a major concern if you use a plasma HDTV with your computer. This tutorial shows you how to select and customize your favorite screen saver from the Personalization window.

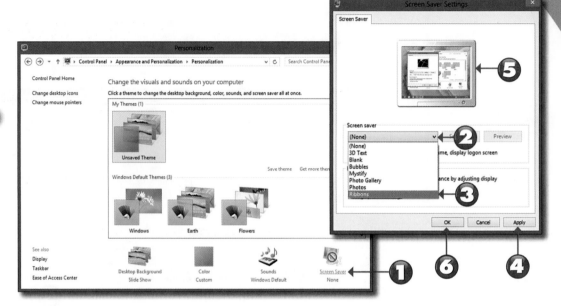

 Start

1 Click **Screen Saver**.

2 Open the **Screen saver** menu.

3 Select a screen saver.

4 Click **Apply**.

5 A preview of the screen saver.

6 Click **OK**.

End

TIP

Keeping Your System Secure with Screen Saver You can also select an option to display your logon screen after the screen saver works. Enable this option in the Screen Saver Settings dialog box if you use your computer where someone might want to snoop around its contents. ■

SAVING A DESKTOP THEME

A desktop theme is the combination of desktop background, window color, sound effects, and screen saver. After you have made changes to any or all of these settings, you can save your selections as a new theme from the Personalization window. Here's how.

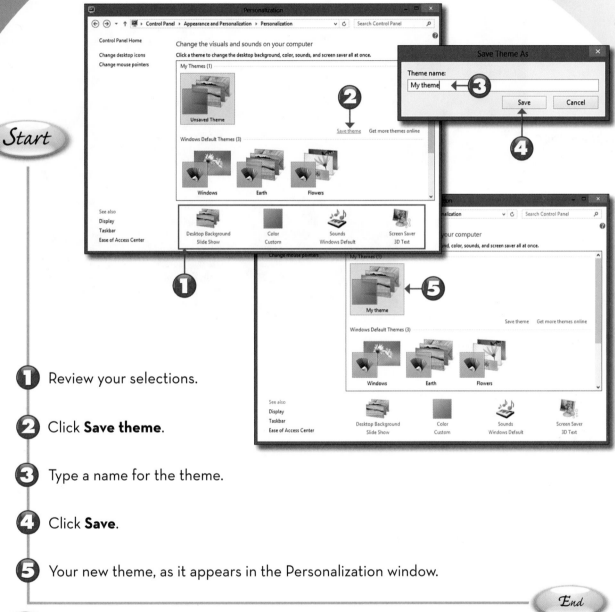

Start

1 Review your selections.

2 Click **Save theme**.

3 Type a name for the theme.

4 Click **Save**.

5 Your new theme, as it appears in the Personalization window.

End

NOTE

Choosing Sound Effects You can select different sound effects for Windows events—such as startup, shutdown, errors, and so on—by clicking the Sounds option shown in step 1 and selecting different sounds for listed actions. The sound scheme you select is also saved as part of your theme. If you download a theme, custom sound effects might be included as part of the theme. ■

SNAPPING APPS

If you have a widescreen display that runs at 1366x768 or higher resolution, you can use a new Windows 8 feature called Snapping Apps. Snapping Apps lets you view two Windows 8 apps or one Windows 8 app and the Windows classic desktop at the same time. Here's how it works.

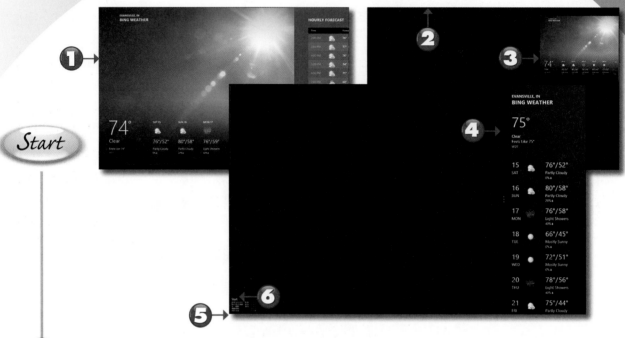

Start

1 Open a Windows 8 app from the Start screen.

2 Click the top edge of the program display.

3 Drag the program display to the left or right edge of the screen.

4 Release the mouse. The program snaps to the left or right edge of the screen.

5 Hover the mouse over the lower-left corner of the screen.

6 Click **Start**.

Continued

NOTE

Adjusting Display Resolution If you need to change the resolution on your display to 1366x768 or higher (you should normally use the Recommended resolution), refer to the first section of this chapter, "Adding and Using an Additional Display." ■

7 Open an app or the Desktop from the Start screen.

8 Drag the Windows 8 program to the other edge of the screen.

9 Release the mouse. The program snaps to the other edge of the screen.

10 To switch a program to full-screen view, drag the border of one program toward the program you want to hide.

End

MANAGING DEVICES AND PRINTERS FROM THE WINDOWS DESKTOP

If you need to diagnose device problems, update drivers for a device, revert to older drivers (rollback drivers), or manage devices and printers, use Control Panel's Devices and Printers window. In this example, we use the Devices and Printers window to adjust mouse settings and power options.

1. Right-click the bottom of the Start screen.

2. Click **All apps**.

3. Click **Control Panel**.

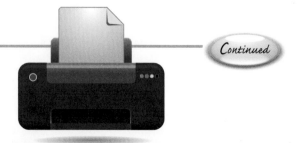

Continued

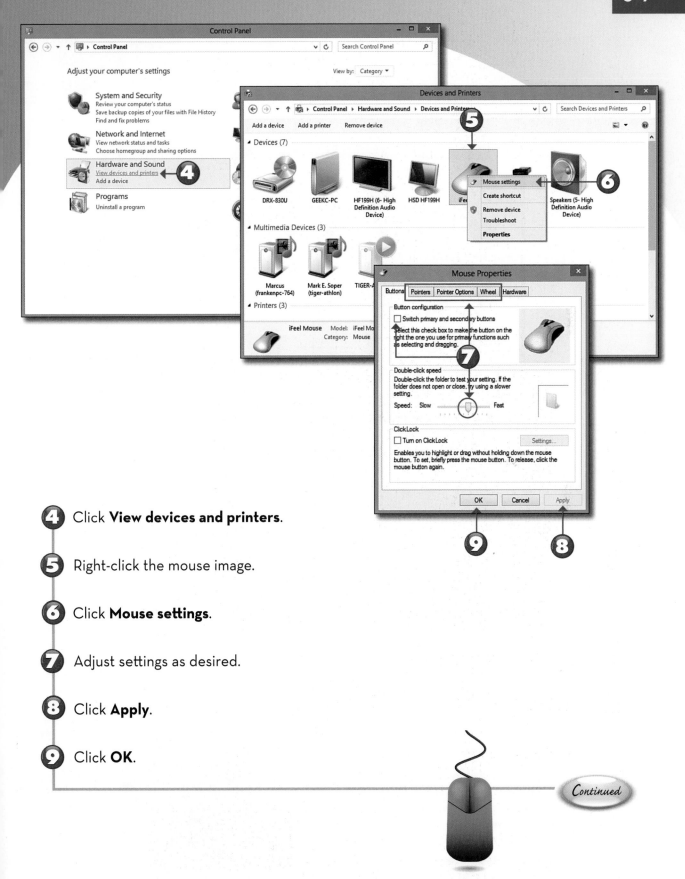

4 Click **View devices and printers**.

5 Right-click the mouse image.

6 Click **Mouse settings**.

7 Adjust settings as desired.

8 Click **Apply**.

9 Click **OK**.

Continued

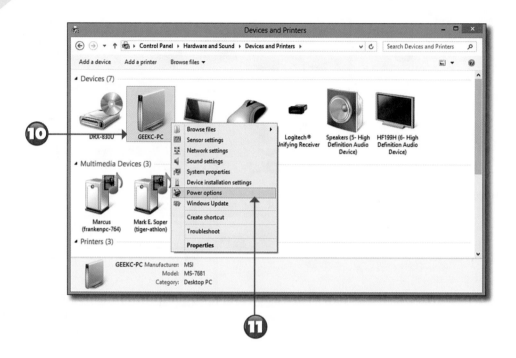

10 Right-click your computer.

11 Select **Power options**.

Continued

NOTE

Menu Options Vary with the Device You Select The options next to
Add a Device and Add a Printer above the Devices section of the window
change according to the item you select. For example, if you select the
optical drive, you can also eject the media or adjust AutoPlay settings. ■

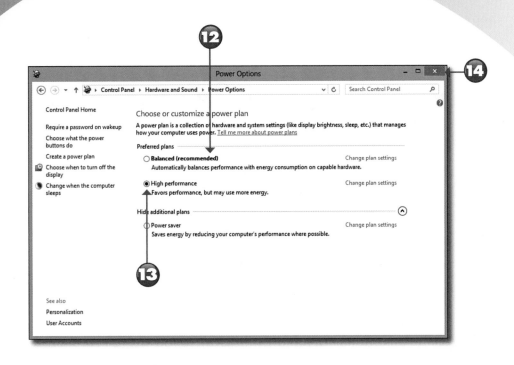

12 Balanced is the default setting.

13 Click **High performance** for fastest system performance.

14 Click **Close**.

End

TIP

Saving Power for Longer Battery Life Use the Power saver option if you are running a laptop on battery power or if you want to reduce power consumption on a desktop computer. Note that the screen is dimmer and the system is slower when you use this option. Click the Show Additional Plans arrow to see other power settings. ■

CHANGING DEFAULT SETTINGS FOR MEDIA AND DEVICES

What happens when you plug in your digital camera, flash memory card, or USB flash drive? How about when you insert a music CD? You can choose what happens when different types of devices and media are inserted. In this example, you use the Control Panel to specify what happens when you insert flash memory cards from digital cameras, music CDs, and blank CDs.

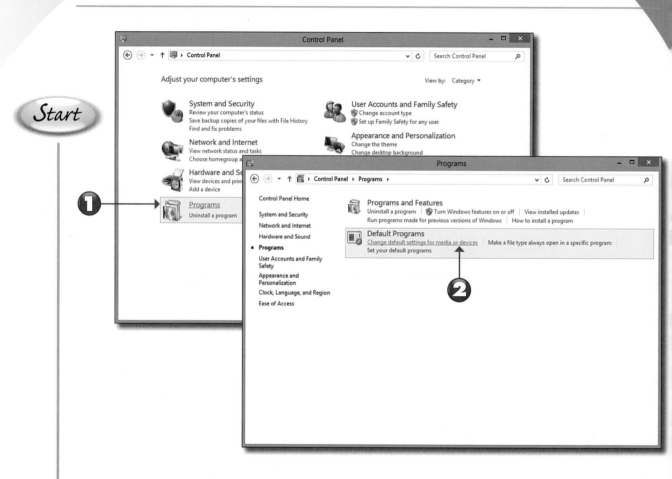

1 From Control Panel, click **Programs**.

2 Click **Change default settings for media or devices**.

Continued

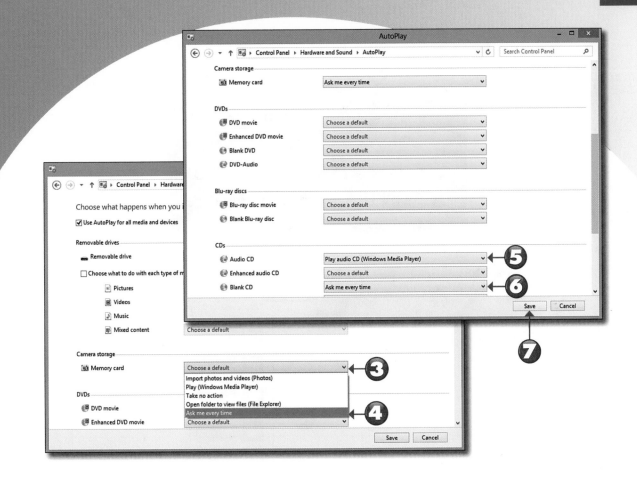

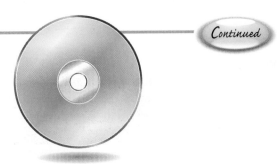

3 Open the Memory card menu.

4 Click **Ask me every time**.

5 Select **Play audio CD (Windows Media Player)** from the Audio CD menu.

6 Select **Ask me every time** from the Blank CD menu.

7 Click **Save**.

Continued

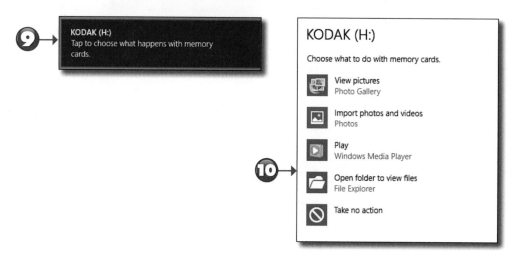

8 Insert a flash memory card or drive into your computer's card reader.

9 Click or tap the message screen.

10 Choose the option you prefer from the AutoPlay menu.

Continued

NOTE

Second Chances to See AutoPlay If you didn't move quickly enough to click or tap the message shown in step 9, open File Explorer, right-click the drive, and then select AutoPlay to see the menu again. ■

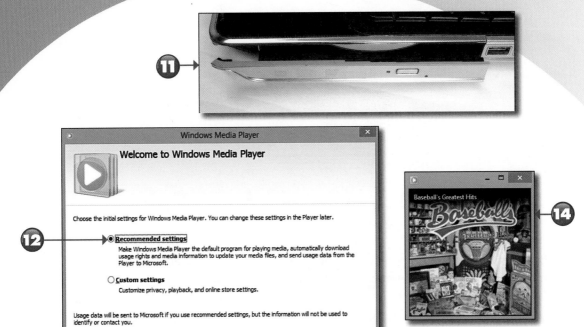

11 Insert a music CD into your computer's optical drive.

12 Click **Recommended settings**.

13 Click **Finish**.

14 The music CD plays automatically.

End

NOTE

Windows Media Player One-Time Settings The dialog box shown in steps 12 and 13 appears the first time you use Windows Media Player. If you have already run Windows Media Player, this dialog box will not appear. ■

Chapter 19

USER ACCOUNTS AND SYSTEM SECURITY

Windows 8 provides new ways to log in to your system, keep it secure, and monitor what younger members of the family are doing. Like its predecessors, Windows 8 is designed to support multiple users, and with features such as Administrator versus Standard accounts and Family Safety, you can provide users of different ages and capabilities just the right level of access to Windows 8 features and the Internet.

Logging In to
Windows 8 with a PIN

Asking a Parent or
Administrator for Permission

Family Safety
Settings

Setting Up
a Picture
Password

Time
Restrictions

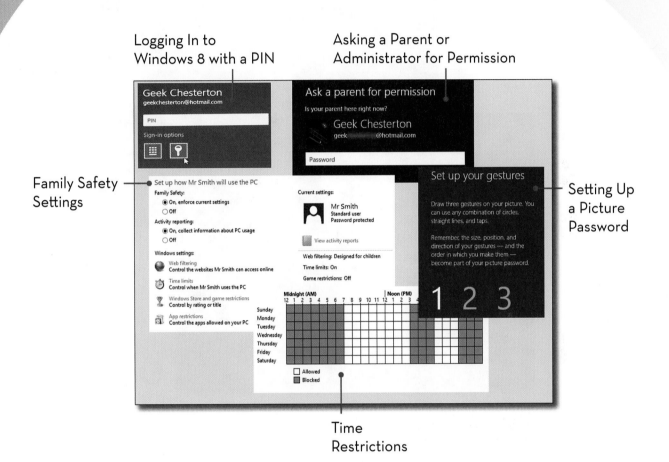

SETTING UP AN ADDITIONAL USER WITH WINDOWS 8

Windows 8 makes setting up an additional user account simple. As this lesson shows, this task is performed from the Windows 8 Start screen.

Start

1 Hover the mouse over the lower-right corner of the display.

2 Click **Settings**.

3 Click **Change PC settings**.

Continued

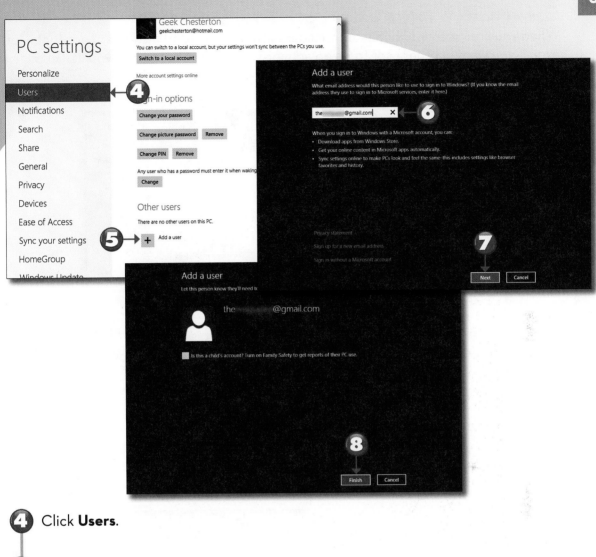

4 Click **Users**.

5 Click **Add a user**.

6 Enter the user's email address.

7 Click **Next**.

8 Click **Finish**.

End

NOTE

Family Safety In step 8, you also have the option to turn on Family Safety. The Family Safety feature is covered later in this chapter. ■

CHANGING AN ACCOUNT TYPE

When you create an additional user account in Windows 8, it's a standard account. However, if you want another user to be an administrator of the computer, you can change their account type. Here's how.

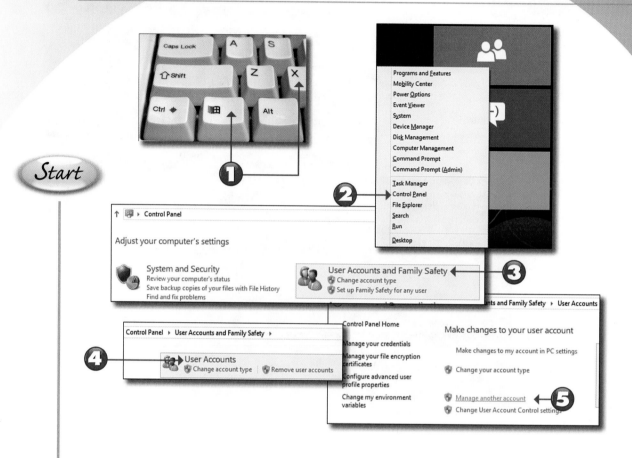

Start

1. Press **Windows key+X**.

2. Select **Control Panel**.

3. Click **User Accounts and Family Safety**.

4. Click **User Accounts**.

5. Click **Manage another account**.

Continued

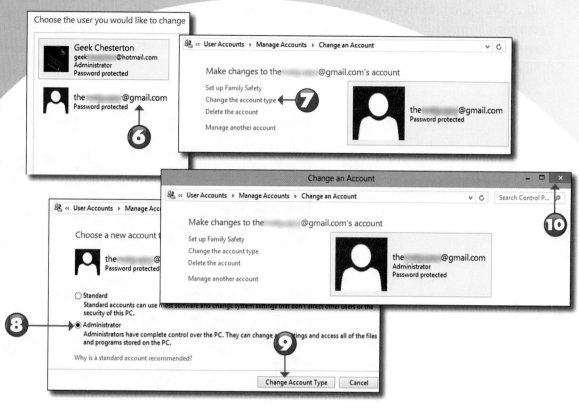

6 Click the account you want to change.

7 Click **Change the account type**.

8 Click **Administrator**.

9 Click **Change Account Type**.

10 Click **Close**.

End

NOTE

Why You Might Need Two Administrators When would you want to create more than one administrator account for a computer? There might be times when the original administrator is not available while the computer is in use, and when systemwide changes need to be made—such as new programs or hardware installations. Be sure that the user you select is trustworthy and not likely to mess around with the computer just for fun. ∎

SETTING UP PIN NUMBER ACCESS

Windows 8 enables users with Microsoft accounts to set up a PIN number as an alternative to a regular password. You must set a regular password before you can set up PIN number access. Using a PIN number for login can be easier for tablet users or users with limited typing ability. Here's how to do it.

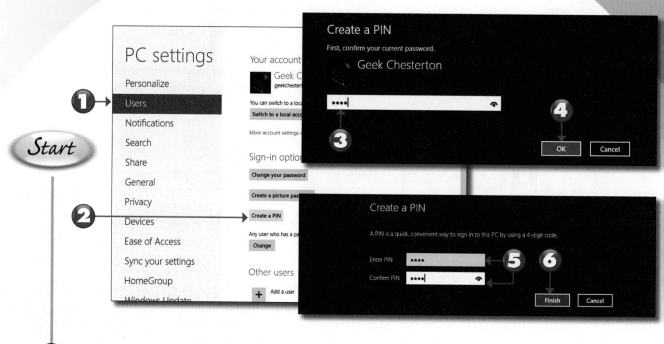

① From the PC Settings screen, click **Users**.

② Click **Create a PIN**.

③ Enter your password.

④ Click **OK**.

⑤ Enter and reenter a four-digit PIN.

⑥ Click **Finish**.

Continued

TIP

How to "Peek" at Your Login Information As soon as you begin typing login information, a stylized eye icon appears (refer to steps 3 and 5 for examples). Click the eye icon, and you can see the characters you type. This feature is handy if your typing skills aren't great—but make sure nobody else is peeking. ■

7 Type your PIN in the login screen.

8 Click to display sign-in options.

9 Click to use a password for login.

End

NOTE

PINs, Passwords, and Waking Up the Computer You must use a password to wake up the computer from sleep, even if the PIN login option is enabled and used. If you disable the password requirement to wake up the computer (see step 2), anyone can wake up the computer. ■

ENABLING PARENTAL CONTROLS WITH FAMILY SAFETY

Windows 8 enables you to keep a watchful eye on how children use a computer through its Parental Controls (Family Safety) feature. Here's how to set up this feature from the Control Panel.

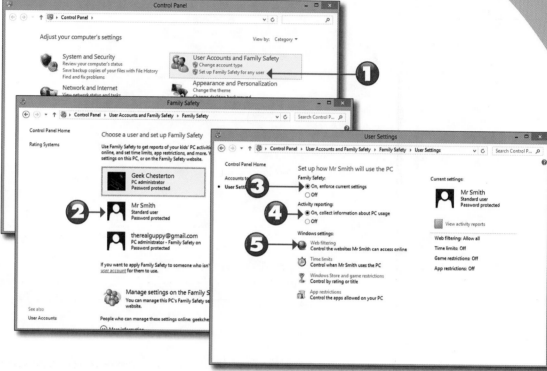

Start

1. Click **Set up Family Safety for any user**.

2. Click a user.

3. Select **On** for Family Safety.

4. Select **On** for Activity reporting.

5. Click **Web filtering**.

Continued

 NOTE

Family Safety Settings Vary By User Each user on a PC can be set up with Family Safety controls. You can use different Family Safety settings for each user. ■

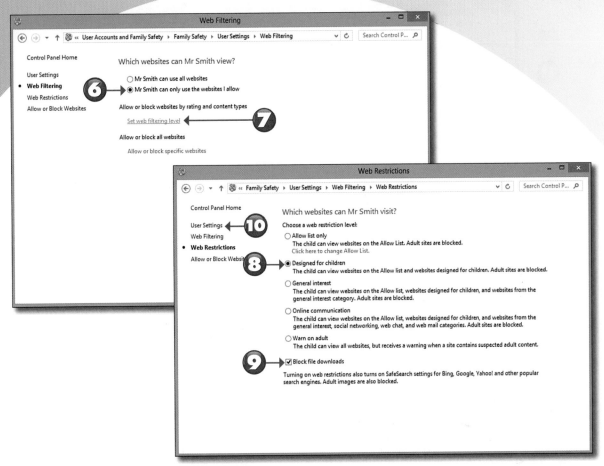

6 Click to restrict access to websites.

7 Click to set web filtering level.

8 Select a web restriction level.

9 Click the empty checkbox to block file downloads.

10 Click **User Settings**.

Continued

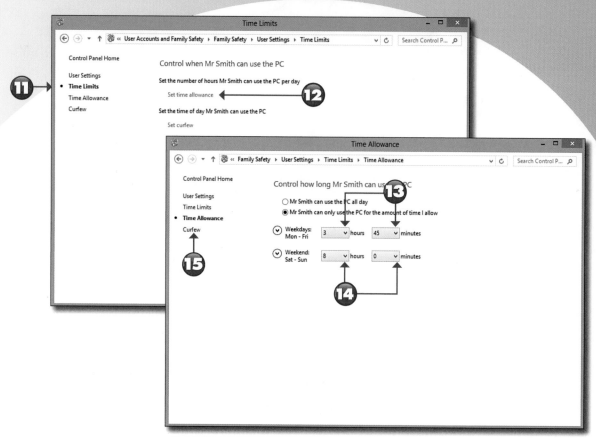

 Click **Time Limits**.

 Click **Set time allowance**.

Select hours and minutes per weekday.

Select hours and minutes per weekend day.

Click **Curfew**.

Continued

TIP

Customizing Amount of Use on a Daily Basis You can also select a separate time for each weekday and weekend day. ■

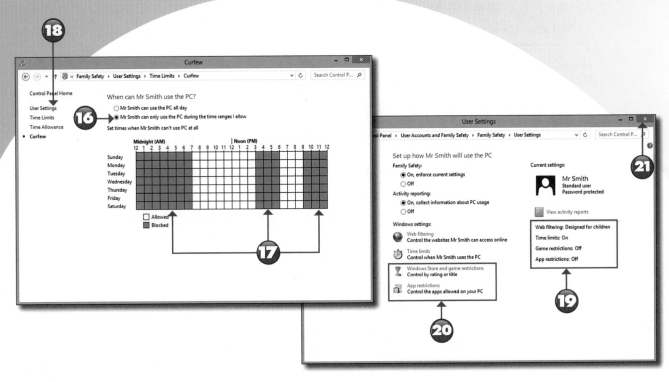

16 Click **...can only use the PC during the time ranges I allow**.

17 Drag across the calendar to specify blocked time periods (shown in blue).

18 Click **User Settings**.

19 The current settings appear here.

20 Other restrictions you can apply.

21 Click **Close**.

End

NOTE

Restricting Games and Apps The game restrictions window uses the ESRB game ratings system. You can also choose to block unrated games. The app restrictions window lets you specify which apps the user can run from the Windows Store. The Browse button lets you add Windows desktop apps to the list. ∎

REVIEWING PARENTAL CONTROLS (FAMILY SAFETY) LOGS

When you enable the Parental Controls (Family Safety) monitoring for a user, you can view activity reports through the Control Panel or via the Internet. In this tutorial, we cover using the Control Panel method.

Start

1 Click **User Accounts and Family Safety**.

2 Click **Family Safety**.

3 Click a user monitored by Family Safety.

Continued

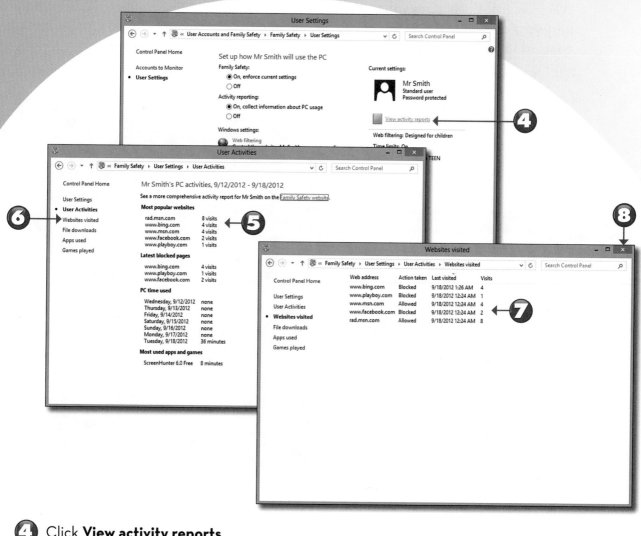

4 Click **View activity reports**.

5 An overview of the activities.

6 Click an item to see details.

7 Detailed usage report.

8 Click **Close**.

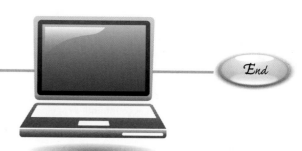

End

SETTING UP AND USING A PICTURE PASSWORD

Windows 8 not only gives you a choice of account types and the option to type in your password or a PIN number, but if you have a touchscreen computer, tablet, or multitouch-enabled touchpad, you can also create a picture password. This tutorial starts in the PC settings screen.

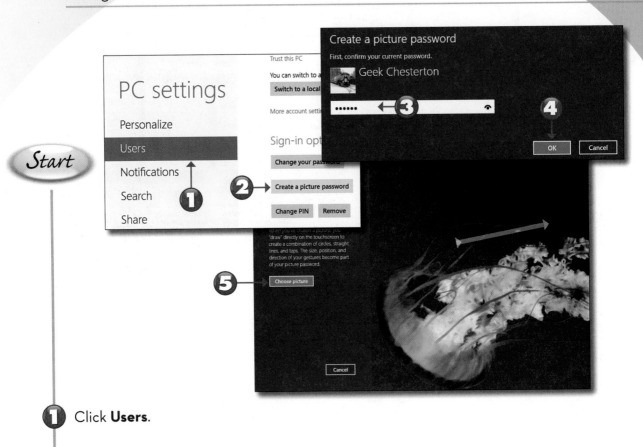

Start

PC settings

Personalize

Users

Notifications

Search

Share

Trust this PC

You can switch to a
Switch to a local

More account setti

Sign-in opt

Change your password

Create a picture password

Change PIN   Remove

When you've chosen a picture, you "draw" directly on the touchscreen to create a combination of circles, straight lines, and taps. The size, position, and direction of your gestures become part of your picture password.

Choose picture

Cancel

Create a picture password

First, confirm your current password.

Geek Chesterton

OK   Cancel

1 Click **Users**.

2 Click **Create a picture password**.

3 Enter your current password.

4 Click **OK**.

5 Click **Choose picture**.

Continued

TIP

Passwords First, Then Picture Passwords You cannot create a picture password for an account until a regular password has been created. ∎

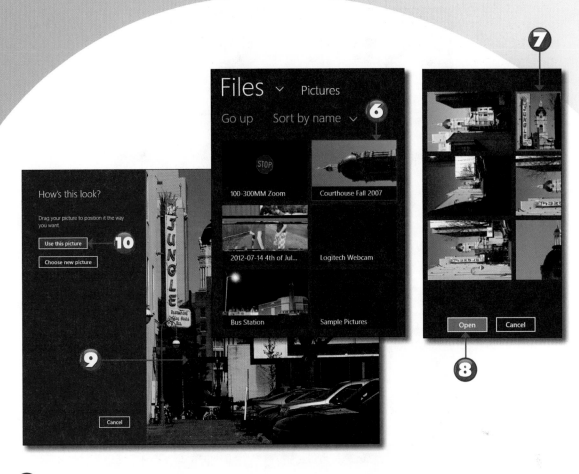

6 Click a folder.

7 Select a photo.

8 Click **Open**.

9 Click the photo and drag it into the desired position.

10 Click **Use this picture**.

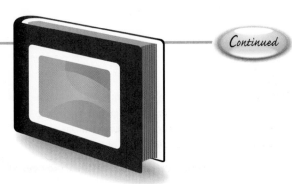

Continued

11 Draw three gestures (taps, circles, or straight lines) on your touch surface.

12 Confirm your gestures.

Continued

NOTE

Your Picture, Your Choice In this example, we used one of each of the allowable gestures (tap, circle, and straight line). You can use any combination of these gestures that you want, but they must be performed in the same order and on the same areas of the picture. ■

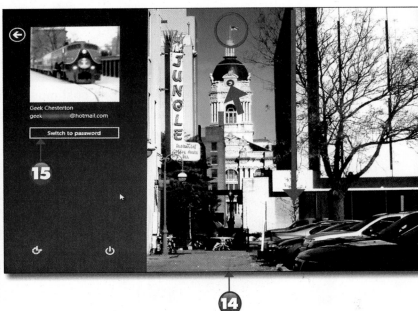

13 Click **Finish**.

14 On the next login screen, log in using the picture password gestures.

15 Click **Switch to password** if you prefer not to use the picture password.

End

TIP

Changing or Removing Your Picture Password Return to the Users section of the PC Settings screen if you want to change or remove your picture password. ■

Chapter 20

PROTECTING YOUR SYSTEM

Today's computers and storage devices don't cost much to buy or replace, but the information you store on them—from documents to photos, video, and music—is priceless. In this chapter, you learn about a variety of easy-to-use features in Windows 8 that are designed to help you protect your computer's contents.

Windows Update from
PC Settings Screen

File History After
Being Turned On

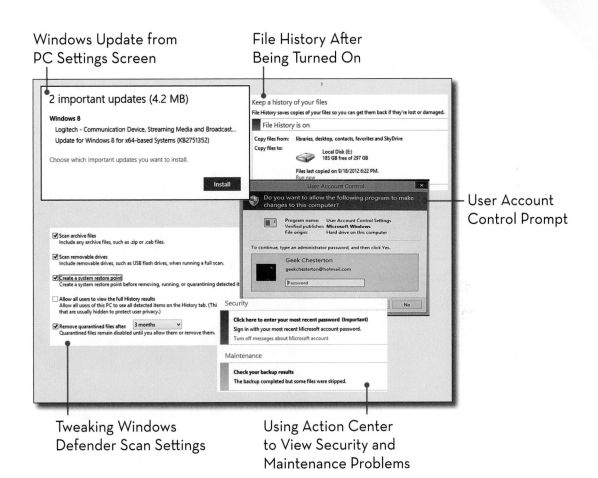

User Account
Control Prompt

Tweaking Windows
Defender Scan Settings

Using Action Center
to View Security and
Maintenance Problems

LOOKING AT USER ACCOUNT CONTROL

User Account Control (UAC) is a feature that helps protect your system from unwanted changes. Program installations and Windows tasks marked with a shield might prompt an administrator to approve the operation. They will also prompt a standard user to get permission from an administrator to perform that task. Here's how User Account Control works and what the prompts look like.

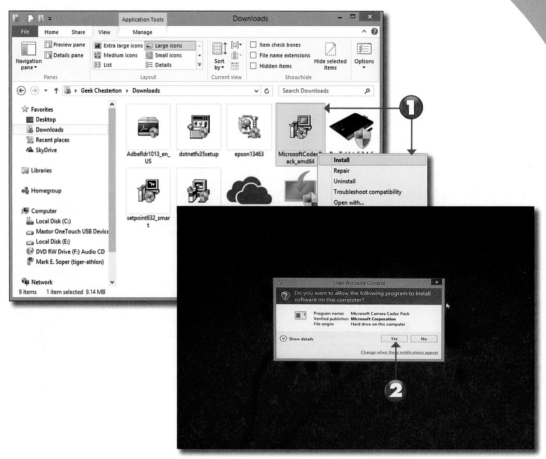

 Start

1 If you are logged in as administrator, right-click a downloaded program file and select Install.

2 The UAC dialog box appears. Click **Yes** to continue.

Continued

NOTE

Changing UAC Settings The normal (default) UAC settings are suitable for most systems; however, UAC settings can be modified in Control Panel. Click the Change User Account Control Settings link under Action Center in Control Panel's System and Security window (see step 3). ■

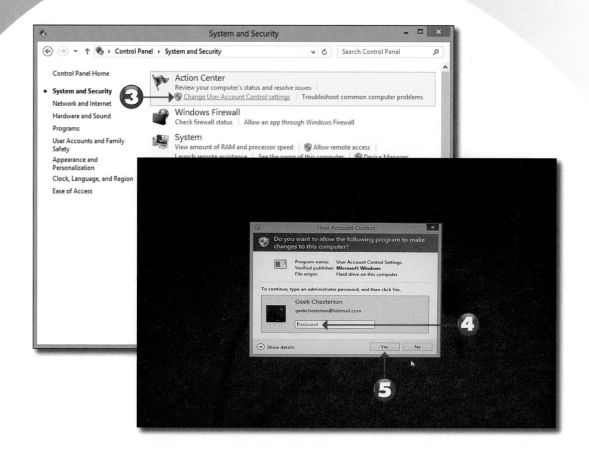

If you are logged in as a standard user, click a task marked with a shield.

Enter the administrator password.

Click **Yes** to continue.

End

NOTE

Two Administrators, No Waiting If your system has two or more administrators, you will see each administrator listed in the UAC dialog box shown in steps 4 and 5. You need only one administrator password to continue. ■

CONFIGURING WINDOWS UPDATE

Windows Update is normally set to automatically download and install updates to Microsoft Windows 8 and to other Microsoft apps such as Office. However, you can change the default settings if you need to install updates on your own schedule. Here's how to tweak Windows Update settings from the Control Panel.

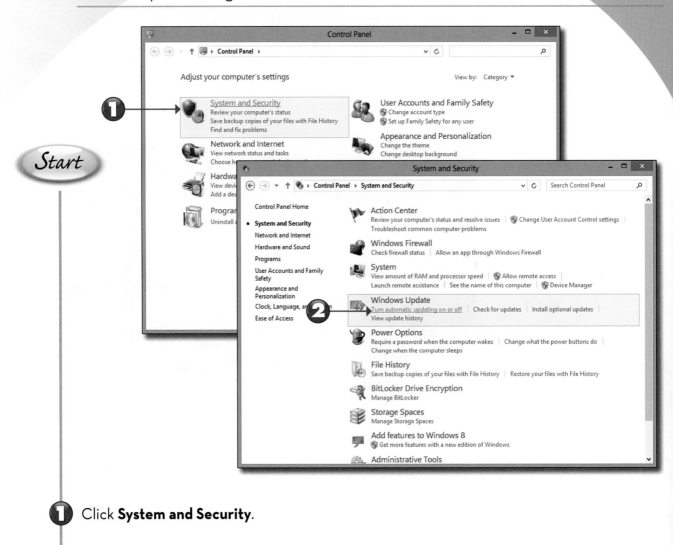

Start

1 Click **System and Security**.

2 Click **Turn automatic updating on or off**.

Continued

NOTE

When Changing from Automatic Updates Makes Sense If you connect remotely with your computer or your computer runs backups on a regular basis, keep in mind that some Windows updates will cause the computer to reboot. This can prevent these operations from taking place. In those situations, it makes sense to control when updates will be installed. ∎

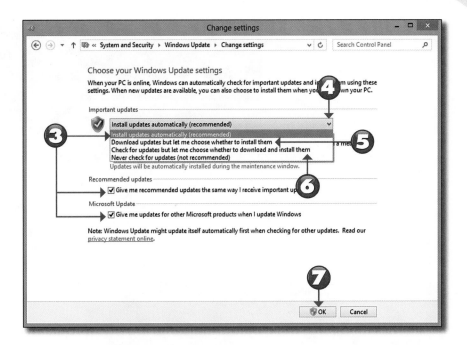

3 Notice the default Windows Update settings.

4 Click to change the automatic update setting.

5 Choose this option if you want to specify when your system is updated.

6 Choose this option if you want to specify whether to download updates.

7 Click **OK** to accept and use your settings.

End

CAUTION

The No Updates Option Is Not Recommended The dialog box shown in steps 3–7 also includes an option to Never Check for Updates. This option is intended primarily for corporate computers whose updates are managed centrally. At home or in a small office, let Windows figure out when to download your updates. ∎

PROTECTING YOUR FILES WITH FILE HISTORY

Previous versions of Windows have included a variety of backup programs, but many users never back up their files. Windows 8's new File History feature makes backing up files in your libraries, favorites, and contacts easy to set up and make automatic. Now, there's no reason to worry about losing your files. Here's how it works.

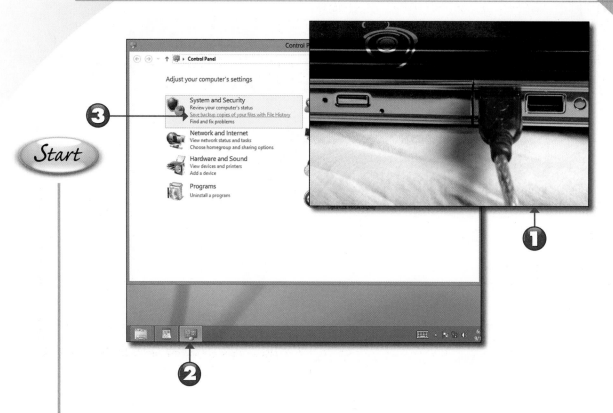

Start

1 Connect an external hard disk to your computer.

2 Open Control Panel.

3 Click **Save backup copies of your files with File History**.

Continued

TIP

Tweaking File History To adjust how often to save files, how much disk space (offline cache) to use, or how long to keep files in File History, click the Advanced Settings link shown in the left pane of the File History window. ■

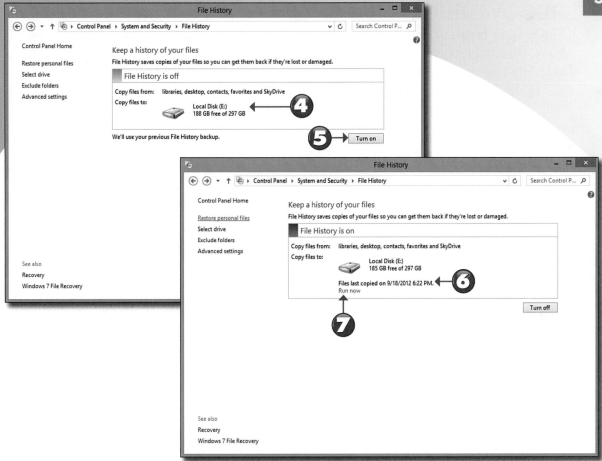

4 The drive recommended by File History.

5 Click **Turn on**.

6 File History backs up your files.

7 Click **Run now** to run File History again immediately.

End

TIP

Choosing Your Preferred Drive If you have more than one external hard disk, the drive selected by File History might not be the one you want to use. Use the Select Drive link in the left pane of the File History window to choose a particular drive before turning on File History. ■

NOTE

Recommending This Drive to Your HomeGroup If your computer is connected to a HomeGroup, you will see a prompt asking whether you want to recommend this drive to other members of the HomeGroup. Click Yes if you want other HomeGroup members to use the drive for File History; otherwise, click No. Clicking the No option is recommended if you expect to use most of the drive's capacity for the computer to which it is connected. ■

RECOVERING FILES WITH FILE HISTORY

File History creates backups of your files so if a file is erased or damaged, you can get it back. If you haven't yet enabled File History in Windows 8, refer to "Protecting Your Files with File History," earlier in this chapter. Here's how to retrieve a lost file or folder.

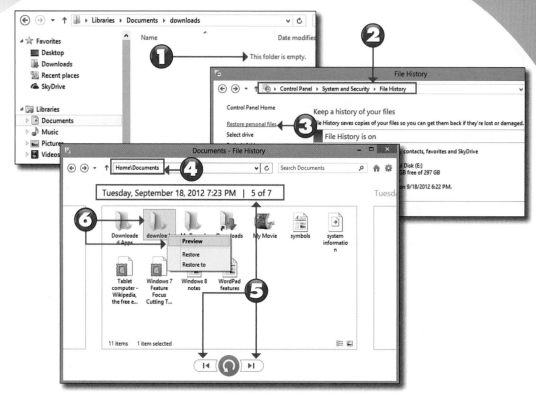

Start

1. The contents of a folder called downloads, in the Documents folder, have been accidentally deleted.

2. Open **File History** from the Control Panel.

3. Click **Restore personal files**.

4. Navigate to the folder's original location.

5. Select a version to restore.

6. Right-click the folder and select **Preview**.

Continued

7 The folder opens. Review its contents to make sure it contains what you want to restore.

8 Click the green **Restore** button.

9 File Explorer opens. The folder and its contents are returned to their original location.

End

NOTE

Restore Options To restore the folder or file to a different location, select the Restore to option in step 6, and then specify the location. ∎

TIP

Restoring Selected Files To restore only selected files, click the first file you want to restore, and then use Ctrl+Click to select additional files. Click the Restore button—only the files you selected will be restored. ∎

CHECKING SECURITY SETTINGS WITH WINDOWS ACTION CENTER

Windows Action Center keeps an alert eye on security and maintenance issues that might happen and gives you specific instructions on how to fix them. Here's how to use Windows Action Center to keep your system safe.

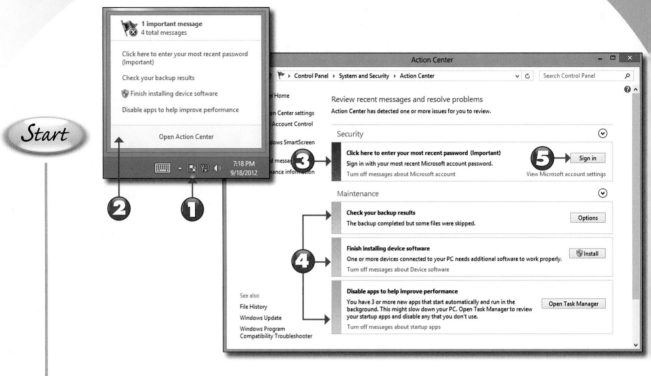

1. Click the **Windows Action Center** icon in the notification area of the taskbar.

2. Click **Open Action Center** for more information.

3. Important issues are marked with a red banner.

4. Other problems are marked with a yellow banner.

5. Click the action button to solve the problem listed.

Continued

NOTE

Running Action Center from Control Panel You don't need to wait for a warning to run Action Center. It's available from the System and Security section of the Control Panel. ■

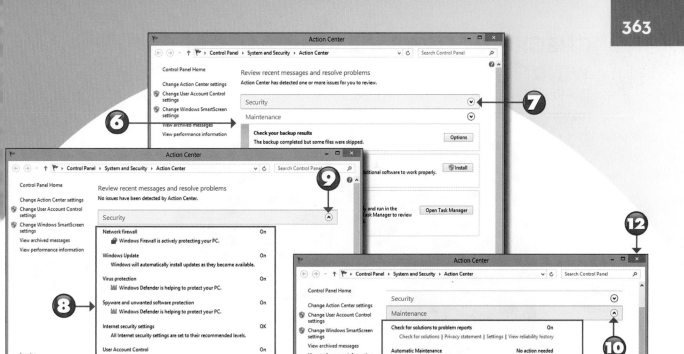

6 After you resolve the problem, the problem is removed from the list.

7 Click to see other security items monitored by Action Center.

8 The status of monitored security items.

9 Click to collapse the Security category.

10 Click to expand the Maintenance category.

11 The status of Maintenance items.

12 Click **Close**.

End

CHECKING FOR VIRUSES AND SPYWARE WITH WINDOWS DEFENDER

The Windows Defender program included with Windows 8 provides protection against spyware and viruses. Here's how to open Windows Defender and run a scan.

1 From the Start screen, type **defe** and Windows Search opens automatically.

2 Click **Windows Defender**.

3 The current status.

4 The last scan details.

5 Choose a scan type.

6 Click **Scan now** to start a scan.

End

SETTING WINDOWS DEFENDER OPTIONS

Windows Defender's normal (default) options provide suitable protection for most users, but if you want to check additional locations for spyware or make other changes to Windows Defender, this lesson shows you how.

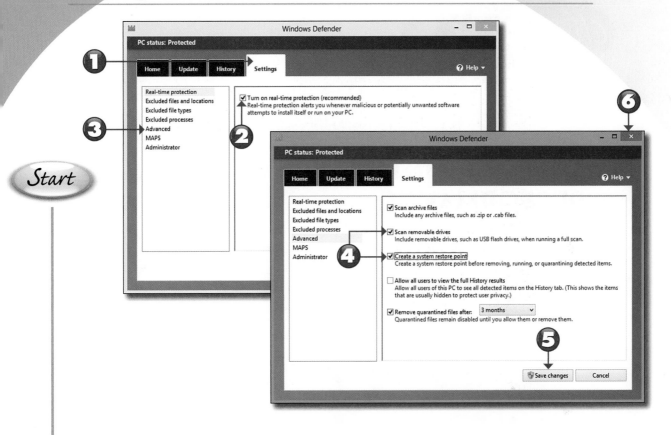

Start

1 From Windows Defender, click the **Settings** tab.

2 Select this option to turn on real-time protection.

3 Click **Advanced**.

4 If these boxes are empty, click them to enable these settings.

5 Click **Save changes**.

6 Click **Close**.

End

Chapter 21

SYSTEM MAINTENANCE AND PERFORMANCE

Windows 8 includes new system maintenance features, improved disk repair features, and familiar programs with new ways to run them—such as System Restore, Disk Cleanup, and others. In this chapter, you learn how to keep your computer system running at peak performance.

Hardware Details from Windows
Experience Index (WEI)

Windows 8 Warns About
a Drive with Problems

Windows
Memory
Diagnostics
Testing System
Memory

Preparing to
Run System
Restore

Refreshing Your PC

Creating a New
Power Plan

DISPLAYING SYSTEM INFORMATION

Windows programs often specify required amounts of RAM, processor speed, and other requirements. Use the Windows Experience Index menu and report in Windows 8 to discover these facts and other important information about your system. In this chapter, we assume that you have added Control Panel to your taskbar. To learn how to do this, see "Adding an App to the Desktop Taskbar" in Chapter 11, "Running Desktop Apps."

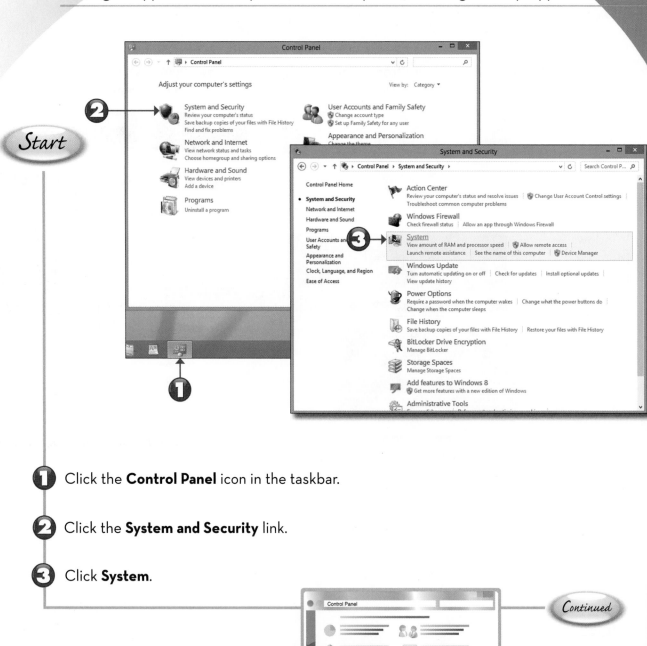

1 Click the **Control Panel** icon in the taskbar.

2 Click the **System and Security** link.

3 Click **System**.

Continued

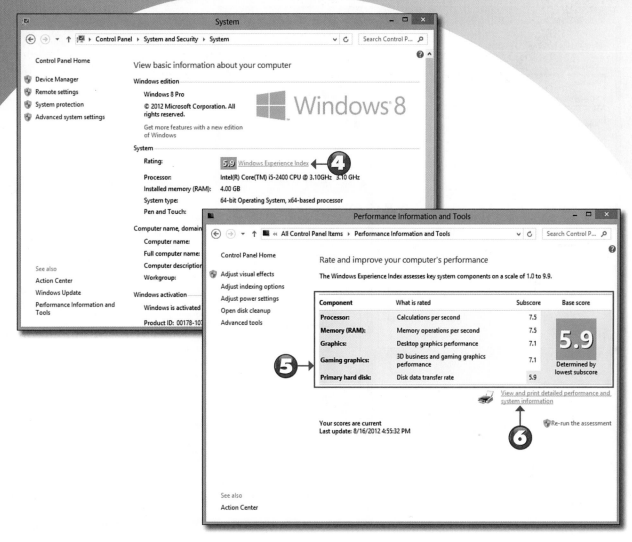

4 Click the **Windows Experience Index** link.

5 The subsystem and overall WEI scores.

6 Click for detailed hardware information.

Continued

NOTE

More About the WEI Scores The Windows Experience Index (WEI) score shown in steps 5 and 6 rates your system on a scale from 1.0 to 9.9—the higher the score, the faster the system. The WEI scores shown in steps 5 and 6 are typical of a mid-range system. ■

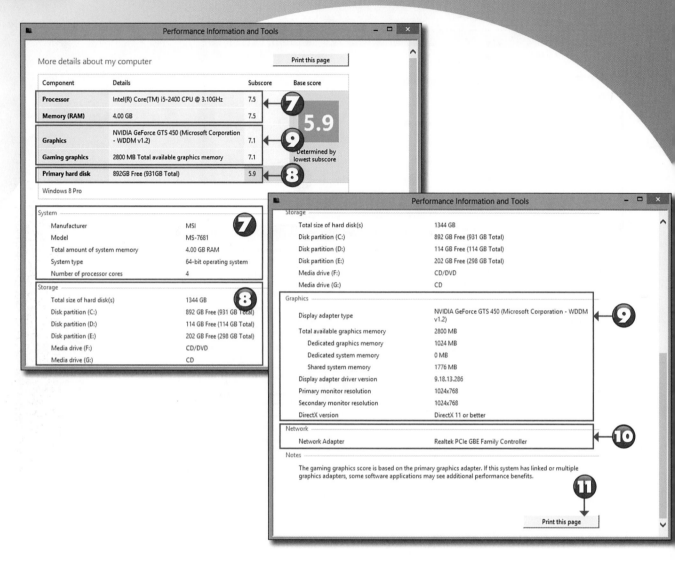

7 System information—motherboard, RAM, and processor cores.

8 Storage information—hard and optical disk sizes.

9 Graphics adapter information.

10 Network adapter information.

11 Click to print a report.

Continued

12 Select a printer.

13 Click **Print**.

14 A portion of the printed report.

End

NOTE

Selecting a Printer Other Than the Default Printer Skip step 12 if you want to use your normal (default) printer. However, if you want to save the report rather than print it, select Microsoft XPS Document Writer. This option creates an Open XPS file that you can read with the XPS Reader from the Windows desktop or with Reader from the Windows 8 Start screen. ■

SELECTING A POWER SCHEME

You can select a power scheme in Windows 8 that will stretch battery life as far as possible or keep your system running at top speed all the time. Here's how to select the power scheme you want from the Windows 8 desktop.

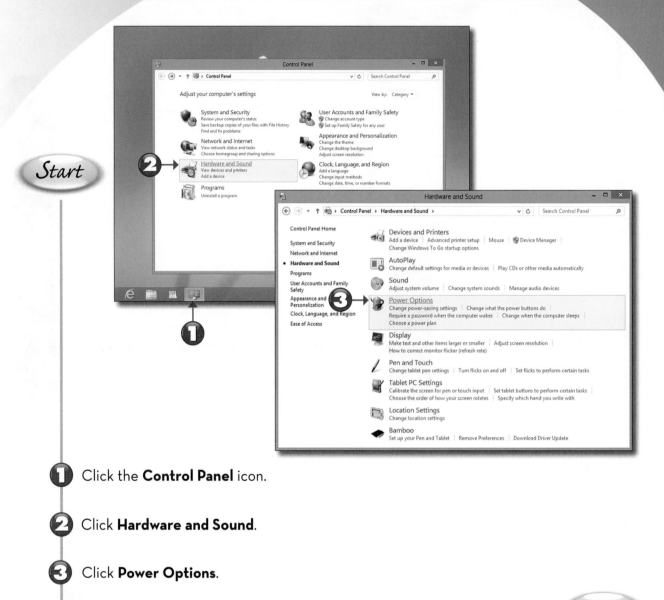

Start

① Click the **Control Panel** icon.

② Click **Hardware and Sound**.

③ Click **Power Options**.

Continued

NOTE

Paths to Power Options Power Options is also available from the System and Security section of Control Panel. ■

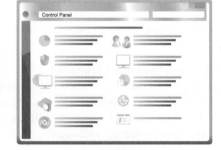

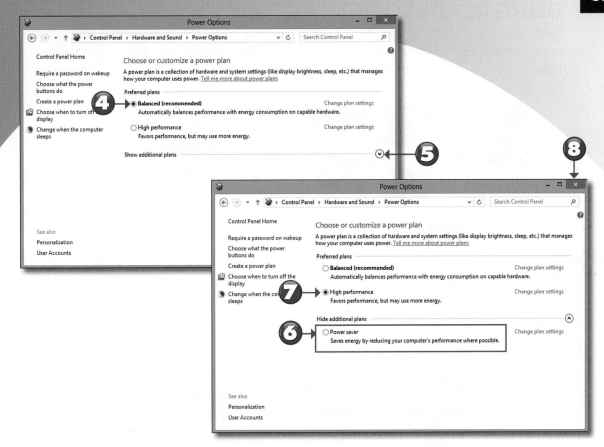

The **Balanced** power plan is the default setting for desktop and laptop computers.

Click to see additional plans.

Additional plans appear here.

Click your preferred plan.

Click **Close**.

End

NOTE

Easy Access to Power Options for Laptops On laptops, you can also select Power Options from the notification area next to the clock in the taskbar. Click the battery icon (displayed when your device is running on battery power) or AC plug (displayed when your device is plugged in to a wall outlet or surge suppressor). If you don't see either icon, click the up arrow to display hidden icons. ■

USING READYBOOST

By plugging in a USB flash drive or a flash memory card, you can improve disk drive read performance if the drive or card is ReadyBoost-compatible. Here's how to set up ReadyBoost.

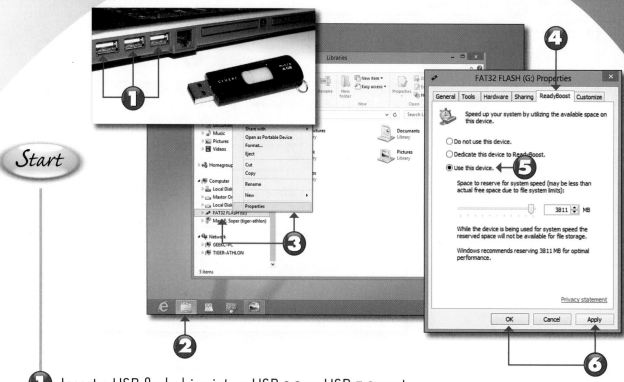

Start

1. Insert a USB flash drive into a USB 2.0 or USB 3.0 port.

2. Click **File Explorer**.

3. Right-click the drive and select **Properties**.

4. Click the **ReadyBoost** tab.

5. Click **Use this device**.

6. Click **Apply**, and then click **OK**.

End

 NOTE

Slow Flash Memory—No ReadyBoost for You! If Windows ReadyBoost is not offered as an option, your drive is not fast enough to support ReadyBoost. ■

VIEWING DISK INFORMATION

How much space is left on your drive? What drive letter is being used by your external hard disk? Use the Computer view in File Explorer for answers to these and other questions about the drives built in to and connected to your computer.

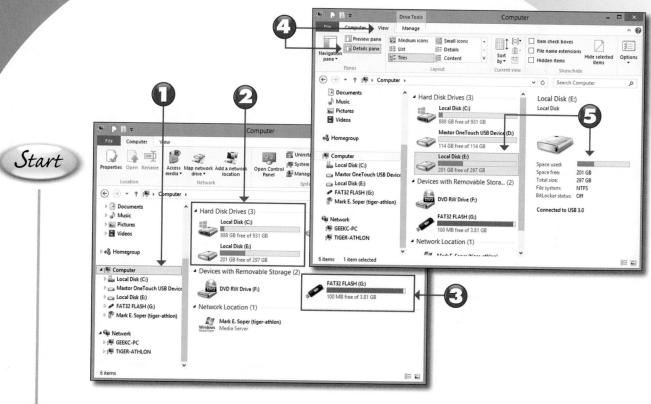

Start

1 Click **Computer**.

2 The blue bar indicates the drive has more than 10% free space.

3 The red bar indicates the drive has 10% or less free space.

4 On the **View** tab, select **Details pane**.

5 Click the drive to view the drive details.

End

NOTE

Drive Tools After you click a drive (step 5), the Drive Tools tab is available. Click this tab to access options for setting up BitLocker disk encryption (Windows 8 Pro only), Optimize, Cleanup, Format, AutoPlay, Eject, Erase, and Finalize Burning. Some options are available only with optical media. ■

CHECKING DRIVES FOR ERRORS

Checking drives for errors periodically makes sense, and is especially important if you need to turn off your computer or if your computer has had a blue screen error. Here's how to find out whether your drive has errors, and how to fix those errors.

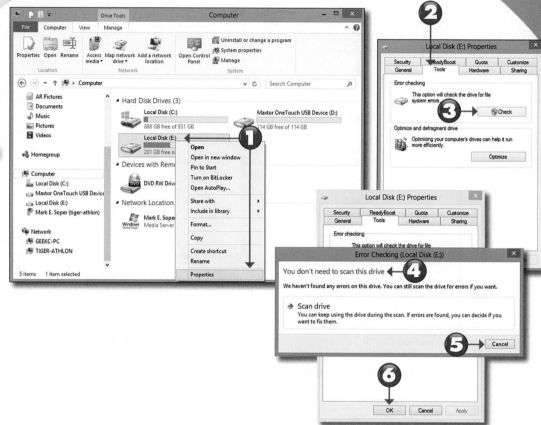

Start

1 Right-click a drive in File Explorer and select **Properties**.

2 Click the **Tools** tab.

3 Click **Check**.

4 This drive does not need to be scanned.

5 Click **Cancel**.

6 Click **OK** to close the drive's Properties dialog box.

Continued

7 This just-inserted flash drive has a problem—click the notification.

8 Click **Scan and fix**.

9 Click **Repair drive**.

10 View the results. On drives with minor errors, you might see a message like this one.

11 If the drive has significant problems, click **Show Details**.

12 Click **Close**.

End

NOTE

Miss the Notification? No Problem! The notification window shown in step 7 stays on-screen for just a few seconds. If it disappears before you can click it, use steps 1–3 to scan the drive from File Explorer. ■

TESTING MEMORY

Reliable memory is essential for reliable operation of any computer. Unexpected lockups, system crashes, and corrupt files can be caused by defective memory (RAM) modules. Use Windows Memory Diagnostics to determine whether your memory is working correctly.

1 Click **Control Panel**.

2 Click **System and Security**.

3 Click **Administrative Tools**.

4 Double-click **Windows Memory Diagnostic**.

Continued

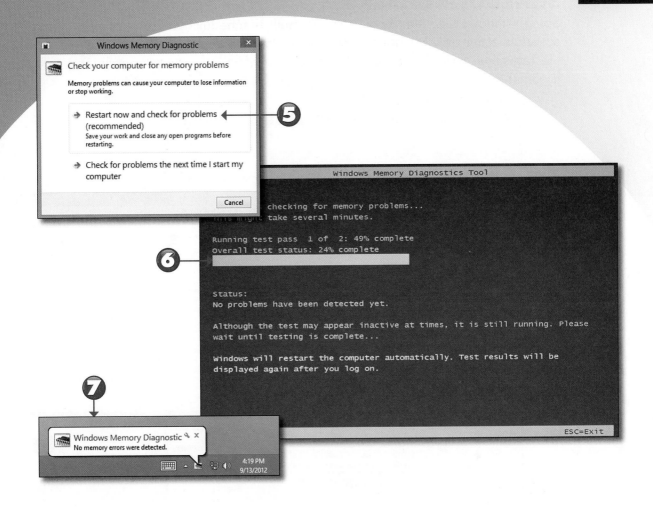

5 Click **Restart now and check for problems**. Be sure to save all open files and close programs.

6 The progress bar during the memory diagnostics test.

7 The memory diagnostics results appear after you log in to Windows and go to the desktop.

End

NOTE

Changing Memory Diagnostic Options To change settings, press the F1 (Options) key as shown in step 6, and then use the Tab and Enter keys to select other testing options. Press F10 to apply changes. ∎

SCHEDULING TASKS

Some Windows 8 utilities have their own built-in scheduling features. However, you can schedule other tasks, such as starting a program you use every day, with the built-in Schedule Tasks feature in Control Panel. This lesson shows you how to open Internet Explorer automatically when you start your computer.

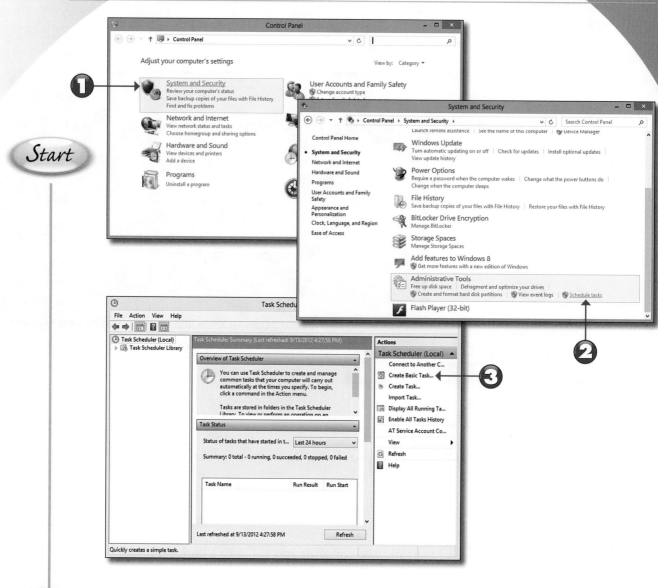

Start

① Click **System and Security** in Control Panel.

② Click **Schedule tasks**.

③ Click **Create Basic Task**.

Continued

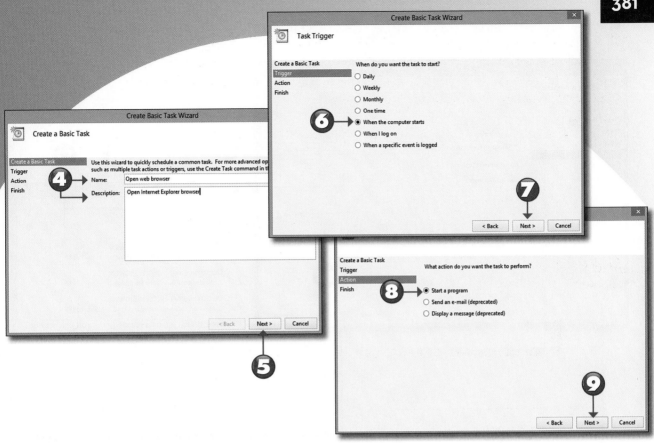

4 Enter a name and a description for the task.

5 Click **Next**.

6 Select **When the computer starts**.

7 Click **Next**.

8 Select **Start a program**.

9 Click **Next**.

Continued

NOTE

Different Intervals, Different Options If you choose a different interval (daily, monthly, one time, and so on) in step 6, the options in this dialog box vary. ■

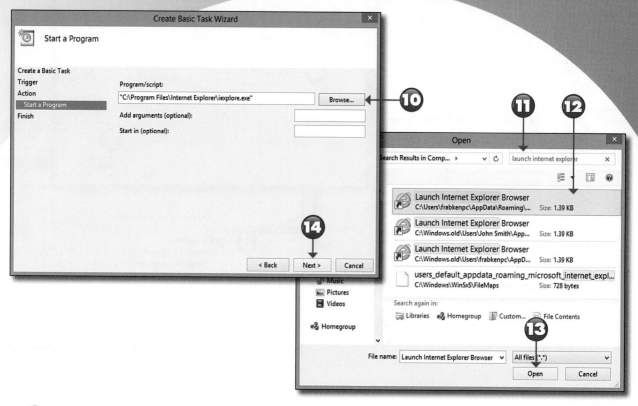

10 Click **Browse**.

11 Type **launch internet explorer** and press **Enter**.

12 Click the **Internet Explorer** program shortcut.

13 Click **Open**.

14 Click **Next**.

Continued

NOTE

Tracking Down the Correct Match The icon for a program shortcut has a curved arrow, as shown in step 12. If you have more than one shortcut, use the one stored in C:\Users\ and not one stored in C:\Windows.old (the folder created when you upgrade from Windows 7). ■

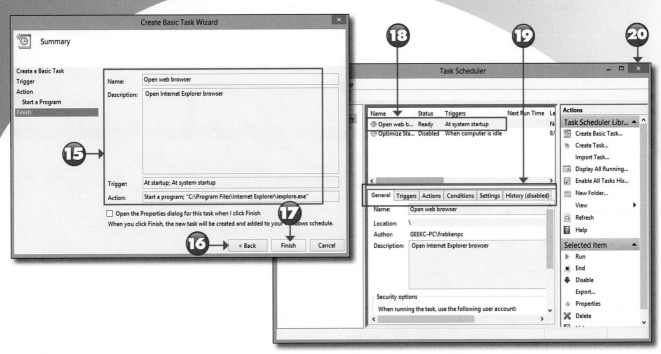

15 Review the settings.

16 Click **Back** if you need to change settings.

17 Click **Finish**.

18 The new task appears here.

19 Click a tab to review or change settings.

20 Click **Close**.

End

NOTE

Viewing and Editing Tasks To view the task, click the Task Scheduler (local) folder in the left pane. Run Task Scheduler again if you need to delete or edit an existing task or create a new task. ■

USING WINDOWS TROUBLESHOOTERS

Windows 8 includes a number of troubleshooters you can run from Control Panel to help solve problems with your system. Here's how to use a troubleshooter to fix an audio playback problem. In this example, the speaker cable was disconnected before running the troubleshooter.

Start

1 Click **System and Security** in Control Panel.

2 Click **Troubleshoot common computer problems**.

3 Click **Troubleshoot audio playback**.

Continued

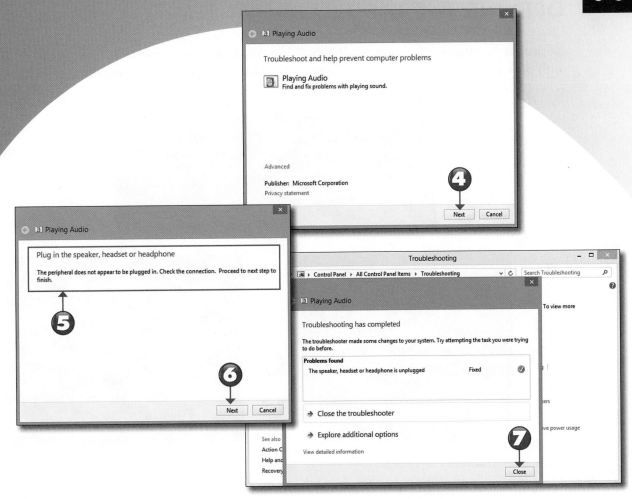

4 Click **Next**.

5 Follow the directions given to fix the problem.

6 Click **Next**.

7 Review the results. If the problem was fixed, click **Close**.

End

NOTE

Audio Troubleshooting x2 If your system has separate connectors for speakers and headsets, you might be prompted to choose which connection to troubleshoot after step 3 and before step 4. ■

OPENING THE TROUBLESHOOT STARTUP MENU

Like previous Windows versions, Windows 8 features special startup options you can use to fix problems with your system. However, Windows 8 offers more and different options than with previous versions. Here's how to open the startup troubleshoot menu.

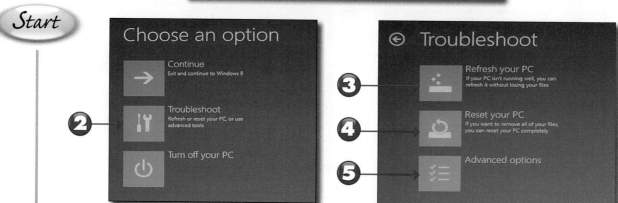

Start

1 After logging in to Windows, click **See advanced repair options**.

2 Click **Troubleshoot**.

3 Click to refresh your system.

4 Click to reset your PC.

5 Click to see advanced options.

Continued

NOTE

Getting to Advanced Repair Options Windows displays the Recovery screen in step 1 if there are serious problems with your system, but it will still boot (start). If Windows can't start, use a rescue disc to start your system. When you start the system with a rescue disc, you are prompted to select a keyboard layout, and then you'll see the screen in step 2. ■

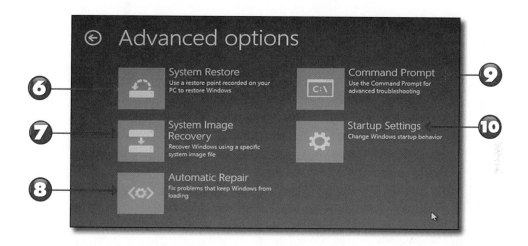

6 Restores your system to an earlier state.

7 Restores a backup image created with Windows File Recovery.

8 Automatic startup repair.

9 The command prompt for advanced repair and file copy operations.

10 Adjusts Windows startup options.

End

USING SYSTEM RESTORE

If you made a recent change to your system, such as installing a new program or a new device, and problems began after the installation, the System Restore feature can help get your system back into working condition. To see how to access this and other advanced options at startup, refer to step 6 in the previous tutorial, "Opening the Troubleshoot Startup Menu." In this section, you learn how to run System Restore from Control Panel.

Start

① Click **System and Security**.

② Click **System**.

③ Click the **System Protection** tab.

④ Click **System Restore**.

Continued

NOTE

Create Your Own Restore Point If you are planning to install new hardware or software, don't assume that Windows 8 will create a restore point for you before the process begins. Use the Create button to create a restore point manually. ■

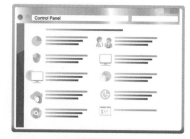

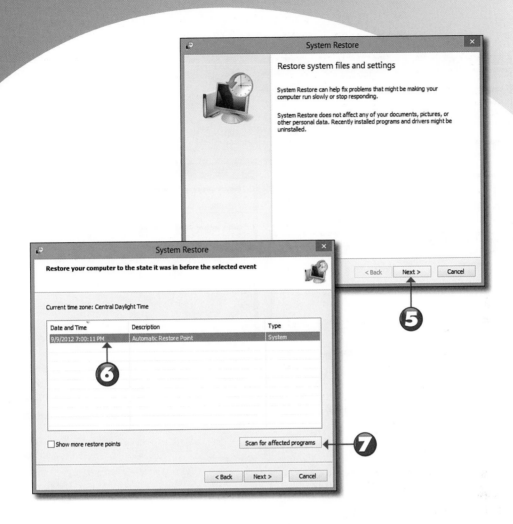

5 Click **Next**.

6 Select a restore point.

7 Click **Scan for affected programs**.

Continued

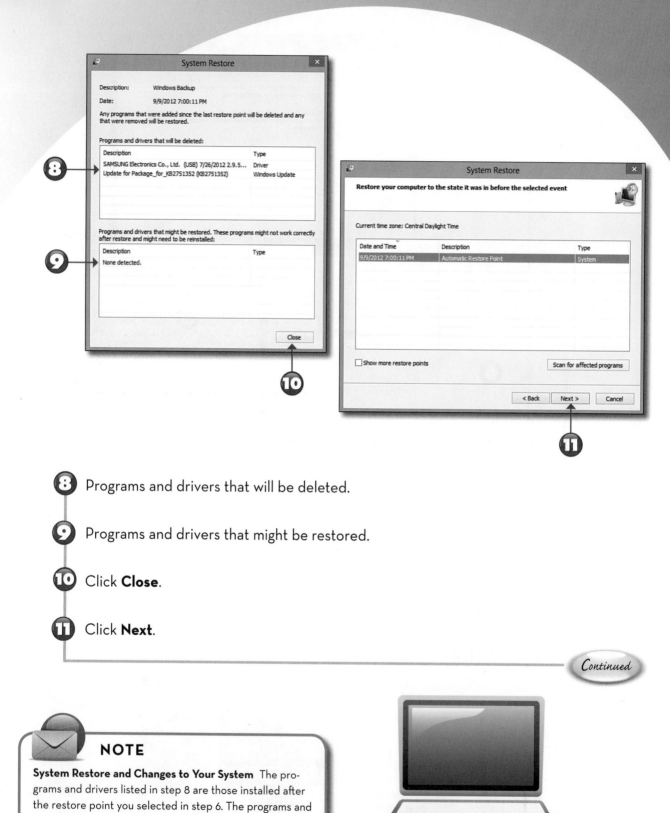

8 Programs and drivers that will be deleted.

9 Programs and drivers that might be restored.

10 Click **Close**.

11 Click **Next**.

Continued

NOTE

System Restore and Changes to Your System The programs and drivers listed in step 8 are those installed after the restore point you selected in step 6. The programs and drivers listed in step 9 might need to be reinstalled. ∎

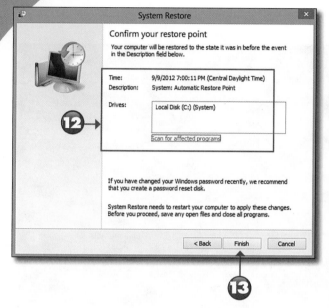

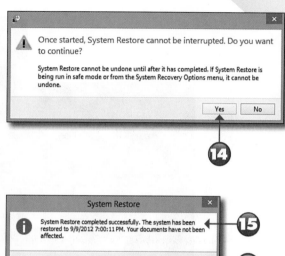

12 Review the changes that System Restore will make.

13 Click **Finish**.

14 Click **Yes**.

15 System Restore displays a status report on the Windows desktop indicating success or failure.

16 Click **Close**.

End

NOTE

Undoing System Restore If System Restore indicates that it didn't work correctly in step 15, you can undo it by running System Restore again and selecting the Undo option when it is presented. ■

USING REFRESH

If you're not sure why Windows 8 isn't running correctly, but you don't want to risk losing your personal files, use the new Refresh option. Refresh wipes out programs that you installed manually (such as from downloads or optical media) but keeps programs obtained from the Windows Store. In this tutorial, you learn how to run Refresh after starting Windows 8.

1. A program from the Windows Store.

2. A program installed from other sources.

3. Point to the lower-right edge of screen.

4. Click **Settings**.

5. Click **Change PC settings**.

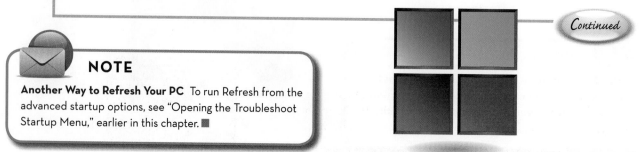

NOTE

Another Way to Refresh Your PC To run Refresh from the advanced startup options, see "Opening the Troubleshoot Startup Menu," earlier in this chapter. ■

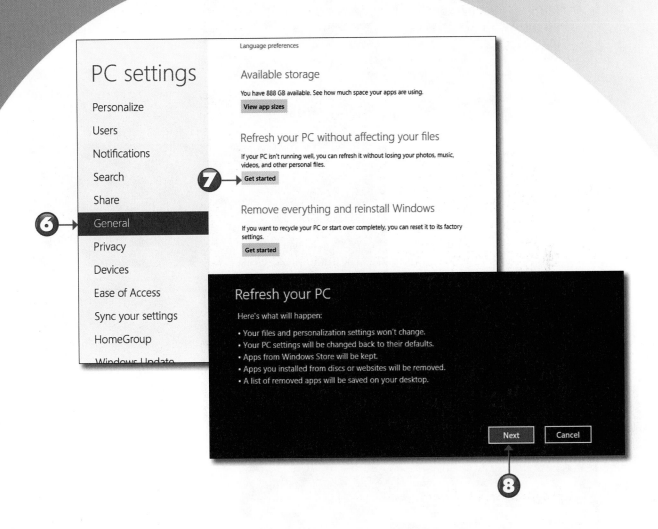

PC settings

Personalize
Users
Notifications
Search
Share
General
Privacy
Devices
Ease of Access
Sync your settings
HomeGroup
Windows Update

Language preferences

Available storage

You have 888 GB available. See how much space your apps are using.

View app sizes

Refresh your PC without affecting your files

If your PC isn't running well, you can refresh it without losing your photos, music, videos, and other personal files.

Get started

Remove everything and reinstall Windows

If you want to recycle your PC or start over completely, you can reset it to its factory settings.

Get started

Refresh your PC

Here's what will happen:

- Your files and personalization settings won't change.
- Your PC settings will be changed back to their defaults.
- Apps from Windows Store will be kept.
- Apps you installed from discs or websites will be removed.
- A list of removed apps will be saved on your desktop.

Next   Cancel

6 Click **General**.

7 Scroll down, and click **Get started** under Refresh your PC....

8 Click **Next**.

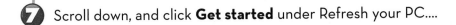

Continued

TIP

Protecting Your Downloaded Apps If you don't want to download non-Windows Store apps again, save your downloads in a folder within My Documents and use File History to make a copy of those files before you run Refresh. ■

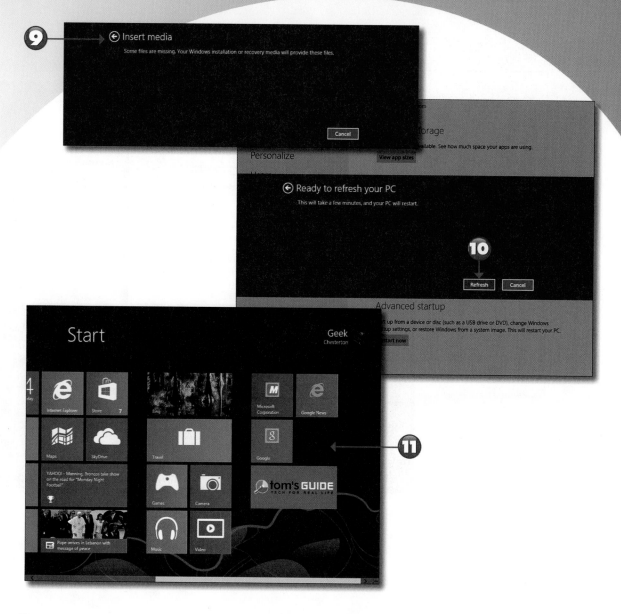

⑨ If prompted, insert your Windows 8 installation disc or recovery media.

⑩ Click **Refresh**.

⑪ After logging back into Windows, the Start screen no longer lists non-Windows Store programs.

Continued

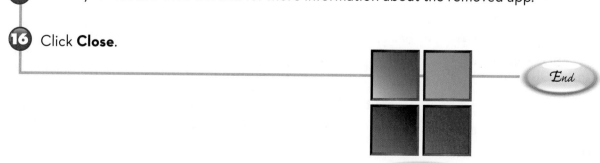

12 Click **Desktop**.

13 Double-click **Removed Apps**.

14 The list of removed apps.

15 Hover your mouse over the link for more information about the removed app.

16 Click **Close**.

End

Glossary

Use this section to bring yourself up to speed on important concepts and terms relating to Windows and to your computer. Definition terms that appear in *italics* are also listed in the glossary.

A

Accelerator A feature of Internet Explorer 10 that enables you to highlight text in a web document and map, search, or perform other activities using that text without opening up a separate browser window.

access point Device on a Wi-Fi network that provides a connection between computers on the network. Can be combined with a router and a switch.

ActiveX Microsoft technology for interactive web pages; used with Internet Explorer.

administrator Windows term for the manager of a given computer or network; only users in the administrator's group can perform some management tasks. Other users must provide an administrator's name and password for tasks marked with the Windows security shield icon.

application program Program used to create, modify, and store information you create. Microsoft Word, Adobe Photoshop, and CorelDRAW are all application programs.

archive attribute Indicates a file has not yet been backed up; automatically set when a file is created or modified.

B

backup Making a copy of a file for safekeeping, especially with a special program that must be used to restore the backup when needed; backups can be compressed to save space. Full backup backs up the entire contents of the specified drive or system; a differential backup backs up only the files that have changed since the last full backup.

Bluetooth A short-range wireless networking standard that supports non-PC devices such as mobile phones and PDAs, as well as PCs. Bluetooth uses frequencies ranging from 2.402 to 2.480GHz with a range up to about 30 feet. Data transmission runs at 1Mbps or 2Mbps, depending on the version of the technology supported by the devices. Windows 8 includes Bluetooth support.

boot Starting the computer. A *warm boot* is restarting the computer without a reset or shutdown. A *cold boot* is shutdown or reset before startup.

boot disk A disk with operating system files needed to start the computer. Windows 8 DVDs are bootable.

boot sector The starting location of operating system files on a floppy disk or hard disk.

boot sequence The procedure followed by the system during the startup process; also called bootstrapping.

Broadband Internet Internet connections with rated download speeds in excess of 100Kbps. Most common types include cable modem and DSL, but ISDN, fixed wireless, FIOS, and satellite Internet services are also broadband services.

browser A program that interprets HTML documents and allows hyperlinking to websites. Windows 8 includes Internet Explorer 10 as its standard (default) web browser.

BSOD Blue Screen of Death. This is a fatal system error in Windows that stops the system from starting; it is also called a stop error, and is named after the blue background and the white text error message.

C

CD Compact Disc.

CDFS Compact Disc File System.

CD-R Recordable CD. Contents of CD-R can be added to but not changed.

CD-ROM Compact Disc-Read-Only Memory. Standard optical drive. Most can read CD-R media, but drives require MultiRead capability and a UDF reader program to read CD-RW media.

CD-RW Compact Disc-Rewritable. Rewritable CD. The contents can be changed. A CD-RW drive can also use CD-R media.

Charms bar Windows 8 interface that appears on the right side of the display. Includes charms for search, share, Start screen, devices, and settings.

clean boot Booting the system without device drivers; Windows 8 uses Safe Mode boot options to boot with only essential drivers.

CMYK Cyan, Magenta, Yellow, Black. Refers to a four-color model for graphics and printing; these are the ink colors used by most inkjet printers; compare to

RGB (Red, Green, Blue), a three-color model used for on-screen graphics.

cold boot Starting a system from power-down or with the reset button; memory count and other hardware tests are performed.

Compact Flash A popular flash-memory storage standard used by digital cameras. It can be attached to desktop and portable PCs by means of a card reader or PC Card adapter.

Control Panel A Windows feature that sets Windows options.

D

DAE Digital Audio Extraction. The process of converting tracks from a music CD to a digital format, such as MP3 or WMA, at faster than normal 1x analog speeds. Windows 8's Windows Media Player and Windows Media Center use DAE to rip (convert) audio into digital form.

defragment Reorganizing the files on a drive to occupy contiguous sectors to improve retrieval speed; a defragmenting utility is included in Windows 8.

desktop Windows 8 uses the desktop for program shortcuts, access to components such as the Recycle Bin, and for program windows.

device driver A program used to enable an operating system to support new devices.

Device Manager The Windows portion of the system properties

sheet used to view and control device configuration. These include drivers, power management, PnP settings, and other configuration options.

Devices and Printers A Windows 8 feature that displays all devices and printers in a single window for quick access to the management features for each device.

dpi Dots per inch. The resolutions of a printer, scanner, or monitor are commonly defined in dpi. Higher values provide sharper images and text but use more memory or disk space to store.

drag and drop Windows term for clicking and holding on an object, such as a file or a tile on the Start screen, dragging it to another location, and releasing it.

driver See *device driver*.

DUN Dial-Up Networking. Using an analog (phone line) modem to connect to other computers.

DVD Digital Video Disc. Also known as Digital Versatile Disk. High-capacity replacement for CD-ROM.

DVD-R Digital Video Disc-Recordable.

DVD-RAM Digital Versatile Disc-Random Access Memory. A rewritable *DVD* standard developed by Panasonic and supported by the DVD Forum. A few of these drives also support DVD-R write-once media.

DVD-ROM Digital Video Disc-Read Only Memory. Retail and upgrade editions of Windows 8 are distributed on DVD-ROM media, as are many other application and utility programs from major publishers.

DVD-RW Digital Video Disc-Rewritable. A rewritable *DVD* standard developed by Pioneer Electronics and supported by the DVD Forum. These drives also support *DVD-R* write-once media.

DVD±RW Refers to drives that support both *DVD-R*/RW and *DVD+R*/RW media.

DVD+RW A rewritable *DVD* standard supported by the DVD+RW Alliance and sold by HP, Philips, Sony, and other vendors. Most of these drives also support DVD+R write-once media.

DVI Digital Visual Interface. Replaced DFP as the standard for support of LCD displays on desktop computers. DVI-D is for digital displays only; DVI-I supports digital and analog displays.

E

email Electronic mail. The contents of email can include text, HTML, and binary files (such as photos or compressed archives). Email can be sent between computers via an internal computer network, a proprietary online service such as AOL, or via the Internet.

executable file .exe file; a machine-readable program file that can be run in any area of memory or any type of program file, including .com and .bat files.

F

FAT File Allocation Table. The part of the hard disk or floppy disk that contains pointers to the actual location of files on the disk.

FAT12 12-bit file allocation table. FAT method used for floppy disk drives only.

FAT16 16-bit file allocation table. FAT method used by MS-DOS and Windows 95; also supported by Windows 7 and earlier versions; allows 65,535 (2^{16}) files maximum per drive and drive sizes up to 2GB (4GB in Windows 7 and some other versions). Windows 7 supports FAT16 for data drives only.

FAT32 32-bit file allocation table. FAT method optionally available with Windows 8 and earlier versions. It allows 2^{32} files maximum per drive and drive sizes up to 2TB (terabytes). Windows 8 supports FAT32 for data drives only.

file attributes Controls how files are used and viewed and can be reset by the user. Typical file attributes include hidden, system, read-only, and archive; Windows 8 also supports compressed and encrypted file attributes when the NTFS file system is used.

file extension Up to four-character alphanumeric after the dot in a filename; indicates file type, such as .html, .exe, .docx, and so on. Windows 8 does not display file extensions by default, but you can make them visible through the Control Panel's Folder Options utility.

file system How files are organized on a drive; FAT16, FAT32, and NTFS are popular file systems supported by various versions of Windows.

firewall A network device or software that blocks unauthorized access to a network from other users. Software firewalls such as Zone Alarm or Norton Internet Security are sometimes referred to as personal firewalls. Routers can also function as firewalls. Windows 8 includes a software firewall.

font A particular size, shape, and weight of a typeface. 12-point Times Roman Italic is a font; Times Roman is the typeface. Windows 8 includes a number of different typefaces, and you can select the desired font with programs such as WordPad, Paint, and others.

format Can refer to document layout or the process of preparing a disk drive for use.

FORMAT A Windows program to prepare a drive for use; hard disks must be partitioned first.

G

GB Gigabyte. 1 billion bytes.

GHz Gigahertz.

GUI Graphical User Interface. The user interface with features such as icons, fonts, and point-and-click commands; Windows and Mac OS are popular GUIs.

H

hard drive A storage device with rigid, nonremovable platters inside a case; also called hard disk or rigid disk.

hardware Physical computing devices.

HDD Hard Disk Drive. Windows 8 is typically installed to an HDD.

HDMI High Definition Media Interface. HDMI cables and ports can carry HDTV video and audio signals.

Hi-Speed USB Another term for USB 2.0.

hidden attribute A file attribute that makes a file invisible to the default File Explorer view.

high-level format A type of format performed by the Windows Format program on hard drives and floppy drives; it rewrites file allocation tables and the root directory but doesn't overwrite existing data on the rest of the disk surface.

HomeGroup A Windows network feature that enables two or more Windows 8 or Windows 7 systems to belong to a secure, easy-to-manage network.

I

icon An on-screen symbol used in Windows to link you to a program, file, or routine.

install The process of making a computer program usable on a system, including expanding and copying program files to the correct locations, changing Windows configuration files, and registering file extensions used by the program.

Internet The world-wide "network of networks" that can be accessed through the World Wide Web and by Telnet, FTP, and other utilities.

J

jump list A Windows 8 feature that enables programs and documents to be started from taskbar shortcuts.

L

LAN Local Area Network. A network in which the components are connected through network cables or wirelessly; a LAN can connect to other LANs via a router.

landscape mode A print mode that prints across the wider side of the paper; from the usual proportions of a landscape painting.

lock screen This screen appears when Windows 8 is started or locked. The user must press the spacebar, click a mouse, or press the touch interface to see the login screen. This screen displays the date, time, and a full-screen image.

logging Recording events during a process. Windows 8 creates logs for many types of events; they can be viewed through the Computer Management Console.

M

mastering Creating a CD or DVD by adding all the files to the media at once. This method is recommended when creating a music CD or a video DVD. Windows 8's built-in CD and DVD creation feature supports mastering.

media Anything used to carry information, such as network cables, paper, CD or DVD discs, and so on.

memory module Memory chips on a small board.

Microsoft account Account setup option supported by Windows 8. Log in with a Microsoft account (example: somebody@hotmail.com), and your settings are synchronized between systems. This was previously known as a Windows Live ID.

Microsoft Knowledge Base The online collection of Microsoft technical articles used by Microsoft support personnel to diagnose system problems. Can also be searched by end users by using the http://support.microsoft.com website.

MMC Microsoft Management Console. The Windows utility used to view and control the computer and its components. Disk Management and Device Manager are components of MMC.

monitor A TV-like device that uses either a CRT or an LCD screen to display activity inside the computer. Attaches to the video card or video port on the system. Windows 8 supports multiple monitors.

mouse A pointing device that is moved across a flat surface; older models use a removable ball to track movement; most recent models use optical or laser sensors.

MP3 Moving Picture Experts Group Layer 3 Audio. A compressed digitized music file format widely used for storage of popular and classical music; quality varies with the sampling rate used to create the file. MP3 files can be stored on recordable or rewritable CD or DVD media for playback and are frequently exchanged online. The process of creating MP3 files is called ripping. Windows Media Player and Windows Media Center can create and play back MP3 files.

MPEG Motion Picture Experts Group; creates standards for compression of video (such as MPEG 2) and audio (such as the popular MP3 file format).

multi-touch A Windows feature that enables icons and windows on touch-sensitive displays to be dragged, resized, and adjusted with two or more fingers.

N

netbook A mobile computing device that is smaller than a laptop and has a folding keyboard and screen (usually no more than about 10 inches diagonal measurement). Netbooks have lower-performance processors, less RAM, and smaller hard disks (or solid state drives) than laptop or notebook computers. Windows 8 runs on netbooks as well as more powerful types of computers.

network Two or more computers that are connected and share a resource, such as folders or printers.

network drive A drive or folder available through the network; usually refers to a network resource that has been mapped to a local drive letter.

Network and Sharing Center The Windows control center for wired, wireless, and dial-up networking functions.

NTFS New Technology File System. The native file system used by Windows 8 and some earlier versions of Windows. All NTFS versions feature smaller allocation unit sizes and superior security when compared to FAT16 or FAT32.

O

objects Items that can be viewed or configured with File Explorer, including drives, folders, computers, and so on.

optical Storage such as CD and DVD drives, which use a laser to read data.

OS Operating system. Software that configures and manages hardware and connects hardware and applications. Windows 8, Linux, and Mac OS are examples of operating systems.

P

packet writing A method for writing data to an optical disc in small blocks (packets). This method is used by UDF programs. Packet-written media requires a UDF reader, unlike media created with a mastering program, which can be read without any additional software. Windows 8's CD and DVD writing feature can use packet writing (UDF formatting).

PAN Personal Area Network. Bluetooth is an example of a network technology that supports PANs.

password A word or combination of letters and numbers that is matched to a username or resource name to enable the user to access a computer or network resources or accounts.

path A series of drives and folders (subdirectories) that are checked for executable programs when a command-prompt command is issued or a drive/network server and folders are used to access a given file.

peer server A client PC that also shares drives or other resources on a Windows network.

peer-to-peer network A network in which some or all of the client PCs also act as peer servers.

personal firewall Software that blocks unauthorized access to a computer with an Internet connection. Can also be configured to prevent unauthorized programs from connecting to the Internet. The free Shields Up! service at Gibson Research (http://grc.com) tests the protection provided by personal firewalls and recommends specific products. Windows 8 includes a personal (software) firewall.

Photo Viewer A Windows 8 utility for photo viewing and printing.

physical drive Same as a hard drive or hard disk; all physical drives must be partitioned and high-level formatted before they can be used by Windows.

PIN Personal Identification Number. Windows 8 supports PIN numbers as an optional login method.

pinning The act of locking a program or document to the Windows taskbar or Start menu. You can use this feature along with jump lists to create shortcuts to your most commonly used programs in either location.

PnP Plug and Play. A Windows technology for using the operating system to detect and configure add-on cards and external devices such as modems, monitors, scanners, and printers. PnP hardware can be moved to different resource settings as needed to make way for additional devices.

POP Post Office Protocol.

POP3 Post Office Protocol 3.

portrait mode The default print option that prints across the short side of the paper; it gets its name from the usual orientation of portrait paintings and photographs.

power management BIOS or OS techniques for reducing power usage by dropping CPU clock speed, turning off the monitor or hard disk, and so on during periods of inactivity.

PowerShell A Windows utility for automating system tasks and creating system management tools. Included in some editions of Windows 8 as an optionally installed feature.

primary partition A hard disk partition that will become the C: drive on a single-drive system.

print spooler A program that stores and manages print jobs on disk and sends them to the printer; an integral part of Windows.

properties sheet A Windows method for modifying and viewing object properties. Accessible by right-clicking the object and selecting Properties or by using Control Panel.

protocol The common language used by different types of computers to communicate over a network.

Q

QWERTY The standard arrangement of typewriter keys is also used by most English or Latin-alphabet computer keyboards; the name was derived from the first six letter keys under the left hand.

R

RAM Random Access Memory. Memory whose contents can be changed.

read-only Storage that is protected from changes.

read-only attribute A file attribute used to protect a file from unauthorized changes; it cannot be overridden or altered and can be deleted only by explicit user override.

read-write caching A method of disk caching that uses RAM to hold data being saved to disk as well as data being read from disk for faster performance. Windows uses read-write caching for hard drives by default.

Recovery Environment Special Windows 8 repair mode used for restoring damaged systems; can be launched at startup or from the Windows 8 DVD or recovery disc.

Recycle Bin Windows holding area for deleted files, allowing them to be restored to their original locations; can be overridden to free up disk space.

Refresh New Windows 8 system recovery feature; enables system and Windows Store software to be reset to its original settings without losing settings or files.

registration The Windows process of matching file extensions with compatible programs.

Registry The Windows structure that stores information on programs and hardware installed on the system and user configuration settings.

removable-media Any drive whose media can be interchanged; floppy disk, CD-ROM, optical, tape, and USB flash memory card drives.

Reset New Windows 8 system recovery feature; resets Windows to its as-installed state. All user changes (new programs, files, and settings) are also wiped out.

resolution The number of dots per inch (dpi) supported by a display, scanner, or printer. Typical displays support resolutions of about 96dpi, whereas printers have resolutions of 600dpi to 2,400dpi (laser printers). Inkjet printers might have even higher resolutions.

RF Radio Frequency. Different versions of Wireless Ethernet use different radio frequencies.

RGB Red, Green, Blue.

Ribbon toolbar The program interface used by many Windows 8 components. Click a tab on the Ribbon to display related commands.

ripping The process of converting CD audio tracks into digital music formats, such as MP3 or WMA.

ROM Read Only Memory. Memory whose contents cannot be changed.

root directory The top-level folder on a drive that stores all other directories (folders); the root directory of C: drive is C:\. Sometimes referred to as a root folder.

router The device that routes data from one network to another. Often integrated with wireless access points and switches.

S

safe mode Windows troubleshooting startup mode; runs the system using BIOS routines only. Can be selected at startup by pressing the F8 key repeatedly and then selecting it from the startup menu that appears.

SD card Secure Digital card. Popular flash memory card format for digital cameras and other electronic devices. See also *SDHC card*.

SDHC card Secure Digital High Capacity card. Popular flash memory card format for digital cameras and other electronic devices. Devices that use SDHC cards can also use SD cards; however, devices made only for SD cards cannot use SDHC cards.

SETUP The common name for installation programs.

shared resource A drive, printer, or other resource available to more than one PC over a network.

shortcut A Windows icon stored on the desktop or in a Windows folder with an .lnk extension; double-click the icon to run the program or open the file.

SkyDrive A Windows online file and photo storage and sharing site. Requires a free Microsoft account (formerly known as a Windows Live ID). Windows 8 provides access to SkyDrive from the Start screen and Windows desktop.

SMTP Simple Mail Transport Protocol.

SNMP Simple Network Management Protocol.

software Instructions that create or modify information and control hardware; must be read into RAM before use.

SOHO Small Office/Home Office.

solid state drive A hard disk equivalent that uses nonvolatile memory for storage instead of a disk mechanism. Used in many netbooks and some laptops. Windows 8 includes support for solid state drives.

SP Service Pack. A service pack is used to add features or fix problems with an operating system or application program.

spam Unsolicited email. Named after (but not endorsed by) the famous Hormel lunch meat. Many email clients and utilities can be configured to help filter, sort, and block spam.

SSD See *solid state drive*.

SSID Service Set Identifier. The name for a wireless network. When you buy a wireless router, the vendor has assigned it a standard SSID, but you should change it to a different name as part of setting up a secure network.

standby The power-saving mode in which the CPU drops to a reduced clock speed and other components wait for activity.

start page The web page that is first displayed when you open a web browser; can be customized to view any web page available online or stored on your hard disk.

Start screen The new Windows 8 user interface that uses tiles for apps and is designed for touchscreens, but can also be navigated with a keyboard, mouse, or touchpad.

startup event File loading and other activities during the startup of Windows.

storage Any device that holds programs or data for use, including hard disks, USB drives, DVD drives, and so on.

suspend The power-saving mode that shuts down the monitor and other devices; it saves more power than standby. Windows 8 calls suspend mode sleep mode.

swapfile The area of a hard disk used for virtual memory; Windows uses a dynamic swapfile (called a paging file in Windows 8) that can grow or shrink as required.

system attribute The file attribute used to indicate whether a file or folder is part of the operating system; boot files are normally set as system and hidden.

System Restore A feature built in to Windows 8 that enables the user to revert the system back to a previous state in case of a crash or other system problem. System Restore points can be created by the user and are created automatically by Windows when new hardware and software is installed or by a predefined schedule.

T

taskbar A Windows feature that displays icons for running programs, generally at the bottom of the primary display. In Windows 8, the taskbar also contains jump list shortcuts to frequently used programs.

TB Terabyte. 1 trillion bytes.

TCP/IP Transmission Control Protocol/Internet Protocol. The Internet's standard network protocol that is also the standard for most networks.

temp file Temporary file. A file created to store temporary information, such as a print job or an application work file. It may be stored in the default Temp folder (such as \Windows\Temp) or in a folder designated by the application. Temp files may use the .tmp extension or start with a ~ (tilde).

tile The Windows 8 term for the icons on the Start screen. They can be moved to different places on the Start screen by using drag and drop.

touchpad A pressure-sensitive pad that is used as a mouse replacement in some portable computers and keyboards.

touchscreen A touch-sensitive screen built in to some desktop and most tablet computers. Windows 8's Start screen is designed for touchscreens, but can also be navigated with a mouse or touchpad.

TrackPoint An IBM-designed pointing device that is integrated into the keyboards of portable computers made by IBM and Lenovo and is licensed by Toshiba and other firms. Also referred to as a pointing stick, it resembles a pencil eraser that is located between the G and H keys; the buttons are located beneath the spacebar.

Trojan horse A program that attaches itself secretly to other programs that usually has a harmful action when triggered. It is similar to a computer virus but cannot spread itself to other computers, although some Trojan horses can be used to install a remote control program that allows an unauthorized user to take over your computer. Antivirus programs can block Trojan horses as well as true viruses.

typeface A set of fonts in different sizes (or a single scalable outline) and weights; Times New Roman Bold, Bold Italic, Regular, and Italic are all part of the Times New Roman scalable typeface.

U

UDF Universal Disk Format. A standard for CD and DVD media to drag and drop files to compatible media using a method called packet writing. Windows 8 supports various UDF versions.

uninstall The process of removing Windows programs from the system.

Universal Disk Format See *UDF*.

upgrade Replacing an old version of software or hardware with a new version.

upgrade version A version of a program (such as Windows 8) that requires proof of ownership of a previous version before it can be installed.

UPS Uninterruptible Power Supply. The term for battery backup that uses a battery at all times to power the system.

URL Uniform Resource Locator. The full path to any given web page or graphic on the Internet. A full URL contains the server type (such as http://, ftp://, or others), the site name (such as www.markesoper.com), and the name of the folder and the page or graphic you want to view (such as /blog/?page_id=38). Thus, the URL http://www.markesoper.com/blog/?page_id=38 displays the "About Mark" page on the author's website.

USB Universal Serial Bus. High-speed replacement for older I/O ports; USB 1.1 has a peak speed of 12Mbps. USB 2.0 has a peak speed of 480Mbps; USB 3.0 has a top speed of 5Gbps. USB 2.0 ports also support USB 1.1 devices. USB 2.0 devices can be plugged in to USB 1.1 devices but run at only USB 1.1 speeds. USB 3.0 ports support USB 2.0 and 1.1 devices, which run at their original speeds.

username Used with a password to gain access to network resources.

utility program A program that enhances day-to-day computer operations but doesn't create data.

V

VGA Video Graphics Array. The first popular analog video standard; the basis for all current video cards. A 15-pin port found on most laptop and many desktop computers.

virus A computer program that resembles a Trojan horse that can also replicate itself to other computers.

VoIP Voice over Internet Protocol. Enables telephone calls to be transmitted or received over an IP network.

W-Z

WAN Wide Area Network. A network that spans multiple cities, countries, or continents. Network sections may be linked by leased line, Internet backbone, or satellite feed; routers connect LANs to WANs and WAN segments to each other.

warm boot Restarting a computer with a software command; no memory or hardware testing.

WAV A noncompressed standard for digital audio. Some recording programs for Windows can create and play back WAV files. However, WAV files are very large, and are usually converted into other formats for use online or for creating digital music archives.

wavetable A method of playing back MIDI files with digitized samples of actual musical instruments.

Web Slice An Internet Explorer 10 feature that displays content from other websites while you view a website in the main window.

WEP Wired Equivalent Privacy. A now-obsolete standard for wireless security. Replaced by *WPA*.

Wi-Fi The name for IEEE-802.11a, IEEE-802.11b, IEEE-802.11g, or IEEE-802.11n wireless Ethernet devices that meet the standards set forth by the Wi-Fi Alliance.

wildcard A character used to replace one or more characters as a variable in DIR, Windows Find/Search, and File Explorer. * = multiple characters; ? = a single character.

Windows Action Center A Windows 8 feature that combines security and system warnings and notifications into a single interface.

Windows Essentials 2012 An optional addition to Windows 8 that provides support for photo management and light editing, blogging, family safety, instant messaging, email, and video editing.

wireless network The general term for any radio-frequency network, including *Wi-Fi*. Most wireless networks can be interconnected to conventional networks.

WLAN Wireless Local Area Network. Instead of wires, stations on a WLAN connect to each other through radio waves. The IEEE 802.11 family of standards guide the development of WLANs.

WMA Windows Media Audio. This is the native compressed audio format created by Windows Media Player. Unlike *MP3*, WMA files support digital rights management.

WPA Wireless Protected Access. Replaced WEP as the standard for secure wireless networks. Original WPA uses TKIP encryption. An improved version known as WPA2 uses the even more secure AES encryption standard.

WWW World Wide Web. The portion of the Internet that uses the Hypertext Transfer Protocol (http://) and can thus be accessed via a web browser, such as Microsoft Internet Explorer, Google Chrome, and Mozilla Firefox.

Zip The archive type (originally known as PKZIP) created when you use Send To Compressed (Zipped) folder. A zip file can contain one or more files and can be created, viewed, and opened in File Explorer. Formerly also referred to the Iomega Zip removable-media drive.

Index

easy
Microsoft® Windows® 8
See it done. Do it yourself.

Mark Edward Soper

FREE
Online Edition

Safari
Books Online

Your purchase of *Easy Windows 8* includes access to a free online edition for 45 days through the **Safari Books Online** subscription service. Nearly every Que book is available online through **Safari Books Online**, along with thousands of books and videos from publishers such as Addison-Wesley Professional, Cisco Press, Exam Cram, IBM Press, O'Reilly Media, Prentice Hall, Sams, and VMware Press.

Safari Books Online is a digital library providing searchable, on-demand access to thousands of technology, digital media, and professional development books and videos from leading publishers. With one monthly or yearly subscription price, you get unlimited access to learning tools and information on topics including mobile app and software development, tips and tricks on using your favorite gadgets, networking, project management, graphic design, and much more.

Activate your FREE Online Edition at
informit.com/safarifree

STEP 1: Enter the coupon code: LFMRUWA.

STEP 2: New Safari users, complete the brief registration form.
Safari subscribers, just log in.

If you have difficulty registering on Safari or accessing the online edition,
please e-mail customer-service@safaribooksonline.com
